W9-CZU-113

CRIME AND CRIMINALITY

Causes and Consequences

Ronald D. Hunter

State University of West Georgia

Mark L. Dantzker

University of Texas–Pan American

WARNER MEMORIAL LIBRARY
EASTERN UNIVERSITY
ST. DAVIDS, 19087-3696

Prentice
Hall

Upper Saddle River, New Jersey 07458

12-21-01

Library of Congress Cataloging-in-Publication Data

Hunter, Ronald D.
    Crime and criminality : causes and consequences / Ronald D. Hunter, Mark L. Dantzker.
      p. cm.
    Includes bibliographical references and index.
    ISBN 0-13-324872-0
    1. Criminal psychology. 2. Criminal behavior. 3. Criminology. I. Dantzker, Mark L.,
  1958—II. Title.

HV6080 .H85 2002
364—dc21

HV 6080 .H85 2002
Hunter, Ronald D.
Crime and criminality

Publisher: Jeff Johnston
Executive Editor: Kim Davies
Development Editor: Cheryl Adam
Production Editor: Linda B. Pawelchak
Production Liaison: Adele M. Kupchik
Director of Manufacturing and Production: Bruce Johnson
Managing Editor: Mary Carnis
Manufacturing Buyer: Cathleen Petersen
Cover Design Coordinator: Miguel Ortiz
Cover Image: Craig Calsbeek/SIS/Images.com
Marketing Manager: Ramona Sherman
Editorial Assistant: Sarah Holle
Marketing Assistant: Barbara Rosenberg
Composition: Naomi Sysak
Printing and Binding: R.R. Donnelley and Sons, Inc..

Prentice-Hall International (UK) Limited, *London*
Prentice-Hall of Australia Pty. Limited, *Sydney*
Prentice-Hall Canada Inc., *Toronto*
Prentice-Hall Hispanoamericana, S.A., *Mexico*
Prentice-Hall of India Private Limited, *New Delhi*
Prentice-Hall of Japan, Inc., *Tokyo*
Prentice-Hall Asia Pte. Ltd.., *Singapore*
Editora Prentice-Hall do Brasil, Ltda., *Rio de Janeiro*

Copyright © 2002 by Pearson Education, Inc., Upper Saddle River, New Jersey 07458.
All rights reserved. Printed in the United States of America. This publication is protected by
Copyright and permission should be obtained from the publisher prior to any prohibited repro-
duction, storage in a retrieval system, or transmission in any form or by any means, electronic,
mechanical, photocopying, recording, or likewise. For information regarding permission(s),
write to: Rights and Permissions Department.

10 9 8 7 6 5 4 3 2 1
ISBN: 0-13-324872-0

Contents

CHAPTER

The Study of Crime / 22

CHAPTER

Biological and Biosocial Theories of Crime Causation / 44

CHAPTER 9

Holistic Theories of Crime Causation / 149

CHAPTER 10

Victimization Theories / 161

CHAPTER 11

Dealing with Lawbreakers / 173

Preface

In writing *Crime and Criminality*, our desire was to "return to basics" by producing a brief yet thorough primer on crime and criminality that under-graduates can both understand and afford. We have developed a text that covers all significant issues and concepts to which undergraduate sociology, criminology, or criminal justice students taking introductory courses in crimi-nology, criminal behavior, juvenile delinquency, deviancy, or theories of crime causation should be exposed. The breadth of coverage of this primer, in conjunction with its length and reasonable cost, makes it an excellent selection as a primary text within the previously mentioned courses or as a supplemental text in other related courses offered by criminal justice, criminology, psychology, and sociology programs.

The primer is comprised of thirteen chapters. Chapter 1, "The Problem of Crime," is an introductory chapter that defines crime and criminal behavior. In this chapter, the student becomes acquainted with the various perspectives on crime and criminality and how different perspectives influence definitions of crime and criminal behavior, as well as responses to crime and criminal behavior. The various strategies for predicting and measuring crime are then contrasted. Included within this discussion are overviews of the various types of violent crimes, property crimes, occupational crimes, organized crime, public order crimes, and political crimes.

Chapter 2, "The Study of Crime," defines criminology, describes the five models of criminology, and discusses the classical and positive schools of criminology and their impacts on both the study of crime and the adminis-tration of criminal justice. In addition, several current influences on the study of crime are presented and discussed.

Chapter 3, "Biological and Biosocial Theories of Crime Causation," presents a historical assessment of the major biological explanations for human and criminal behavior (genetics, physical abnormalities, neurological disorders, environmental pollution, etc.) and their incorporation into modern biosocial explanations that provide for both nature and nurture.

Chapter 4, "Psychological and Psychosocial Theories of Crime Causation," reviews the major psychological explanations for human and criminal behavior (Freudian psychoanalysis, behavioral theory, cognitive theory, etc.) and the development of social psychological and psychosocial explanations of crime and criminality.

Chapter 5, "Social Structure Theories of Crime Causation," introduces the major class-based sociological theories that emphasize the effects of poverty and the individual's location within the lower class as explanations for crime and criminality.

Chapter 6, "Social Interaction Theories of Crime Causation," investigates the major social psychological and sociological theories for crime and criminal behavior. These theories focus on the social interactions through which criminal and deviant behaviors are learned and reinforced. Social reaction theories are included as the bridge between functionalist and conflict theories.

Chapter 7, "Social Conflict Theories of Crime Causation," presents those theories that explain crime as the product of political and economic struggles between those in power and those who are without power or are seeking power. This chapter includes non-Marxist explanations as well as the Marxist perspectives of critical theory and radical theory. Of particular interest is the inclusion of elitist theory within non-Marxist conflict theories.

Chapter 8, "Integrated Theories of Crime Causation," contrasts the leading efforts to combine different perspectives regarding crime and criminality into more comprehensive explanations that draw from two or more previous theories.

Chapter 9, "Holistic Theories of Crime Causation," reviews contemporary efforts to develop general explanations for crime and criminality. Included is our own identity theory.

Chapter 10, "Theories of Victimization," describes the study of victimology and explores the various theoretical explanations of victimization.

Chapter 11, "Dealing with Lawbreakers," contrasts the various perspectives on how to appropriately deal with those who are found to have committed crimes (including the rationales for retribution, deterrence, incapacitation, reintegration, and rehabilitation). The merits of corporal punishment and capital punishment are also examined.

Chapter 12, "Dealing with Victims," examines the treatment of victims by society and explains how victim justice differs from criminal justice.

Chapter 13, "Dealing with the Law-Abiding," critiques the various views on how the criminal justice system impacts and is affected by the law-abiding public. The influence of politics on the administration of justice is discussed. The different justice perspectives (social responsibility, social problems, and social engineering) are reviewed. In addition, the use of law and punishment as symbolic reassurance is introduced.

The text uses the following pedagogical devices within every chapter: *Key Concepts* and *Learning Objectives* at the beginning, with *Discussion Questions* at the end. In addition, an instructor's manual that includes multiple choice and true-false questions is available.

We hope that you find this primer to be a useful guide in exploring the complexities of crime and criminality.

ACKNOWLEDGMENTS

No text would ever be published were it just the authors' efforts. We have several people to whom we need to express our appreciation. The Prentice Hall editorial team is a group of dedicated professionals to whom we are greatly indebted: then Senior Editor, now president of Prentice Hall's Career, Health, Education, and Technology Division, Robin Baliszewski, who initially saw the merit in publishing such a primer; Executive Editor Kim Davies, who encouraged us to return to a concept that had previously given way to other projects; Development Editor Cheryl Adam, who worked with us throughout the writing and production process; and Production Liaison Adele Kupchik, Manufacturing Buyer Cathleen Petersen, Proofreader Muriel Adams, and Page Makeup Editor Naomi Sysak, who performed all those vital tasks needed to turn a raw manuscript into a finished product. We especially thank Copy Editor Laura Starrett and Production Editor Linda Pawelchak for their excellent editorial work. In addition, we wish to thank Melton E. Beane, Tidewater Community College; Chuck Brawner, Heartland Community College; Stephen Brodt, Ball State University; and Nicholas Irons, County College of Morris for the valuable insights and recommendations provided in their reviews.

We also want to thank our colleagues at the State University of West Georgia and the University of Texas–Pan American for their encouragement.

We particularly thank Dr. Florence Ferguson of the State University of West Georgia for coauthoring Chapters 3 and 4.

Last, we wish to thank our wives, Vi Hunter and Dr. Gail Dantzker, for their love, tolerance, and support.

Ronald D. Hunter
State University of West Georgia

Mark L. Dantzker
University of Texas–Pan American

CHAPTER 1

The Problem of Crime

▦ KEY CONCEPTS ▦

assault
burglary
codes of criminal procedure
conflict perspective
consensus perspective
corporate crime
crime statistics
criminal law
felony
index crimes
interactionist perspective
mala in se
mala prohibita
misdemeanors
morality
National Crime Victimization Survey
  (NCVS)

occupational crimes
organized crimes
political crimes
procedural law
professional crimes
property crimes
public order crimes
robbery
self-report surveys
sexual assault
state organized crimes
substantive law
theft-larceny
typologies
Uniform Crime Reports (UCR)
victimless crimes
violent crimes

▦ LEARNING OBJECTIVES ▦

After reading this chapter, the student should be able to:

1. Present and discuss the three perspectives on the nature of crime.

2. Define crime, criminal behavior, and criminality.

3. Define substantive law and procedural law and explain their relationship.

4. Define *mala in se* and *mala prohibita* offenses and provide examples of each.

5. Discuss the leading means of determining the extent of crime in the United States and describe their limitations.

6. Discuss the various costs of crime endured by citizens.

7. Present and discuss the various types of violent crime.

8. Present and discuss the various types of property crime.

9. Present and discuss the other types of crime categories in addition to violent and property crimes.

10. Present and discuss the various types of criminal offenders.

CRIME AS PHENOMENON

Crime is one of the most fascinating events or phenomena in our country. The media, in particular, seem to delight in regaling us with stories related to crime. For example, the cover of the April 21, 1997, issue of *U.S. News and World Report* pictures a baby in a striped prison uniform with the large-type words "Born Bad?" to draw attention to its story on how certain factors, particularly biology, may influence criminality. A little over a year later in its May 25, 1998, issue, the same publication's cover displayed a pair of handcuffs and cited a special report inside entitled "Why Crime Is Down: The Real Story." Their December 6, 1999, cover story was on crimes of the century.

The media perpetuate stories on crimes because the public is extremely interested in this subject. Among many citizens, crime is perceived as a major problem. For example, the Gallup Organization conducts numerous opinion surveys yearly. A consistent question in the surveys asks the respondent what he or she thinks is the most important problem facing this country today. The results from four surveys taken December 1997, April 1998, September 1998, and January 1999 showed that crime was among the top three public concerns along with education and ethical issues (www.gallup.com/poll/trends/ptproblem.asp).

There is little doubt that crime is an interesting subject. In addition to the criminal act itself and theories as to why crime occurs, interest exists in the characteristics of crime as well as in the characteristics of criminal behavior.

The Nature of Crime

What causes crime? Why does a person commit a crime? What is the best way to prevent crime? These are all important questions. However, to be able to truly answer these questions is a difficult task. Frank Hagan (1998) suggests that answering these types of questions is similar to asking "What causes sickness?" (p. 92). It is difficult primarily because there are so few common-alities other than that the criminal act is "a violation of criminal law" (p. 92).

Have you ever heard someone say, "That ought to be a crime" or "There should be a law against that" usually in conjunction with some type of behavior or action the individual has observed and of which he or she disapproved? While there are many unethical or immoral actions that might be considered criminal, not all are or can be. An interesting issue in the study of crime is the lack of consensus surrounding its development and why it occurs. This has lead to the development of three differing views of crime.

It is probably safe to say that the majority of people in this country believe that the intentional taking of another's life is murder, whereas not everyone would agree that smoking marijuana should be illegal. It is clear that there are many different perspectives on what constitutes a crime and how to respond to criminal behavior. These differences provide us with the three major categories of views regarding crime: consensus, interactionist, and conflict (Vold, Bernard, and Snipes, 1998).

The individual viewing crime from a *consensus perspective* views crimes as behaviors that are essentially harmful to the majority of citizens and agrees that these crimes should be controlled or prohibited by the existing criminal law. The consensus view looks at criminal law as a set of rules that expresses the norms of society, the will of the "majority," and that serves a social control function in restraining individuals who would take advantage of others for personal gain. The question with this view is whether those acts designated as criminal truly express the norms of the majority of society or of a select few (Roberson and Wallace, 1998).

The *interactionist perspective* accepts that criminal law defines the actions (or omissions) constituting a crime. However, the interactionist challenges the belief that the law represents the will of a majority of society. Instead, the interactionist views criminal law as being influenced by people who hold social power and use it to mold the law to reflect their interest. For example, the interactionist would say that the insurance industry has strongly influenced the creation of seat belt and child car seat laws (Vold, Bernard, and Snipes, 1998).

From the *conflict perspective,* criminal law is a means of protecting the power of the upper class at the expense of the poor. The conflict view is based on the premise that society is a collection of diverse groups that are in constant conflict and that certain groups are able to assert their power and use the criminal law to advance their interests. Ultimately, social conflict theorists believe that criminal law protects the "haves" from the "have nots" (Hagan, 1998).

How one defines crime and criminality is largely determined by how one views society. Each of these perspectives sees society and its laws in different lights. Furthermore, within these perspectives there are numerous disagreements on what constitutes crime and how society should respond to it.

Defining Crime

Many definitions of crime are used by criminologists, attorneys, and laypersons. From them, we have developed the following definition, which will be used throughout this text (the reader should note that this definition is limited to crime within democratic societies): *Crime is that which a democratically selected legislative body has determined to be unlawful activity (commission) or inactivity (omission), for which there is a proscribed legal sanction.*

To be criminal, one must have committed an unlawful act or failed to act in a manner required by law. *Criminal behavior may be viewed as any action or failure to act as defined by criminal laws.* These actions do not have to be heinous crimes such as murder or rape. Indeed, many of the activities that an ordinary citizen may have engaged in (or failed to engage in) would qualify as criminal behaviors. Many of us have willingly or unknowingly participated in behaviors that were criminal. This does not necessarily mean that we are "bad people." However, it does demonstrate that defining criminal laws and enforcing them is a more complex issue than many realize.

Criminality is said to occur when "certain behaviors have been transformed by society into crimes and people engaging in those behaviors have been identified as criminals" (Barlow, 2000, p. 17). In other words, when crime and criminal behavior occur, a state of criminality exists. Whether a serious felony or a simple misdemeanor, crimes occur on a regular basis within our society and are committed by all types of people (often unknowingly). It is this constancy of criminality within all regions of our nation and impacts of crime upon all levels of society that makes the problem of crime such a fascinating topic. In order to understand the nature of crime, we must first understand the nature of criminal law. For it is the legal definition of crime that ultimately creates crime.

The Nature of Criminal Law

One of the most difficult questions in criminal justice is, why are certain behaviors criminal while others are not? As discussed earlier, based on the differing views of crime, no clear-cut answer to this question exists. However, at least one common theme determines what is criminal: moral behavior (Lilly, Cullen, and Ball, 1995). Since the beginning of time, societies have tried to regulate morality, initially drawing from their religions. Because of these moral imperatives, societies eventually legislated laws and sanctions against certain activities. The issue, as societies developed and modernized, was deciding what was moral and acceptable behavior.

While today many would argue that determining what is criminal is still steeply based in religious and moral imperatives, the reality is that the decisions of those who pass laws (state and federal legislators) determine what is criminal. Often their decisions are influenced by lobbyists and special interest groups and are not necessarily a moral imperative but rather a desired behavior. Nonetheless, much of what is considered criminal behavior is either based on moral beliefs or social beliefs that the action in question is not acceptable. When such an action has been deemed unacceptable by a legislative body and made "criminal," then those who still participate in that action must be sanctioned.

Characteristics of Criminal Law

Criminal law is the legal code that attempts to control public behavior by defining what constitutes a crime. Criminal law has the following features: *Criminal law is political in its origins* (because government is charged with creating and enforcing criminal laws and government is by nature political). *Criminal law is specific in its construction* (criminal laws are very clear and to the point about which behaviors are acceptable and which are not). *Criminal law is uniform in its application* (meaning that, theoretically, the law is applied equally to everyone). Finally, *criminal law contains provisions for penal sanctions* (it directs how a person who has committed a crime should be dealt with).

Ultimately, the reasons we have criminal law are to avoid or prevent society from degenerating into anarchy and chaos, to promote widely shared social values, and (according to conflict perspective proponents) to express the more narrow interests of the powerful segments of society. How law is imposed and enforced is based on two types of criminal law: substantive and procedural (Dantzker, 1998).

Substantive law explains what is criminal and what the sanctions for violations will be. Substantive laws are commonly called *felonies* (any offense punishable by more than one year of incarceration in a state or federal prison) and *misdemeanors* (offenses punishable by a fine or one year or less of incarceration in a city or county jail). The classification of a crime, as well as the punishment, is determined by statute. The substantive law spells out all the requisite information needed by governmental agents (police, prosecutors, and judges) to define a behavior as criminal and to provide sanctions for such behavior.

Procedural law regulates how to uphold or enforce substantive law. All states and the federal government have *codes of criminal procedure.* These codes delineate how government officials will enforce the substantive laws. The failure of government officials to follow procedural law can often result in the dismissal of a case. Within U.S. society, citizens are protected by both state constitutions and the U.S. Constitution.

Sources of Crime Statistics

Although a variety of sources of crime statistics exist, the best known and most often used source is the *Uniform Crime Reports* (UCR) compiled and reported by the Federal Bureau of Investigation. Each month, local law enforcement agencies voluntarily submit the number of offenses reported by their agency to the FBI. However, since there are several hundred types of crimes due to the variety of laws from state to state, not all crimes can be included. Therefore, the UCR is primarily concerned with *index crimes.* These include murder and non-negligent manslaughter, forcible rape, robbery, aggravated assault, burglary, larceny-theft, arson, and auto theft. These crimes are reported even if there are no arrests and no recovery of property and whether or not prosecution occurs.

Other data reported in the UCR are arrest rates, which include age, gender, and ethnicity/race of offender. Using the UCR, we can examine (albeit tentatively) a variety of crime trends in the United States. (as discussed previously). Although the UCR provides us with a variety of crime data, the following flaws must be acknowledged:

1. Reporting practices by the police

2. Lack of reporting by victims

3. Improper classification

4. Downgrading charges/plea bargaining

5. Under/overreporting by police

6. Political manipulation

7. Technical flaws (inaccurate volume of crime, population base)

Although the UCR is perhaps the most popular source of crime data, its potential inaccuracies have lead to questions of its validity and an accusation that it leaves a "black hole" of criminality (Dantzker, 1998). In an attempt to offset that lack of knowledge, there are two other major sources of crime data: The National Crime Victimization Survey and self-reports.

The National Crime Victimization Survey

The shortcomings of the UCR led to the creation of a survey that bypasses the police and goes directly to victims. The *National Crime Victimization Survey* (NCVS) is believed by some (e.g., Doerner and Lab, 1998) to provide a more credible set of data on the type and frequency of criminal victimization than the UCR. The UCR relies on the collection and reporting of data to the FBI; the NCVS directly contacts a representative sample of people to determine whether they have been victims. From this information, data are extrapolated to fit the general population.

Unlike the UCR, the NCVS provides characteristics of victims (age, sex, race/ethnicity, marital status, annual family income, employment status, and occupational group). However, it is not a good source for characteristics of offenders. The NCVS is believed to provide a better indication of the incidence, seriousness, and cost of the types of crime that permits us to gauge fluctuations in the rates of these crimes over time and across geographical areas more precisely than the UCR.

Self-Report Surveys

Self-report surveys supplement the other two sources and provide an alternative to obtaining data that cannot be derived from official statistics. In these types of reports, individuals (often young people) are asked whether they have ever engaged in criminal behaviors. Advocates of self-report studies argue that they enable us to learn more about crimes not reported to official sources. The findings of self-report studies were instrumental in the development of labeling theory, an influential theory that will be described in chapter 6. Flaws of these studies include the population (usually juveniles attending school who are coerced into participating), honesty (resulting from distrust of the researchers and fears regarding anonymity), and incompleteness (inability to ask about all types of crimes).

National Incident-Based Reporting System

In 1982, a Bureau of Justice Statistics and FBI task force conducted a study on how to improve the UCR program. The results of the study led to the creation of a more comprehensive data collection system, the *National Incident-Based Reporting System* (NIBRS) (Reaves, 1993). Unlike the UCR, which primarily focused on index crimes, the NIBRS looks at more categories of crimes divided into two major groups of offenses (Table 1–1). The NIBRS is designed to collect

TABLE 1–1   The NIBRS Offense Categories

Group A Offenses	
Arson	Homicide offenses
Assault offenses	Murder/nonnegligent manslaughter
Aggravated assault	Negligent manslaughter
Simple assault	Justifiable homicide
Intimidation	Kidnaping/abduction
Bribery	Larceny/theft offenses
Burglary/breaking and entering	Pocketpicking
Counterfeiting/forgery	Purse snatching
Destruction/damage/vandalism	Theft from building
Drug/narcotic offense	Theft from coin-op machines
Drug/narcotic violations	Theft from motor vehicle
Drug equipment violations	Theft of motor vehicle parts
Embezzlement	All other larceny
Extortion/blackmail	Motor vehicle theft
Fraud offenses	Pornography/obscene materials
False pretenses/swindles	Prostitution offenses
Confidence games	Prostitution
Credit card/ATM fraud	Assisting/promoting prostitution
Impersonation	Robbery
Welfare fraud	Sex offense, forcible
Wire fraud	Forcible rape
Gambling offenses	Forcible sodomy
Betting/wagering	Sexual assault w/an object
Operating/promoting	Forcible fondling
Assisting gambling	Sex offenses, nonforcible
Gambling equipment violations	Stolen property offenses
Sports tampering	Weapons law violations

TABLE 1–1   The NIBRS Offense Categories *(Continued)*

Group B offenses

Bad checks
Curfew/loitering/vagrancy
Disorderly conduct
Driving under the influence
Drunkenness
Liquor law violations
Nonviolent family offense
Peeping Tom
Runaway
Trespassing
All other offenses

Source: Adapted from Reaves, 1993.

more information than the UCR and will eventually replace the UCR. Whether the NIBRS will eliminate the problems currently observed among the various data sources is yet to be seen.

The Extent of Crime

As we saw in the previous section, several means are available to determine the incidences of crime. Despite these efforts, there is still a great deal of uncertainty among scholars as to the true extent of crime and the actual number of crime victims in the United States within any particular period of time. Fortunately, we can track trends by reviewing the changes within the various methods of data gathering. The good news at the time of this writing is that crime rates for both property offenses and violent crimes continue to decline.

According to the Uniform Crime Reports (Federal Bureau of Investigation, 1999), 12,475,634 crimes were reported in 1998. Of these incidents, 12 percent were violent crimes and 88 percent were property crimes (Table 1–2). The National Crime Victimization Survey (Bureau of Justice Statistics, 1999) yielded a much higher finding of 31.3 million crimes that were said by victims to have occurred in 1998. Of these 26 percent were reported to be violent crimes and 73 percent were said to be property offenses. While the numbers in themselves may appear impersonal, they represent individuals who have been harmed financially, physically, and/or emotionally as crime victims.

TABLE 1–2 UCR Crime Incidents for 1998 (in percentages)

Total Number of Crimes	12,475,634
Murder	0.1
Rape	0.7
Robbery	3.6
Aggravated Assault	7.8
Burglary	18.7
Larceny/Theft	59.1
Auto Theft	9.9

Source: Crime in the United States (Federal Bureau of Investigation, 1999).

To put the incidents of crime in perspective, one should consider that the UCR crime figures in Table 1–2 reflect an average national incidence of 4,615 crimes per 100,000 persons. In particular they signify the following victimization rates: 1 in 12 of children 12 to 15, 1 in 357 of elderly aged 65 and over, 1 in 24 of blacks, 1 in 28 of whites, 1 in 23 of males, and 1 in 33 of females. In addition 47 percent of murder victims are black, 49 percent are white, and 2 percent are from other racial groups. Seventy-five percent of murder victims were male, and 63 percent were under age 35 with 11 percent under the age of 18 (Federal Bureau of Investigation, 1999). It is obvious from these data that despite the decline in criminal occurrences, millions of Americans are victimized each year.

The Cost of Crime

Regardless of how it is reported, the fact is that crime is a problem and has dire consequences on society and citizens (Doerner and Lab, 1998). According to the Federal Bureau of Investigation (1999), the costs of criminal victimization in the United States exceeded $15.8 billion in 1998. Of this amount, only about 35 percent was recovered by law enforcement officials. These costs reflect only the value of property taken and do not reflect the costs of medical treatment for victims of violent crimes. Nor do they reflect the costs of property and/or injuries in incidents not reported to the police. It is not unreasonable to assume that the financial consequences of crime victimizations in America could be several times higher. The cost of crime is high, and it is therefore imperative to restrict criminal behavior. Chapter 12 provides a more detailed discussion regarding the costs of crime.

CRIME TYPOLOGIES

While there is considerable agreement that certain behaviors should be termed *crimes*, there is even greater disagreement as to whether other behaviors should be termed *criminal*. Nor is there consensus on how society should respond to the various types of crime and criminal behaviors. In classifying crime and criminal behavior it is helpful to make use of typologies. *Typologies* have been described as a "framework and theoretical construct used to describe and compare different forms of criminal behavior" (Vito and Holmes, 1994, p. 228). Hagan (1998, p. 92) suggests that typologies have two purposes: to be used as (1) a scientific classificatory system or (2) a heuristic scheme (an educational tool). It is for the second purpose that we offer the use of typologies. An interesting issue is that except for classifying a crime as either a felony or misdemeanor, property or violent, little consensus exists as to how to classify crime. The purpose of the following sections is to acquaint the reader with the many types of crime and criminal behavior that exist within a democratic society.

In this text we offer a broad typology of crimes adapted from Marshall Clinard and Richard Quinney's (1986) typology of criminal behaviors. The typology includes violent, property, public order, political, occupational, corporate, organized, and professional crimes. These crimes are known as *mala in se* crimes because most lawmakers and the public agree that these behaviors should be criminalized.

Violent Crimes

Violent crimes are viewed as *any type of intentional action that causes some form of bodily injury or death to another.* Murder is the leader in this area but is most certainly not the only violent crime (Doerner and Lab, 1998). Murder may range from a thoughtless blow struck while under emotional distress to killings by hired professional "hitmen." Murders may be as simple as "crimes of passion" committed by angry lovers or complex serial killings by sexual sadists.

Probably the second best known violent crime is sexual assault. Although many of today's statutes refer to rape as just one form of sexual assault, forcible rape is the only one tracked in the FBI crime index. *Sexual assault, in any form, is the uninvited touching of the genitals, the unwilling touching of the genitals of another, or the penetration of another in a sexual manner.* Because it is against the victim's will and requires physical contact between the offender and victim, sexual assault is a violent crime regardless of the degree of injury sustained (Schmalleger, 1999). Sexual assault offenses may include sexual abuse of children, the elderly, the mentally incompetent, and the physically challenged. It may include the actions of serial rapists, pedophiles, and sexual sadists, who inflict severe physical harm or death on their victims. Sexual assault most definitely includes "date rape" whether committed by force or with the use of drugs to overcome the victim's resistance.

Another well-known violent crime is assault. While today much attention is paid to domestic assault, *any unwanted, intentional contact made by one person against another is an assault.* Because of the varying degrees of assault (simple unwanted touching to severe bodily injury), every state has its own assault typology (for example, in Texas an assault can range from a Class C misdemeanor to a first-degree felony).

Finally, the last violent crime we discuss is robbery. Many people find it difficult to think of a robbery as being violent, in comparison to say murder or assault. However, *the act of robbery requires the physical taking of property from another either by threat of or by use of force.* Even though it is done for economic motives, it is the use (or threat) of force that places robbery in the violent crime category.

Undoubtedly, some people might suggest that other crimes could be placed under the violent crime category. However, if one closely examines the four crimes listed here, one might conclude that each crime could be a typology in itself (i.e., assault).

Property Crimes

As with violent crimes, numerous property crimes exist. Regardless of their particular natures, *property crimes are any crime in which one person has intentionally deprived another person of his or her right to that property by either destroying or taking the property.* Many different crimes appear within this category, but three of the most common are: arson, burglary, and theft-larceny (Albanese, 2000).

Arson is the intentional destruction of property by flammable process (e.g., gasoline or dynamite). Arson is often committed for profit (e.g., insurance fraud) or for destroying evidence (of another crime previously committed). *Burglary involves the unlawful entry into a building, vehicle, or machine with the intent to commit some type of criminal action,* such as stealing property or assaulting someone. *Theft-larceny is simply the unlawful taking of another's property in order to deprive that individual of the item.* Some of the more commonly recognized types of theft include shoplifting, pickpocketing, embezzlement, passing bad checks, and motor vehicle theft (Barlow, 2000).

Public Order Crimes

Although violent and property crimes are the two most prevalent categories of crime, a variety of other activities can be identified and classified. One such set of activities might be referred to as public order crimes. *Public order crimes are those activities that would disrupt or interfere with socially acceptable behavior.* Two of the best known public order crimes are disorderly conduct and riots. Both crimes can be committed in a variety of ways, but regardless of how they are committed, the question of criminality ultimately comes down to whether the activity is disturbing or interfering with acceptable behavior. Additionally, behavior or activity that could lead to harm to others may be included (e.g., yelling "fire" in a crowded movie theater) (Siegel, 1998).

Still another group of public order crimes includes victimless crimes. *Victimless crimes do not have direct victims but are criminalized because they have been deemed to be socially unactable.* Prostitution, drug use, and unauthorized gambling are the main victimless crimes. These crimes are also known as *mala prohibita crimes* in that they are crimes solely because of a ban imposed by a legislative body that felt such activities to be hazardous to society. They differ from *mala in se* crimes, such as the violent crimes discussed earlier, for which there is a consensus among the population that they are evil actions in and of themselves.

Political Crimes

In 1972 individuals broke into a room in the Watergate Hotel, in Washington, D.C., that housed information about the Democratic Party. That break-in eventually led to the resignation of then-President Richard M. Nixon. Although the act itself was a burglary (property crime), the purpose of the act had political ramifications, thus making it a political crime. *A political crime involves any activity that violates the laws of government.* The attaining of information about one political party by another using illegal means could be viewed as a political crime (Schmalleger, 1999). Social conflict theorists also argue that political crimes include the use of lawmaking and enforcement to maintain political power.

Occupational Crimes

Occupational crimes are committed in the course of one's employment. Again, because almost all crimes can be either violent or property, they may carry the corresponding label (i.e., theft, burglary, assault), but because they are committed as part of one's work, the acts can be viewed as occupational crimes

(Siegel, 1998). A mailperson who, rather than delivering the mail, throws it in the trash or a police officer who in response to a burglary call steals items from the scene would be examples of occupational crime. Embezzlement of a client's funds by an attorney or accountant would also classify as occupational crime.

Corporate Crime

Perhaps one of the most difficult of crimes to prosecute falls under the category of corporate crimes. *Corporate crimes are criminal activities conducted during the course of doing business or that result from inappropriate business practices* (Hagan, 1998). Corporate crimes differ from occupational crimes in that occupational crimes are committed by an individual or a group for self-gain, whereas corporate crimes are committed by groups of individuals on behalf of their company or organization. While corporate crimes are *white-collar crimes* (involving professionals or administrators), occupational crimes may be either white-collar or blue-collar crimes (involving lower level employees).

The problem with corporate crimes is that prosecution of those responsible is often difficult because the crime was committed under the umbrella of the corporation. An example of this dilemma was that of the Ford Motor Company and the exploding Ford Pinto gas tank. The company was aware of the danger in how and where the gas tank was mounted and that a rear-end collision could cause a rupture of the tank and possible fire, but it continued to manufacture the vehicle in that way. An accident did occur in which the occupant was killed because the car exploded into flames. Ford Motor Company was prosecuted and found guilty of negligent manslaughter, the penalty for which generally includes a term in prison. However, in this case no one did any jail time; instead Ford paid a hefty fine. Similar investigations have taken place in regard to recent deaths from faulty Firestone tires.

Organized Crime

Organized crime can be any criminal activity that is committed in an orderly and continuous fashion by a group or organization created to accomplish that purpose. The victimless crimes of prostitution, drug use, and gambling are three of the most common activities that can be a function of organized crime. Whereas the majority of crimes in the other categories are committed by individuals, organized crime is committed by several individuals acting in concert (Hagan, 1998). The majority of organized crimes involve the provision of goods or services to those desiring them despite their illegality and are deemed to be public order crimes.

Professional Crimes

The last category we offer is *professional crimes.* Like corporate, occupational, and organized crimes, the crimes committed here may be found within the previous categories. Almost any crime found elsewhere can fit here, the qualifier is that *the crime is being committed as the primary means of financial support for the offender.* An example would be burglaries in which only easily saleable or negotiable items (e.g., cash or jewelry) are taken by people who sell such goods to support themselves.

Eight categories were offered within our typology of crimes. However, it should be evident from these categories that several other typologies are possible. For most of us, there may be little need or desire to type crime beyond the misdemeanor/felony and violent/property dichotomies. However, typologies are useful for criminologists and criminal justice practitioners in understanding and responding to the myriad of crimes found within our society.

CRIMINAL TYPOLOGIES

Earlier we noted that the interest in typologies extends more to criminal behavior than the crimes. In the preceding section, a typology of crimes was presented. Now we present a typology of criminal behaviors. As with our crime typology, our criminal typology is adapted from Clinard and Quinney's (1986) typology.

Violent Personal Criminals

The violent personal criminal is someone who is unable to control hostility or allows anger toward others to erupt into violence. Although this person may have a long history of violent behaviors toward others, because crime is not a part of his or her career, the violent offender usually does not see him- or herself as a criminal. The violence is often viewed as a justifiable response to another's behavior. Thus, the violent offender frequently does not accept that what he or she has done is criminal. Domestic abusers blame their spouses for "provoking them." Mean drunks often engage in barroom brawls but "really didn't intend to hurt anyone." Pedophiles were "seduced" by their young victims. Racists who commit a "hate crime" did so because they have been "wronged by society." The list could go on ad nauseam, but the reader can see how a history of violent behaviors is often rationalized by the offender.

Occasional Property Criminals

Occasional property criminals do not engage in theft or burglary on a regular basis. They will commit their crimes as a means of obtaining thrills, to strike back against perceived wrongs done to them, to obtain desired items that they could not legitimately afford, or to augment their incomes. As with violent criminals, property criminals may also rationalize their behavior as necessary. Oftentimes the behavior is said to be committed as a means of survival and as such criminals do not identify or associate themselves with "real" criminals, that is, those who commit crime as a way of life or for the thrill.

Public Order Criminals

Public order criminals live in a state of ambiguity. They neither regard their behavior as criminal nor do they have a clearly defined criminal career. Public order criminals disagree with local, state, and/or national prohibitions against a specific victimless crime. They may be totally conformist in their other activities but frequently engage in what they believe should be legitimate behaviors. Purchasing drugs, soliciting prostitution, or participating in illegal gambling operations are but three of the more common public order crimes in which many otherwise "law-abiding citizens" participate. The problems that arise from such participation are that it supports organized crime organizations and creates a disrespect for other legal prohibitions on the part of both those who participate and those who view the offenders as role models.

Political Criminals

Like violent, property, and public order criminals, political criminals do not identify with being a criminal or believe that they have committed any crimes. Two types of political criminals exist. The first type is the person employed as a governmental official who abuses his or her position for personal benefit, to cause harm to those perceived to be enemies, or to provide undeserved aid or preferential treatment to associates. While such political criminals may fall within another category of offender (i.e., drug use in their private lives), they are criminal only when a violation of law regulating the government is committed. Your position in the debate about former President Clinton's alleged behavior with several female accusers and his relationship with Monica Lewinsky was based on whether or not you thought his behaviors were private actions or violations of his office.

The second type of political criminal believes that the government itself has acted in an unjust or illegal way, provoking his or her response. This person engages in opposition actions deemed to be criminal by the government which may involve simple sit-ins or banned demonstrations, or may result in actual terrorist activities, such as the bombing of the federal building in Oklahoma City. It is the perception of this offender that the criminal label is attached solely because of the perceived threat he or she may pose against the government.

Occupational Criminals

The occupational criminal may commit petty theft by stealing pens and paper from work. This individual can easily rationalize such behavior as inconsequential and will often consider it as a perk of the job. This type of occupational criminal (and there are many) usually accepts the conventional norms and values of society and has little or no self-conception of being criminal. Indeed, most would be enraged if they were accused of being criminals. On the opposite end of the spectrum are those people who use their positions to obtain considerable fortunes by selling information and/or by granting favors to others for personal gain. Like the offender who "borrows" items from work, this occupational criminal may also see his or her actions as being merely perks of the job.

Corporate Criminals

As discussed in the previous section, corporate crimes are among the most difficult crimes to prosecute. Corporate criminals are generally white-collar criminals (professionals or administrators) who seek to advance their company or organization by engaging in illegal practices. These practices may involve such activities as bribing government officials to get lucrative grants, circumventing state or federal environmental regulations, conspiring to fix prices, or developing an illegal monopoly. Often these offenders are unrepentant, they consider what they did as merely "good business." In addition, the prosecutions that occur often nab only underlings who will or must "take the heat" on behalf of their superiors. Last, many such criminals may see the fines imposed as being worth the profits attained through their illegal actions.

Organized Criminals

All of us have seen movies or televison programs that depict organized criminals. These may range from the old Mafia movies—from *Some Like It Hot* to *The Godfather* to *Goodfellas*—to depictions of the violent worlds of contemporary drug lords. These depictions are distorted in that they tend to overstate the amount of violence used and the luxuriant lifestyles of organized criminals. However, they are accurate in that they demonstrate the difficulties law enforcement faces in thwarting the illegal behaviors demanded by the numerous public order criminals within our society.

Despite pretensions to the contrary ("I just provide a service for the public"), organized criminals generally accept their criminality. Crime is pursued as a way of life. The criminal activity may often begin as minor but usually progresses to major criminality. The progression aids in the development of isolation from mainstream society, and this isolation, along with the huge sums of money that can be made by those in the higher echelons of the organization, ensures continued involvement.

Professional Criminals

Other than the organized criminal, the professional criminal is probably the only criminal type who not only recognizes and accepts his or her status as a criminal but actually takes pride in it. Generally this individual has a well-developed criminal career engaging in specialized crimes. The desired outcome of the criminality is primarily economic gain. Professional criminals include the romantic-sounding "cat burglars" who steal from the homes of the affluent despite the presence of high-tech security systems, as well as their less talented colleagues who burglarize small businesses in order to "earn" their living. Other professional criminals might include bank robbers, con artists, shoplifters, blackmailers, or any others who make a living from their criminal activities.

These typologies provide insights into the varieties of crimes and criminals found within U.S. society. The first typologies offered brief insights into what may influence specific types of crime. The second explored how certain types of criminals might perceive their criminality. From an applied perspective, neither is of much value unless we understand what originally led to the criminal behavior and what may be done in response to it. We explore these issues in the following chapters.

▨▨▨ SUMMARY ▨▨▨

There is little doubt that crime is an interesting subject. In addition to the criminal act itself and theories as to why crime occurs, there is an interest in characteristics of crime and how to label and classify it. While there are some actions people might wish were criminal, not all are. Crime is defined as *that which legislative bodies define as activities (commission) or failures to act (omission) that are unlawful.* Participation in such an act or failure (to act) means an individual has committed a crime. An interesting issue in the study of crime is the lack of consensus surrounding its development and its causes. This has lead to the development of three differing views on the nature of crime: consensus, interactionist, and conflict.

Regardless of the view, the reality is that when a criminal act has been committed, punishing or sanctioning the offender is a priority. However, determining what is criminal must be accomplished first. Much of what is considered criminal behavior is either based on moral or social beliefs that the action is not acceptable. When such an action has been deemed unacceptable and made "criminal," then those who still participate in that action must be sanctioned.

Criminal offenders exist because of criminal law, which can be viewed as being political in its origins, specific in its construction, and uniform in its application and contains provisions for penal sanctions. Criminal law, with respect to policy and process, is divided into substantive and procedural law. Substantive law explains what is criminal. Procedural law explains how to uphold or enforce substantive law.

Because law is the basis of societal interaction, the occurrence of crimes creates public interest. Of particular interest is the extent of crime. We attempt to determine how much crime exists through crime statistics. The best known and most frequently used source of crime statistics are the Uniform Crime Reports (UCR). The National Crime Victimization Survey (NCVS) and self-surveys are other means of gathering crime statistics. The newest attempt to collect crime data is the National Incident-Based Reporting System (NIBRS), which has been designed to collect more information than the UCR and will eventually replace it.

Last, we presented several examples of crime and criminal offenders based on our adaptions of Clinard and Quinney's typologies. The first included violent crimes, property crimes, public order crime, political crimes, corporate crimes, organized crimes, and professional crimes. The second provided a brief overview of the criminals who engage in those crimes.

▩▩▩ DISCUSSION QUESTIONS ▩▩▩

1. Considering the three views of crime, which one seems to best represent current societal views? Which view seems the most prudent? Is there another way to view crime?

2. There are many reasons why society sanctions criminal behavior. Are these reasons valid? Are there other reasons? Do the reasons seem to truly reflect today's s society?

3. Using only the index crimes, identify at least five characteristics you would use to describe crime.

4. Of what value are crime trends? What types of trends would you look for if the information was wanted by a police department? A prosecutor's office? The mayor?

5. How would you classify criminal behavior? What would be the focus of your typology?

REFERENCES

Albanese, J. (2000). *Criminal justice 2000 update.* Needham, MA: Allyn & Bacon.

Barlow, H. D. (2000). *Criminal justice in America.* Upper Saddle River, NJ: Prentice Hall.

Clinard, M. B., and Quinney, R. (1986). *Criminal behavior systems: A typology,* 2nd ed. Cincinnati, OH: Anderson.

Cannon, A. (1999, December 6). Crimes of the century. *U.S. News and World Report,* pp. 40–51.

Dantzker, M. L. (1998). *Criminology and criminal justice: Comparing, contrasting, and intertwining disciplines.* Woburn, MA: Butterworth-Heinemann.

Doerner, W. G., and Lab, S. P. (1998). *Victimology,* 2nd ed. Cincinnati, OH: Anderson.

Federal Bureau of Investigation. (1999). *Crime in the United States, 1998.* Washington, DC: U.S. Government Printing Office.

Gallup Organization Website. (2000). www.gallup.com/poll/trends/ptproblem.asp.

Hagan, F. E. (1998). *Introduction to criminology,* 4th ed. Chicago: Nelson-Hall.

Lilly, J. R., Cullen, F. T., and Ball, R.A. (1995). *Criminological theory: Context and consequences,* 2nd ed. Thousand Oaks, CA: Sage.

Reaves, B. A. (1993). "Using NIBRS data to analyze violent crime." *Bureau of Justice Statistics Technical Report.* Washington, DC: U.S. Department of Justice.

Roberson, C., and Wallace, H. (1998). *Introduction to criminology.* Incline Village, NV: Copperhouse.

Schmalleger, F. (1999). *Criminal justice today,* 5th ed. Upper Saddle River, NJ: Prentice Hall.

Siegel, L. J. (1998). *Criminology: Theories, patterns and typologies,* 6th ed. Belmont, CA: West.

Sourcebook of Criminal Justice Statistics. (1998). Washington, DC: U.S. Government Printing Office.

Vito, G. F., and Holmes, R. M. (1994). *Criminology: Theory, research, and policy.* Belmont, CA: Wadsworth.

Vold, G. B., Bernard, T. J., and Snipes, J. B. (1998). *Theoretical criminology,* 4th ed. New York: Oxford.

Witkin, G. (1998, May 25). Why crime is down (special report): The real story. *U.S. News and World Report,* pp. 28–40.

Wray, H. (1997, April 21). Born bad? *U.S. News amd World Report,* pp. 72–80.

The Study of Crime

▦ KEY CONCEPTS ▦

aggravating circumstances
atavism
classical school
criminological theory
criminologist
criminology
deterrence
determinism
due process
equity
free will
general deterrence
hedonistic calculus
justicology
just deserts
interdisciplinary model

legal model
medical model
mitigating circumstances
neoclassical school
penology
political model
positive school
social contract
social conflict
sociological model
sociology of law
specific deterrence
structural functionalism
Twentieth Century Rehabilitative Ideal
utilitarianism
victimology

▦ LEARNING OBJECTIVES ▦

After reading this chapter, the student should be able to:

1. Define criminology and describe the various issues explored within the study of criminology.

2. Compare and contrast the five models of criminology.

3. Discuss the contributions of Cesare Beccaria.

4. Discuss the contributions of Jeremy Bentham.

5. Describe the tenets and impact of the classical school.

6. Discuss how the neoclassical approach revised the classical school.

7. Explain what is meant by "just deserts."

8. Explain what determinism is.

9. Discuss who Cesare Lombroso was and describe his contributions to criminology.

10. Describe the tenets and impacts of the positive school.

11. Describe the current status of criminology.

12. Explain how current issues impact upon the study of criminology.

INTRODUCTION TO CRIMINOLOGY

Conceptually, criminology has existed for more than two hundred years (Dantzker, 1998). Yet, as an academic field of study, it is still relatively new. For many years, criminology was a subfield within sociology. The majority of early criminologists were sociologists who studied crime and its place in and impact on society. Many of today's criminologists still acquire a sociological education, but because of a movement in the 1950s to separate criminology from sociology, there are existing academic programs that are "strictly criminology. What led to the beginning of the separation, perhaps a catalyst for this movement, was C. Ray Jeffery's (1956) critical analysis of criminology, "The Structure of American Criminological Thinking." Yet, "the truer emergence of criminology appears to have begun in the late 1960s as sociology and other social sciences were undergoing criticisms and change" (Dantzker, 1998, p. 8).

Defining Criminology

Providing a definition of criminology is easy, agreeing on one is not. Every criminology textbook, and a majority of criminal justice textbooks, offers a definition of criminology. While acknowledging the validity of other definitions, this consensus definition of criminology offered by Dantzker

(1998) will serve our purposes: *"Criminology is the scientific approach to the study of crime as a social phenomenon, that is, the theoretical application involving the study of the nature and extent of criminal behavior"* (p. 27).

With this definition, it can be said that a major objective of criminology is developing general and testable principles. These principles are intended to be used as building blocks of the body of knowledge relating to the process of law, crime, punishment, and treatment.

The Study of Criminology

Defining criminology takes us to the next step, the study of criminology. Because criminology encompasses a variety of other social sciences, such as anthropology, biology, economics, history, sociology, psychology, and political science, it tends to project "a multidisciplinary persona" (Dantzker, 1998, p. 28). By studying criminology, one may explore a variety of issues that include:

1. The creation and use of laws in society

2. Examination of the patterns of crime

3. Causation of crime and criminality

4. Societal response and reaction to criminality

5. The administration of justice

6. Custody and punishment of those accused and convicted of criminality

7. Treatment or rehabilitation of those labeled criminal

8. Treatment and consideration for victims of crime

Individuals who study criminology are generally called *criminologists* and may focus on one or all of five speciality areas of criminological study. These areas include

1. *Sociology of law,* which is the understanding of how laws are created and enacted, modified, and applied

2. *Criminological theory,* which focuses on the causes and consequences of crime and criminal behavior

3. *Penology,* which is the study of punishment, treatment, and correctional techniques

4. *Justicology,* which is the study of the criminal justice system, its components and processes

5. *Victimology,* which is the study of crime victims, the relationships with offenders and how society responds to their needs.

The Five Models of Criminology

The study of criminology can be even more specialized by beginning with a *legal model* of criminology, the roots of which may best be found in the *classical school* of criminology. The main tenets of the classical school are that an individual is bound to society by mutual *social contract;* that individuals have free will to make their own choices to act, that decisions are rationally made based upon the seeking of pleasure and avoidance of pain; and that punishment should be used as a deterrent to criminal behavior, meting out identical punishments for identical crimes (Albanese, 2000).

Criminologists who take the legal approach to criminology accept that individuals freely choose to commit crimes. They are interested in how the legal system deals with violators, an approach much different from that of the medical approach to criminology. (The *classical school of criminology* is discussed in detail later in this chapter.)

The *medical model* of criminology primarily centers on the *positive school of criminology,* which attributes criminal behavior to internal and external influences that limit or prohibit rational thinking and/or freedom of choice. The medical model focuses on biological elements that include physical structure, heredity, and genetic and biochemical explanations for criminal behavior. This approach could encompass psychological reasons for criminal behavior. This approach also offers one of the oldest explanations for crime and criminality. Rather than using punishment based upon the severity of the offense to deter criminals, the medical model emphasizes treatment based upon the needs of the offender. While biological explanations have been unpopular with sociologically trained criminologists, the concepts of limited choice and treatment for offenders have been widely accepted. The medical model is used to provide individualized treatment for offenders and has seen a resurgence among theorists as biosocial explanations for criminal behavior have emerged. (This model is discussed later in the chapter.)

The *sociological model* is similar to the medical approach in that it focuses on reasons for criminal behavior, usually finding that such behaviors arise from some type of social error or problem (Schmalleger, 1999). This approach is probably the most popular among contemporary criminologists because it allows them to study a wide variety of possible causes for criminality, such as upbringing, environment, economics, peer socialization, social structure, and other societal issues. Numerous theories have been developed to help provide explanations for crime and criminal behavior within the sociological approach to criminology.

Within the sociological explanations there are two distinct theoretical categories. *Structural functionalism* holds that society as a whole is sound but that there are anomalies that impact upon individuals and groups, leading to criminality. The emphasis of structural functionalism is to identify those conditions within society that may cause criminal behavior and seek to eliminate them.

A second perspective that evolved within the sociological model is known as the *social conflict* or *political model* of criminology. Social conflict theorists argue that crime is the product of conflicts among members of society. Rather than seeking to address social issues that might impact on individual and group criminality, social conflict theorists either see crime as the natural product of societal power struggles or call for the restructuring of society (such as the elimination of capitalism) in order to achieve a just and equitable social order.

Finally, many criminologists are interested in looking at a mixed group of reasons for criminality and how the legal system affects this behavior. This is an *interdisciplinary model* of criminology, where more than one possible area of inquiry is considered. This multifactor approach emphasizes the interaction of various individual and environmental influences on crime and criminality (Jeffery, 1990). The various models of criminology are displayed within Table 2–1.

Overall, regardless of which approach to the study of criminology is taken, all are steeped in theory. These theories have been formed based on research conducted by criminologists. More thorough explanations of the many theories are provided within the next several chapters. The final chapters then explore their applications in dealing with crime and criminality.

THE CLASSICAL SCHOOL OF CRIMINOLOGY

As previously noted, criminology, as a formal field of study, has only existed since the late 1950s. However, as a field of interest or a social question, it has existed much longer. W.V. Pelfrey (1980) advised that "criminology, as a social focus, emerged with the publication of Cesare Beccaria's *Essay on Crimes and Punishment* in 1764" (p. 1).

TABLE 2–1 The Five Models of Criminology

	Legal Model	Medical Model	Sociological Model	Political Model	Interdisciplinary Model
School	Classical school	Positive school	Positive school	Positive school	Mixture of schools
Orientation	Legal orientation	Biological/psychological orientation	Sociological orientation	Sociological/political orientation	Integrated orientation
View on Reason	Rational thinking	Limited reason	Limited reason	Limited reason	Rationality varies with approach used
View on Free Will	Freedom of choice	Limited or no choice	Limited or no choice	Limited or no choice	Amount of choice varies
Solution to Crime	Punishment based upon offense	Treatment based upon offender need	Treatment based upon offender need	Social change based upon societal needs	Combination based upon approach used

THE CONTRIBUTIONS OF CESARE BECCARIA

Cesare Bonesana the Marchese di Beccaria was an eighteenth-century Italian philosopher and lawyer. In his *Essay on Crimes and Punishment,* Beccaria (1963) suggested that an individual had a "social contract" with society in which he or she was bound to society by consent and vice versa. A key aspect of this social contract was *free will,* one's ability to exercise choice. Beccaria believed that a human being was generally a rational being who sought pleasure and tried desperately to avoid pain (Beccaria, 1963). His writings were in response to the extreme and inequitable nature of punishment during this time. Torture, brandings, mutilation, banishment, and death were common sentences. In addition, punishment was meted out disproportionately, with the nobility receiving light, if any, punishments for offenses while the poor were severely punished for the same offense.

Based upon Beccaria's writings, the first recognizable criminological approach to criminal behavior and society's response would emerge. Beccaria identified three types of crimes that warranted punishment: crimes that threatened the security of the state; crimes that injured citizens or their property; and crimes that ran contrary to the social order. In responding to these offenses, he argued that the punishment should fit the crime: Property offenses warranted payment of monetary fines; crimes inflicting personal injuries demanded corporal punishment; serious crimes against the state might warrant the death penalty, but only in exceptional cases. Beccaria viewed excessive use of the death penalty as "war waged by society against its citizens" (Schmalleger, 1999, p.159).

In addition to making punishment appropriate to the crime, Beccaria (1963) called for equal justice under the law, stressing that punishment for an offense should be the same regardless of a person's position in society. Furthermore, he called for the abolition of torture to elicit confessions (a common practice in the eighteenth century). And, he argued that the accused's guilt or innocence should be determined by his or her peers.

Last, Beccaria was the first to stress that punishment should not be for retribution but for the purpose of deterrence. The prevention of future crime was seen as being more important than exacting revenge. His views would have an impact on the criminal justice systems of several European nations, most notably France, Russia, Austria, and Prussia (Schmalleger, 1999).

The Contributions of Jeremy Bentham

Beccaria's ideas were refined by the English social philosopher Jeremy Bentham. Bentham was an advocate of *utilitarianism* (the social ideology that in their laws and actions governing bodies should seek to achieve the most utility or good for the greatest number of people). Bentham (1948) argued that people would choose pleasure and avoid pain. Thus punishment for criminal behavior should be sufficient to negate any pleasure to be derived from criminal acts. Ultimately, the belief was that individuals make conscious decisions to commit criminal acts based upon their expected benefits from those acts. If society could impose more pain upon the individual than he or she could gain from commission of the criminal act, that person would be deterred from committing further crimes. This weighing of pain and pleasure came to be known as *hedonistic calculus* (Vold, Bernard, and Snipes, 1998).

In order for hedonistic or moral calculus to work, Bentham (1948) argued that although punishment should be severe enough to offset the benefits of the crime, it should not be excessive. In addition, for the punishment to dissuade the offender and other individuals contemplating similar crimes, it had to be swift and certain. By "swift" he meant that punishment must take place within a reasonable period of time so that the reason for punishment was not forgotten by the offender or observers. By "certain" he meant that the potential for being caught and punished had to be reasonably high or, regardless of the severity of the sanction, there could be no deterrent effect.

Bentham's adaptations of Beccaria's earlier works would become the foundation for the classical school of criminology. Bentham's principles are still found within the justice systems of the world's democracies.

Tenets of the Classical School

The main premise of the classical school is that crime can be controlled by punishing identified offenders in a way that makes potential offenders fearful of the consequences of committing crime. Our adaptation of the primary tenets of the classical school is as follows:

1. The social contract—an individual is bound to society only by his or her own consent and, therefore, society is responsible to him or her.

2. Free will—individuals are free to make their own choices to act.

3. People seek pleasure and avoid pain.

4. Punishment should be used as a deterrent to criminal behavior.

5. Punishment should be based upon the seriousness of the crime.

6. Punishments for identical crimes should be identical.

The Concept of Deterrence

As the reader will have noted, classical criminology is based upon the concept of *deterrence*. This application of punishment to alter behavior or prevent misconduct is sometimes referred to as *deterrence theory*. The application of deterrence theory is thought to be both general and specific in nature. By *general deterrence* we mean that punishing an offender is done so that others in society who might be contemplating similar acts become aware that they risk suffering the same punishment. By *specific deterrence* we mean that the offender who has committed the criminal behavior realizes that the benefits received from the act were not worth the costs of the punishment for the crime.

As we noted in the previous section, in order for either general or specific deterrence to work, punishment must be severe enough to outweigh the benefits of the crime. In addition to severity the punishment must be imposed as swiftly as possible after the crime has occurred in order to make an impression upon the offender and any would-be offenders considering a similar act. Last, the punishment should be certain so that offenders will have cause to fear that their crimes will be discovered, successfully prosecuted, and punished.

In the United States, swiftness (also known as celerity) and certainty are often lacking in our apprehension, adjudication, and punishment of criminals. Therefore the American justice system tends to over rely on severity as a means of gaining compliance. Unfortunately, as pointed out by both Beccaria (1963) and Bentham (1948), severity alone cannot produce conformity.

The Concept of Justice

When criminologists discuss the classical school of criminology they often tend to focus on the concept of deterrence and overlook other aspects of this legal model of justice. However, other important concepts should be emphasized. The first is the concept of the social contract, which was noted in the discussion of Beccaria's contributions and in the tenets of the classical school. It should be understood that there is a two-way commitment between the individual and society: The individual has an obligation to abide by the laws enacted by society's legislative bodies and enforced by appropriate agents of social control, and the state has the responsibility to provide fair and equitable treatment of that individual in exchange for his or her compliance. Failure on the part of the state to treat its citizens properly negates the social contract.

Another important concept of the classical school is equity. By *equity* we mean that the law is applied equally to every member of society regardless of social station. Issues such as race, class, religion, gender, or ideology are not to influence the administration of justice. Failure on the part of the state to provide for equitable treatment could result in dismissal of the charges against the accused. Chronic failure on the part of the state to provide for equitable treatment could result in distrust of the system and nullification of the social contract.

A third concept that must be considered is *due process*—every individual who is charged with violating a criminal law must be accorded the full protection of the law during the investigation, prosecution, and adjudication of his or her case. In addition, the imposition of any sanctions must be in accordance with legal proscriptions (Barlow, 2000). As with equity issues, failure to provide due process could result in acquittal. Chronic failures could seriously impair the state's ability to govern.

THE NEOCLASSICAL SCHOOL OF CRIMINOLOGY

The application of classical criminology during the eighteenth century quickly revealed flaws with the idea of identical punishment for identical crimes, as well as with the concepts of free will and rationality. It was discovered that aggravating or mitigating circumstances sometimes caused similar crimes to differ in significant ways. In addition, while the concept of free will was not abandoned, people recognized that there were sometimes circumstances in which freedom of choice was limited. Likewise, under certain conditions, people did not always act rationally. These issues quickly led nations that had been implementing classical criminology to revise their ideas (Vold, Bernard, and Snipes, 1998). The changes in classical criminology resulting from these realizations developed into *neoclassical criminology*.

In their administration of justice, the nations that use classical tenets now incorporate these neoclassical revisions: allowance for mitigating and aggravating circumstances; consideration of youth, insanity, necessity, duress, self-defense, and, to lesser degrees, ignorance and intoxication (Lilly, Cullen, and Ball, 1995; Roberson and Wallace, 1998; Liska and Messner, 1999).

Rationales for Leniency

Saying that there were "aggravating" or "mitigating" circumstances is quite simply a way of acknowledging that other issues may have played a role in the commission of a crime. *Aggravating circumstances* are those that cause the offender to be punished more severely than they would normally be for a specific crime. For example, conviction for the rape of a child would warrant a more serious punishment than rape of an adult because our society views a child as more vulnerable and helpless. *Mitigating circumstances* are those that would result in a more lenient sentence than would normally be imposed for a similar crime. A first-time offender would normally receive a lesser sentence than someone who has an extensive criminal history.

Immaturity or youth is often a consideration for leniency under neoclassical criminology. The separate juvenile justice system and age limitations on the imposition of adult penalties are modern exemplars of these considerations. In most states juveniles under the age of twelve cannot be adjudicated as adults. Nor can juveniles under the age of sixteen face the death penalty.

Insanity has traditionally been a defense in the U.S. legal system. Offenders must not only have been sane when they committed their crimes, but they must also be mentally competent to stand trial. The determination of what constitutes insanity and competence to stand trial varies considerably among states depending upon the legal criteria that are used. The various standards for insanity are discussed in a later chapter.

Necessity, duress or coercion, and self-defense are also considerations. If someone was forced by circumstances to behave in a manner that might ordinarily be considered criminal, they may be excused based upon the circumstances. For example, if you broke into a remote mountain cabin to escape a blizzard, the necessity of the act of breaking and entering would excuse your actions. However, if you engaged in additional unlawful behaviors that were not necessary, such as defacing the property, those would not be excused. Crimes committed under coercion from others are also excused, but the reasonableness of the coercion in regard to the crime committed would have to be considered. For example, a person who commits a less harmful offense because of physical threats or intimidation would most likely be held blameless, but one who commits a violent crime against others to avoid a similar or lesser injury would most likely be held accountable. In these incidents the reasonableness of one's actions would have to be considered. Also, actions that would be considered unlawful may be excused if they were necessary to defend oneself or others from a greater harm.

Last, criminal acts are committed due to ignorance or while under the influence of drugs or alcohol may receive consideration for leniency. Ignorance of the law is not an excuse for escaping prosecution, but it may be considered as a mitigating circumstance in sentencing. Intoxication or chemical impairment will not excuse criminal behavior but may also be used as a mitigating circumstance if it can be shown that the behaviors were not anticipated.

Just Deserts

In recent years advocates of the neoclassical school have revisited the importance of the social contract in applying punishment. As a result of the perceived failure of rehabilitation, some scholars have argued that criminals should be punished because their actions demand that criminal sanctions be applied. The culpability of the offender and the seriousness of the crime require that punishment be administered (Adler, Mueller, and Laufer, 1998). While critics argue that this is nothing but a return to retribution, advocates insist that the social contract must be enforced for the benefit of both the offender and society (Schmalleger, 1999).

The basic premise of the *just deserts* argument is that even if specific deterrence is not accomplished, society needs to see that criminals receive the punishment they deserve. Such punishments are seen by advocates as effective general deterrents. They insist that failure to exact punishment would be a violation of the social contract and would erode respect for the law. In recent years, Americans who have wearied of stories of criminals going unpunished tend to be drawn to this argument. Some people view such punishments as "symbolic reassurance" (discussed in later chapters) for the law abiding rather than punishment in the name of general deterrence.

The Current Status of the Classical School

Overall, the classical school insisted upon a clear-cut legal definition of acts punishable as criminal and fostered the idea of free will. The classical school of thought would maintain strength and prominence within academia until the early 1900s, when it began to decline because of a more treatment-oriented approach fostered by the positive school of criminology. *It should be noted, however, that the neoclassical school remains the model by which the U.S. criminal justice system operates in the prosecution and adjudication of adult offenders.*

Starting in the 1970s and into the new century, the classical school has seen a resurgence in the areas of sentencing and corrections. This is because of the public's and justice system practitioner's disenchantment with the positive school of thought (primarily, the positive school's emphasis on rehabilitation did not seem to work. Continuing increases in criminal behavior also contributed to a "get tough on crime mentality" that emphasizes punishment. The "war on drugs" and habitual offender laws that emphasize "three strikes and you're out" are products of this reliance on punishment. The result is that the numbers of offenders incarcerated in U.S. prisons and the numbers of individuals sentenced to death continue to rise.

THE POSITIVE SCHOOL OF CRIMINOLOGY

Beginning in the late 1800s, a second school of thought would emerge in criminology. Popularly recognized as the positive school of criminology, its humble beginnings are often attributed to an Italian physician, Cesare Lombroso. This school of thought is believed to have emerged "in opposition to the harshness of the classical school, as well as in response to the lack of concern for the causes of criminal behavior" (Pelfrey, 1980, p. 5).

Members of the positive school of thought believed that external forces—biological, psychological, and sociological—caused criminal behavior. They rejected the legal concept of crime recognized by the classical school. In search of differences between criminals and noncriminals, they focused the individual instead of the law and sought scientific status for criminology. A major shift from the classical school was the emphasis on treatment as opposed to punishment.

Determinism

The positive school is based upon the notion of *determinism,* which means that factors beyond a person's control determine behavior. This perspective also implies that a man or a woman is not a self-determining agent free to do as he or she wishes and as his or her intelligence directs (Vold, 1981, p. 9). In other words, determinism is the opposite of free will. If a person acts on his or her free will to commit a crime, it means he or she made a rational decision to do so. Various forms of determinism are defined by biological or cultural factors. *Grim determinism* is the belief that God has ordained certain behaviors and nothing can prevent them from occurring. This perspective was prevalent during ancient and medieval times. *Hard determinism* the view that behavior often may be programmed at birth. It is mostly natural (e.g., biological) and allows for no or only limited free will. *Soft determinism* views behavior as having biological (nature) or sociological (nurture) characteristics (Gaines, Kaune, and Miller, 2000). In this perspective, an individual's freedom of choice may be limited by nature and/or nurture.

Darwin's Theory of Evolution

In 1859, Charles Darwin published *Origin of Species,* in which he outlined his theory of evolution. His work caused a sensation and was controversial because it attacked the biblical theory of creation and established a new area of science for understanding human behavior and other social and physical phenomena. Scientists were encouraged to explore a different approach in the study of criminal behavior. The debate over free will and determinism was a long-standing issue in philosophy and religion, and some thinkers believed that God determined, or predestined, an individual's fate. In a similar way, the positivist approach raised questions of determinism, in this case scientific rather than religious. Though the positivists looked to worldly forces rather than to God, their ideas challenged everyday assumptions about free will. In essence, the positivists, in their quest for answers, were raising very basic philosophical questions in the social sciences (Hagan, 1998).

In his work, Darwin presented evidence that humans were animals, except that they were more highly evolved or developed than other animals. The ancestors of modern people were less highly evolved and were part of a continuous chain linking humans to the earliest and simplest forms of life. The idea that some individuals might be reversions to an earlier evolutionary stage had been originally suggested by Darwin, who had written, "With mankind some of the worst dispositions which occasionally without any assignable cause make their appearance in families, may perhaps be reversions to a savage state, from which we are not removed by many generations" (Darwin, 1871, p. 137). Darwin's work was also important because it formed the theoretical basis for the early biological explanations of crime.

Lombroso's Theory of Atavism

As previously noted, Cesare Lombroso is recognized as the father of the positivist school. Darwin's theory of evolution heavily influenced much of his work. Lombroso was an Italian physician who was the first criminologist to employ the scientific method (measurement, observations, and the application of generalizations from one's research findings to other similar research) in his work. In 1876, he wrote and published *The Criminal Man,* in which he coined the term *atavism.* The theory of *atavism* asserts that criminals are born—as opposed to made—and their criminal behavior is the result of primitive urges. Criminals were believed to be evolutionary accidents who were throwbacks to more primitive people. By nature they possessed a relatively underdeveloped brain, and this physical shortcoming made them incapable of conforming to the rules and expectations of a complex modern society. They exhibited a lack of guilt or remorse for any wrongdoing and were unable to learn the distinction between good and evil.

Some of the characteristics that Lombroso linked to criminal behavior included deviations in the criminal's head size and shape, asymmetry of the face, large jaws and cheekbones, unusually large or small ears or ears that stood out from the head, fleshy lips, abnormal teeth, receding chin, abundant hair or wrinkles, long arms, extra fingers or toes, or an asymmetry of the brain (Lombroso-Ferrero, 1972). Since many of these characteristics supported his theory, he concluded that criminal offenders had physical characteristics that resembled those of lower animals, such as monkeys and chimpanzees.

Lombroso described the *born* criminal as one who was biologically predisposed to criminal behavior. However, other types of criminal offenders fell within six categories: the *habitual* or *professional* criminals, who engaged in crime as a trade or occupation; the *morally insane; criminoloids;* the *juridical criminal;* the *hysteric;* and those who violated the law in *crimes of passion.* Criminals who fell under the category of the morally insane were mental and moral degenerates, alcoholics, drug addicts, and other similar types of offenders. Criminoloids were described as occasional or situational offenders, whose participation in criminal behavior was determined by environmental factors.

Lombroso believed criminoloids exhibited some degree of atavism and differed from the born criminal in degree only, not in kind. Juridical criminals violated the law usually in an impulsive act. They lacked self-control, care, or any type of forethought. Criminals who engaged in passion crimes responded to intense emotions that may have been provoked by love, jealousy, hatred, or the need to seek vengefulness. The hysteric usually engaged in criminal behavior through some compulsive, neurotic, or schizoid act.

Lombroso's theory of atavism attracted international attention, but it was not long before he and his students began to soften his position. By the time of his death in 1909, he modified his view of atavism. He decided that born criminals constituted only one-third of the total criminal population and the remaining two-thirds comprised two additional types—insane offenders, whose crimes were the result of any one of many complex mental disorders; and criminoloids, whose personalities were somehow warped by a host of environmental factors (Lombroso-Ferrero, 1972).

Lombroso's work did not escape criticism. It was suggested that many differences he found between his prisoners and control group subjects were too small to be statistically significant. It was also suggested that his findings were biased in that many of his subjects were Sicilians (who were at the bottom of Italy's socioeconomic order). Despite these criticisms, the arguments that Lombroso made regarding limited will, the use of scientific methods to study the causes of crime, and treatment rather than punishment of criminals would serve as the foundation for the positive school of criminology (Vold, Bernard, and Snipes, 1998).

Tenets of the Positive School

Although Lombroso's biological approach was rejected by American criminologists, they did accept his positivist tenets (Reid, 2000). Instead of the medical model, however, they developed the sociological model mentioned earlier in the chapter. The positivist tenets are as follows:

1. Denial of the free will concept

2. Multiple causes of criminal behavior

3. Causes are biological and environmental

4. Using scientific methods to look at causes

5. Actions toward the criminal should be to correct the behavior, not punish it

Edwin Sutherland and the criminologists at the University of Chicago who pioneered the development of American criminology were instrumental in promoting the *twentieth-century rehabilitative ideal.* This perspective holds that the causes of crime can be identified and that changes (both social and individual) can be made to reduce the potential for criminality to occur and/or to minimize its impact upon society (Sutherland and Cressey, 1970).

Current Status of the Positive School

While the U.S. system of justice was based upon the classical school of criminology, sentencing and correctional efforts have been based upon positivist tenets since the early part of the twentieth century. Positivist tenets have also been the basis of the juvenile justice system. *We do not suggest that all sentencing considerations and correctional efforts were based upon positive school considerations. The focus on punishment has always been a part of U.S. correctional efforts.*

Today positive school criminology dominates academic studies of crime and criminality. The following chapters demonstrate this influence in their explanations of crime and criminal behavior. Despite the resurgence of classical criminology with its current "get tough on crime" emphasis, positive school ideals continue to be practiced in both adult and juvenile corrections in the United States.

CRIMINOLOGY TODAY

The study of criminal behavior today is as strong and vital as it ever has been. In many respects, it has become an even more important field of inquiry in light of violent episodes such as the recent shootings at schools, in community centers, and in churches. Undersanding why these events occur is vital, particularly for the future protection of life and property.

Influences on Crime

In the chapters to follow we present numerous theoretical explanations for crime and criminal behavior. Before we do so, we wish to note that a number of influences on crime and criminality warrant consideration, regardless of one's theoretical orientation. We conclude this chapter with an overview of several of these influences.

Ecological/geographical differences

Examining national crime data reveals that crime rates in rural and suburban areas tend to be lower than crime in large urban areas. This difference might suggest that crime is influenced by those factors found more often in urban areas, such as overcrowding, poverty, social inequality, drug use, racial conflict, and economic instability. Crime rates are also often higher in the western and southern parts of the country and during the summer, suggesting that warmer climates have some influence on criminal behavior (Doerner and Lab, 1998).

Gender

Does crime discriminate? According to crime data, males are the dominant criminal perpetrators. For example, in 1998, 78 percent of all the persons arrested, 74 percent arrested for index crimes, 83 percent arrested for violent crimes, and 71 percent arrested for property crimes were male (Federal Bureau of Investigation, 1999). Males were arrested most often for drug abuse violations and driving under the influence, while females were most often arrested for larceny-theft.

Despite the fact that males dominate criminal behavior, statistics indicate that female criminality is increasing, while male criminality is decreasing. For example, while there was no change from 1997 to 1998 in the number of females arrested, arrests of males declined by 2 percent. Furthermore, for the period of 1994-1998, while male arrests rose only 2 percent, female arrests rose 12 percent. From 1989 to 1998, male arrests rose only 2 percent, while female arrests rose 28 percent (*Sourcebook of Criminal Justice Statistics,* 1998).

Based on these statistics, it can be said that crime does not discriminate, but that it has welcomed females with open arms. Of course, the concern is why female crime rates have increased. While no one definitive answer has yet been identified, one could argue that the increase in the female population (more than 50 percent of the population is now female) would influence the growing number of females arrested. Furthermore, equal rights and equal application of the law may have some influence. Regardless of the reason, the reality is that females are becoming more and more criminal.

Race/Ethnicity

One of the greatest misnomers in criminal justice is that minorities are arrested more than whites. In 1998, 68 percent of the individuals arrested were white and 30 percent were African American (Federal Bureau of Investigation, 1999). This statistic alone would indicate that minorities are not arrested more than whites. However, this statistic is misleading in that minority group members tend to be arrested disproportionally to their population base. That is, African Americans make up less than 20 percent of the population, yet 30 percent of those arrested are African Americans. This disproportion has created a great debate in criminal justice over racial equality. The question of whether race influences the commission of crime or merely the prosecution of it has yet to be properly addressed.

Age

With respect to age, according to 1998 data, 45 percent of all those arrested were under the age of twenty-five. Fifty-five percent of those arrested for index crimes were under twenty-five. Because 6 percent of those arrested were under fifteen, one could suggest that criminality is greatest among individuals ages fifteen to twenty-four (Federal Bureau of Investigation, 1999). Perhaps immaturity prevents this group from accepting the responsibility of being in a society that requires certain rules to be followed regardless of how doing so might hamper reaching one's goals. The issue of responsibility is easily connected with the idea of free will, which one might argue younger people have more opportunity to exercise.

Another issue in considering age and criminality is the increasing number of elderly offenders who are being tried and sentenced within the criminal justice system. The problems of dealing with elderly offenders in both community and institutional corrections will be of increasing concern within the coming years.

Social Class

Among all the variables one could claim have an influence on criminality, one of the more difficult to quantify is social class. Most commonly, society has been viewed as three-tiered in terms of class; upper, middle, and lower. Each tier can then itself be divided into an upper, middle, and lower. These tiers have long been determined by economic status, which in the United States is usually defined by yearly income. Pundits, politicians, and political activists often claim that crime results from poverty, which is associated with the lower class. However, depending upon one's political ideology, class-interpretations can be used to blame the poor and label them as inherently criminal or to excuse their behaviors as the result of social injustice. We investigate these views in detail within later chapters. Suffice it to say at this point that there are more than enough examples of crime among the upper and middle classes to counter this claim. In truth, criminality is found among all levels of society; it is just that many refuse to acknowledge that factors other than poverty can contribute to crime.

SUMMARY

Criminology was defined as *the scientific approach to the study of crime as a social phenomenon, that is, the theoretical application involving the study of the nature and extent of criminal behavior.* The specialty areas within the study of criminology are *sociology of law,* the understanding of how laws are created and enacted, modified, and applied; *criminological theory,* the causes and consequences of crime and criminal behavior; *penology,* the study of punishment, treatment, and correctional techniques; *justicology,* the study of the criminal justice system, its components and processes; and *victimology,* the study of crime victims, their relationships with offenders, and how society responds to their needs.

The five models of criminology were then presented. These include the *legal model,* which emphasizes how the legal system deals with violators; the *medical model,* which focuses on biological and psychological reasons for criminal behavior; the *sociological model,* which focuses on reasons for behavior as resulting from some type of social error or problem; the *political model,* which views crime as the product of conflicts among members of society; and the *interdisciplinary model,* which emphasizes the interaction of various individual and environmental influences on crime and criminality.

The contributions of Cesare Beccaria and Jeremy Bentham led to the development of the classical school of criminology. The classical school was concerned with the application of law and punishment in order to deter criminal behavior. General deterrence is effective when those contemplating crimes see the severity of punishment that a similar offender received and are dissuaded. Specific deterrence was based upon the offender's deciding that the punishment received for committing the crime was greater than the benefits received from having done so. In order for deterrence to work, punishment had to be severe (greater than the benefits received), swift (occurring within a reasonable time after the crime so that both the offender and the public recalled the details), and certain (the likelihood of being caught and punished was thought to be high).

The necessary revisions of the neoclassical school made allowances for issues that might impact the rationality and/or the free will of offenders. These issues included aggravating and mitigating circumstances; immaturity; insanity; necessity of duress; and to a lesser degree, ignorance and chemical impairment. The modern concept of "just deserts" is seen by proponents as being the needed application of punishment to promote general deterrence.

The concept of determinism and its challenges to the assumptions of free will and rationality were developed in the works of Darwin and Lombroso. While the biological explanation offered by Lombroso have long since been discredited, his arguments were instrumental in development of the positive school of criminology. The positive school called for scientific analysis rather than legal actions. Rather than punishment based upon the severity of the crime, the positive school called for treatment based upon the needs of the offender. The use of science to determine the causes of crime, to reduce the potential for crime by addressing social ills, and to provide appropriate treatments for offenders became the basis for academic criminology.

Utilizing the tenets of the positive school, the chapter concluded with a brief discussion of a variety of issues that are thought to influence crime and criminal behavior. Influences that must be considered in contemporary studies of criminological theory include ecological/geograhic differences, gender, race/ethnicity, age, and social class.

■ DISCUSSION QUESTIONS ■

1. Explain why crime is considered a phenomenon.

2. If you were to become a criminologist, what subfield would you study? Why?

3. The history of criminology is best explained through the various schools of thought. The classical school seems to be the most dominant. Why?

4. What is determinism? Identify and describe the types of determinism and what role they may play in today's criminal behavior.

5. Identify Lombroso's six types of criminals and discuss which types of criminal acts committed today might best match with each type.

6. What are the tenets of the positive school of criminological thought? Explain how they might apply in today's criminal justice system.

■ REFERENCES ■

Adler, F., Mueller, G. O. W., and Laufer, W. S. (1998). *Criminology,* 3rd ed. Boston: McGraw-Hill.

Albanese, J. (1999). *Criminal justice.* Needham, MA: Allyn & Bacon.

Barlowm, H. D. (2000). *Criminal justice in America.* Upper Saddle River, NJ: Prentice-Hall.

Beccaria, C. (1963). *Essay on crimes and punishments.* Translated with an introduction by H. Paolucci. New York: Macmillan.

Bentham, J. (1948). *An introduction to the principles of morals and legislation.* Edited by L. J. Lafleur. New York: Hafner.

Dantzker, M. L. (1998). *Criminology and criminal justice: Comparing, contrasting, and intertwining disciplines.* Newton, MA: Butterworth-Heinemann.

Darwin, C. (1871). *Descent of Man.* London: John Murray.

Doerner, W. G., and Lab, S. P. (1998). *Victimology,* 2nd ed. Cincinnati: Anderson.

Federal Bureau of Investigation. (1998). *Crime in the United States, 1997.* Washington, DC: U.S. Government Printing Office.

_____. (1999). *Crime in the United States, 1998.* Washington DC: U.S. Government Printing Office.

Gaines, L. K., Kaune, M., and Miller, R. L. (2000). *Criminal justice in action.* Belmont, CA: Wadsworth.

Hagan, F. E. (1998). *Introduction to criminology: Theories, methods, and criminal behavior,* 4th ed. Chicago: Nelson-Hall.

Jeffery, C. R. (1990). *Criminology: An interdisciplinary approach.* Englewood Cliffs, NJ: Prentice Hall.

_____. (1956). The structure of American criminological thinking. *Journal of Criminal Law, Criminology, and Police Science* 45 (5): 658-72.

Lilly, J. R., Cullen, F. T., and Ball, R. A. (1995). *Criminological theory: Context and consequences,* 2nd ed. Thousand Oaks, CA: Sage.

Liska, A. E., and Messner, S. F. (1999). *Perspectives on crime and deviance,* 3rd ed. Upper Saddle River, NJ: Prentice Hall.

Lombroso-Ferrero, G. (1972). *Criminal man according to the classification of Cesare Lombroso.* Montclair, NJ: Patterson-Smith.

Pelfrey, W. V. (1980). *The evolution of criminology.* Cincinnati, OH: Anderson.

Reid, S. T. (2000). *Crime and criminology,* 9th ed. Boston: McGraw-Hill.

Roberson, C., and Wallace, H. (1998). *Introduction to criminology.* Incline Village, NV: Copperhouse.

Schmalleger, F. (1999). *Criminal justice today,* 5th ed. Upper Saddle River, NJ: Prentice Hall.

Sourcebook of Criminal Justice Statistics. (1998). Washington, DC: U.S. Government Printing Office.

Sutherland, E. H., and Cressey, D. (1970). *Principles of criminology,* 7th ed. Philadelphia: Lippincott.

Vold, G. B. (1981). *Theoretical criminology,* 2nd ed. New York: Oxford University Press.

_____, Bernard, T. J., and Snipes, J. B. (1998). *Theoretical criminology,* 4th ed. New York: Oxford University Press.

CHAPTER

3

Biological and Biosocial Theories of Crime Causation

██

■ **KEY CONCEPTS** ■

"bad blood"
bio-criminology
biology
biosociology
concordance
determinism
environmental factors
genetics
hard determinism

nature vs. nurture
neurological disorders
physical abnormalities
positivism
psychopathy
sociobiology
soft determinism
somatotypes

■ **LEARNING OBJECTIVES** ■

After reading this chapter, the student should be able to:

1. Describe how early biological theories linked physical features with criminal behavior.

2. Describe how early biological theories linked heredity with criminal behavior.

_____

This chapter was coauthored by Dr. Florence Ferguson of the State University of West Georgia.

3. Describe how early biological theories linked feeblemindedness with criminal behavior.

4. Describe how transitional theories linked body types with criminal behavior.

5. Describe how transitional theories linked genetics with criminal behavior.

6. Describe how transitional theories linked chromosomal abnormalities with criminal behavior.

7. Describe how transitional theories linked intelligence with criminal behavior.

8. Describe how contemporary theories link nutrition with criminal behavior.

9. Describe how contemporary theories link chemical imbalances with criminal behavior.

10. Describe how contemporary theories link allergies with criminal behavior.

11. Describe how contemporary theories link environmental contaminants with criminal behavior.

12. Describe how contemporary theories link neurophysiological factors with criminal behavior.

13. Describe how contemporary theories link hormonal influences with criminal behavior.

BIOLOGICAL EXPLANATIONS

Chapter 2 discussed the positive school of criminology and the contributions of the Italian physician Cesare Lombroso. While the primary focus of this school has been sociological explanations of crime and criminality, early positive school theories revolved around biology and began with the concept of determinism. Because of racial stereotyping and dissatisfaction with hard determinism, these theories fell into disfavor with contemporary criminologists. Today criminologists favor "nurture" (biological factors) over "nature" (sociological and psychological factors), although modern biological explanations have gained some status among criminologists who allow for the influences that nature may have upon nurture in producing crime and criminality.

This chapter discusses the leading biological and biosocial explanations of crime beginning with early theories that were influenced by Lombroso and Darwin. The focus of these biological explanations of crime are displayed in Table 3–1.

Early Biological Explanations

Charles Goring, a student of Lombroso's, measured the degree of correlation between physiological features and the criminal history of his subjects. In 1913, he published the results of his research in *The English Convict.* Goring's data showed that the criminals in his study were shorter and weighed less than the noncriminal control group subjects. The finding was taken as support of Goring's general thesis that criminal behavior, like other physical traits and features, could be inherited.

Goring's work was criticized by others who argued that his findings were flawed because he failed to account for the effect of environment. Despite the questions raised about his methodology, Goring's work was significant because he was the first to claim that criminal behavior might be the result of the interaction between heredity and environment, a view now held by many criminologists. He did not reject the influence of the environment as the cause of crime, but maintained that empirical evidence, evidence not found in his study, was required to support this view (Driver, 1972).

Physical Features and Criminal Behavior

In 1939, Earnest A. Hooten conducted research similar to Lombroso's and Goring's. The findings of his research were published in *Crime and Man.* Hooten evaluated 13,873 inmates from ten states, comparing them along 107 physiological dimensions with 3,203 individuals who were not incarcerated and who formed the control group. He found that prisoners tended to have certain

TABLE 3–1 Biological Theories

Early Theories	Transitional Theories	Contemporary Theories
Physical features	Body types	Nutrition
Heredity	Genetics	Chemical Imbalances
Feeblemindedness	Chromosomal abnormalities	Allergies
Gender	Intelligence	Environmental contaminants
		Neurophysiological factors
		Hormones

physiological characteristics (such as low foreheads, crooked noses, narrow jaws, small ears, long necks, and stooped shoulders) not found in the control group. Hooten labeled these criminals *organically inferior* and concluded that the primary cause of their criminal behavior was their biological inferiority.

Hooten (1939) also believed there was a relationship between criminals' body shapes and the types of crimes they committed. He found that murderers tended to be tall and thin, while rapists were short and heavy. Men with average builds did not specialize in any particular crime because they, like their physical shape, had no specific orientation. Hooten's research was heavily criticized because it suffered from the same methodological flaws as Goring's work. Hooten's work also failed to gain recognition because it was published at the onset of World War II when theories of biological inferiority had come under attack by opponents of Nazism and fascism.

Heredity and Crime

Criminal behavior as an inherited trait received attention after biologists and medical researchers accepted the belief that behavior could be passed from generation to generation. The most famous of these studies were those of the Jukes and the Kallikaks. In 1877, Richard L. Dugdale published a study entitled *The Jukes: A Study in Crime, Pauperism, Disease, and Heredity*. After learning that six members of the Jukes family were incarcerated in rural New York, Dugdale traced the genealogy of the family back two hundred years and found a history of pauperism, prostitution, exhaustion, disease, fornication, and illegitimacy. He attributed these findings to the "degenerate" nature of the family. His research was criticized because it was based on unreliable, incomplete, and obscure information and was filled with value judgments and unsupported conclusions. His work was also criticized because he had no control group to determine whether the Jukeses' level of criminality was higher than that of other families with similar histories.

In 1912, Henry H. Goddard published *The Kallikak Family: A Study in the Heredity of Feeblemindedness*. He attempted to address the shortcomings of the Jukes study by placing the study of deviant families within an acceptable scientific framework that included a control group. For comparison purposes, he studied two branches of the same family. Martin Kallikak, a soldier in the Revolutionary War, had fathered two children with two different women. The first child was illegitimate and the result of a sexual liaison between Kallikak and a barmaid. After he returned home from the war, Kallikak married a "righteous" Quaker girl, and a second lineage was formed. Goddard found a higher proportion of crime and other problems in Kallikak and the barmaid's descendants (Goddard, 1912). Critics of Goddard's findings argue that educational and environmental factors explain his findings better than hereditary in that the "deviant" set of Kallikak descendants lived in poverty, while the "normal" set lived in wealth. They also argued that the claimed differences between the two groups were not as obvious as Goddard claimed (Hagan, 1998).

Feeblemindedness and Crime

During the early part of this century, studies by Goddard (1914) and others (Goring 1912; Zeleny, 1933) found low IQs (intelligence quotients) among prisoners and juveniles in reform schools. This research was later criticized by sociologists because of the small, unrepresentative samples of subjects and because the tests were unreliable. As a result, studies on intelligence and crime lost their popularity by the 1930s (Gould, 1981). Goddard (1914), of the New Jersey Training School for the Feebleminded, popularized IQ tests in the United States, beginning with his study of the Kallikak family. In the Kallikak study, he assumed that low intelligence or "feeblemindedness" was passed on biologically from one generation to the next. Although in his study of the Kallikak family Goddard employed a subjective definition of feeblemindedness, the later investigation identified feeblemindedness based on IQ distribution among those in institutions for the feebleminded, a somewhat more objective standard. These distributions yielded an IQ of seventy-five or less, or a mental age of twelve or below, as the cutoff point for classifying feeblemindedness.

The initial wave of research that followed Goddard's earlier studies reported that feebleminded prisoners constituted 25 to 90 percent of prison populations (Fink, 1938). The validity of this research, however, came into question when the U.S. army began to administer IQ tests to army draftees during World War I. These tests indicated that roughly one-third of the draftees were feebleminded, according to the Goddard's definition of feeblemindedness (Zeleny, 1933). Clearly, this was an unsettling proposition. Consequently, the definition of feeblemindedness was revised downward to an IQ of fifty, or a mental age of eight or below. This readjustment cast doubt on the earlier work of Goddard and others that had so often linked low intelligence and feeblemindedness with delinquency.

Gender and Crime

In addition to his earlier research on atavism, Cesar Lombroso (1920) was one of the first criminologists to study female criminals. In his book *The Female Offender,* he attributed the differences between males and females to variations in evolutionary development. He believed females were more primitive than males and that they possessed many traits common in children, that is, women were more likely to be vengeful, jealous, insensitive to pain, and lacking any sense of morality. According to Lombroso, women had lower rates of criminal behavior than men only because their natural deficiencies were "neutralized by piety, maternity, want of passion, sexual coldness, weakness, and an undeveloped intelligence (Lombroso-Ferraro, 1972, pp. 150–52). Women committed crimes only when they inherited male characteristics—a "virile" cranium, excessive body hair, moles, and other gross features. Lombroso's (1920) theory became known as the *masculinity hypothesis*. With the exception of prostitutes (who were thought to act out of atavistic yearnings), he believed a few masculine females were responsible for the majority of crimes committed by women.

Lombroso (1920) also believed that masculinity among women itself was an anomaly. Conversely, women who were born with feminine features would be protected from crime by their innate physiological limitations and would be predisposed to unimaginative, dull, and conformist lives.

Lombroso reasoned that, like males, the majority of females could be classified as occasional criminals whose physical features contain no signs of degeneration and whose moral character would be similar to that of their "normal sisters" (Lombroso-Ferrero, 1972, pp. 193–95). In addition, he argued that occasional female criminals might be encouraged to commit crime because of the increased frustrations they would meet in life as their educational opportunities increased. Lombroso, therefore, recognized the influences of female criminality that have gained popularity in recent decades. Although Lombroso's philosophy on female criminality was built on sexist and outdated notions of women's biological makeup, it remained influential for many years. Like his concept of atavism, it remains noteworthy for the later studies it generated more so than for its own theoretical contributions. (Chesney-Lind and Sheldon, 1992).

Transitional Biological Explanations

Early biological theories in criminology took the view that nature exerted influences on human beings that overcame socialization (nurture). This perspective assumed that offenders behaved differently because they were physically different from nonoffenders. These views followed the lead of Lombroso and were compatible with hard determinism. Later studies conducted in the 1940s through the 1970s made allowances for psychological and sociological influences. They were believed to be more in line with the soft determinism perspective that came to dominate criminology during the twentieth century. However, many of these later theories remained unpopular with criminologists because they still emphasized biological and psychological factors with little regard for sociological influences. In addition, some studies revisited issues such as race, class, and intelligence resulting in opposition from both within and without criminology. These studies, however, mark the beginning of the transition in understanding crime and criminality from "nature versus nurture" to "nature *and* nurture."

Body Types and Crime

The body-build, or *somatotype,* school was developed by William Sheldon, who theorized that criminals had distinct physiques that made them susceptible to particular types of criminal behavior. Sheldon (1949) maintained that elements of three basic body types could be found in all people: *Endomorphs* are heavy persons with short arms and legs; they tend to be relaxed and extroverted and relatively noncriminal. *Mesomorphs* are athletic and muscular; they tend to be aggressive and particularly likely to commit violent crimes and other crimes requiring strength and speed. *Ectomorphs* are thin, introverted, and overly sensitive.

Sheldon (1949) compared 200 male delinquents in an institution with a control group of some 4,000 male college students. He found that compared to the students, delinquents tended to be mesomorphic. Sheldon theorized that people with athletic bodies were particularly apt to engage in adventurous and aggressive behaviors. As a result, muscular boys were more likely to join juvenile gangs and to be bullies.

Sheldon's work was followed by that of Sheldon Glueck and Eleanor Glueck (1950), who examined the relationship between body type and delinquency in 500 institutionalized delinquents who had persistent brushes with the law. These delinquents were matched with a control sample of nondelinquents. After measuring body types through photographs, they found more than 60 percent of the delinquents were mesomorphic compared with 31 percent of nondelinquents.

In 1956, the Gluecks conducted another study of somatotypes and delinquency. They found that mesomorphs who became delinquent were also characterized by a number of personality traits not normally found in mesomorphs. These included susceptibility to contagious diseases of childhood, destructiveness, feelings of inadequacy, emotional instability, and emotional conflicts (Glueck and Glueck, 1956). In addition, three sociocultural factors—careless household routine, lack of family group recreations, and meagerness of recreational facilities in the home—were strongly associated with delinquency in mesomorphs. Whether the mesomorphic body structure determines these characteristics or whether the personality traits are generated from environmental factors, including being labeled a "delinquent," was addressed by the Gluecks. They concluded that delinquency was caused by a combination of environmental, biological, and psychological factors and that there was no such thing as a "delinquent personality" among mesomorphs (Glueck and Glueck, 1956).

Both Sheldon's and the Gluecks' work was criticized. Sheldon's work was found to suffer from the same methodological flaws of the work of Lombroso, Goring, Hooten, and other early biologists (Vold, Bernard, and Snipes, 1998). Critics argued that even if Sheldon's delinquent subjects were more mesomorphic, he could not rule out the possibility that their muscular, athletic bodies made it more probable that juvenile justice officials viewed them as a threat and hence were more likely to institutionalize them. Criticism of the Gluecks stemmed from their not having a control group for the rapid body changes that occur in adolescence. They were also criticized because their method of somatotyping relied on visual assessments, not precise measurements. Finally, they were criticized because the delinquent population they studied included only institutionalized youths (Hagan, 1997).

Genetics and Crime: Twin and Adoption Studies

Early studies at the beginning of the twentieth century attempting to address the hereditary bases of criminality by examining traditional families, such as the Jukes and Kallikaks, were eventually abandoned because it was essentially impossible to disentangle the effects of nature (such as genes) from those of nurture (environment). Half a century later, researchers found that one way to determine the role of genetics was to compare the incidence and types of criminal convictions of identical and fraternal twins. Theoretically, twin research assumes that the environment exerts similar influences on each member of a twin set. Therefore, any differences between the twins would presumably be due to genetic factors. Therefore the hereditary versus environmental influences on behavior can be accurately determined by comparing concordance rates between identical and fraternal twins. *Concordance* is a key concept in twin study research and is the term used in genetics for the degree to which related pairs of subjects both show a particular behavior or condition.

In the earlier studies conducted on the behavior of twins, researchers generally found greater similarities of criminal behavior between identical twins than between fraternal twins. A review of relevant studies conducted between 1929 and 1961 found that 60 percent of identical twins shared criminal behavior patterns (if one twin was criminal, so was the other), while only 30 percent of fraternal twins were similarly related (Mednick and Christiansen, 1971). This evidence was widely interpreted as supporting a genetic basis for crime.

In another study of twins, Christiansen studied 3,586 male twin pairs and found a 52 percent concordance for identical pairs and 22 percent concordance for fraternal pairs. This result suggests that identical twins may share a genetic characteristic that increases the risk of their engaging in criminality (Christiansen, 1974). Similarly, D. Rowe and D.W. Osgood have analyzed the factors that influence self-reported delinquency in a sample of twin pairs and concluded that genetic influences actually have explanatory power (Rowe and Osgood, 1984).

Critics have argued that other reasons may account for the concordance. Compared to siblings, identical twins spend more time together, tend to have the same friends, are more attached to each other, and tend to think of themselves as alike. They are also more likely than other siblings or even fraternal twins to be treated the same by their parents, friends, and teachers. All these likenesses produce similar attitudes and behaviors among identical twins, including delinquency and crime (Dalgaard and Kringlen, 1976).

Adoption studies yield similar findings to twin studies. It would seem logical that if the behavior of adopted children is more similar to that of their biological parents than to that of their adoptive parents, the idea of a genetic basis for criminality would be supported. If, however, adoptees are more similar to their adoptive parents than their biological parents, an environmental basis for crime would seem more valid. Several studies indicate that some relationship exists between biological parents' behavior and the behavior of their children, even when their contact has been infrequent or nonexistent (Mednick and Christiansen, 1971).

One of the most significant adoption studies was conducted by Barry Hutchings and Sarnoff Mednick (1977), who analyzed 1,145 male adoptees born in Denmark between 1927 and 1941; of these, 185 had criminal records. After following up on 143 of the criminal adoptees and matching them with a control group of 143 noncriminal adoptees, Hutchings and Mednick found that the criminality of the biological father was a strong predictor of the child's criminal behavior. When both the biological and adoptive fathers were criminal, the probability that the youth would engage in criminal behavior greatly expanded. Twenty-five percent of the boys whose adoptive and biological fathers were criminals had been convicted of a criminal law violation compared with only 14 percent of those whose biological and adoptive fathers were not criminals (Hutchings and Mednick, 1995).

Chromosomal Abnormalities and Criminal Behavior

Chromosomal theory has also been used to explain criminal behavior. Within this theory, aggressive behavior is linked with a genetic abnormality wherein a sperm or ovum contains more than one sex chromosome. When conception occurs, the resulting embryo will have an extra sex chromosome.

In 1965, the first well-known study that linked criminal behavior to an abnormal sex chromosome was made by British researchers who examined 197 Scottish prisoners for chromosomal abnormalities through a relatively simple blood test (Jacobs, Brunton, and Melville, 1965). Twelve of the group displayed chromosomes that were unusual, and seven were found to have an XYY chromosome. "Normal" males possess an XY chromosome structure, while "normal" females are XX. The XYY male, whose incidence in the prison population was placed at around 3.5 percent by Patricia Jacobs, was identified as potentially violent and termed a "supermale." The extra Y chromosome was thought to be the cause of violent behavior.

The supermale concept became popular after a number of offenders attempted to use it as a criminal defense for the crimes they committed. For example, in 1969, Lawrence Hannell, who was declared to be a supermale, was acquitted of murder in Australia on the grounds of insanity (Jones, 1986). The XYY defense, however, did not work for Richard Speck, who was convicted of killing eight Chicago nursing students in 1966. It was later learned that Speck did not carry the extra Y chromosome. Speck's case drew much attention after the public became concerned that all XYYs were potential killers and should be closely controlled. As it became clear that most violent offenders actually did not possess the extra Y chromosome, interest in the XYY theory dissipated.

Intelligence and Crime

Intelligence and crime was revisited by T. Hirschi and M.J. Hindelang (1977) when they reviewed many studies using both self-report and official data and found that delinquent's IQs scores were significantly lower than nondelinquent scores. The authors concluded that low IQ was an important predictor of delinquency.

Subsequent studies also linked criminal behavior or delinquency to low IQ. Most of this research focused on delinquency in adolescents with low IQs. First, it was believed that youths with low intelligence did poorly in school. Students with poor performance felt more alienated from school; therefore, poor school performance was thought to contribute to delinquent behavior. Second, it was believed that a lower ability to engage in moral reasoning and to delay gratification increased the likelihood of offending. Finally, adolescents with low intelligence were thought to be less able to fully realize the consequences of their actions; therefore, they were susceptible to the influence of their delinquent friends (Lynam et al., 1993).

Other controversial issues stemmed from research on IQ, race, and crime. On average, African Americans score about 15 percent lower than European Americans on intelligence tests. These findings led some researchers to conclude that low IQ scores were more prevalent among African Americans. This finding was thought to explain why, as a portion of the population, African Americans are arrested more often than whites (Herrnstein and Murray, 1994; Wilson and Herrnstein, 1985).

The intelligence controversy began with a 1967 speech before the National Academy of Sciences by William Shockley, a winner of the Nobel Prize for physics. Shockley maintained that the differences in IQ between African Americans and European Americans might be solely the result of genetic differences, and these genetic differences might also explain the differences in poverty and crime rates between these two groups (Shockley, 1967).

Arthur Jensen (1969) wrote a lengthy article in which he asserted some of the same points Shockley made. Jensen argued that there was a strong possibility that African Americans were endowed with less intellectual capacity than were whites. From his review of the research on IQ, he found that approximately 80 percent of IQ was inherited, while the remaining 20 percent could be attributed to the influence of environmental factors. Jensen hypothesized that because African Americans differ significantly from whites in achievement on IQ tests and in school, the sources of these differences were genetic as well as environmental.

Richard Herrnstein (1973) agreed with Jensen that intelligence is largely inherited. He argued that intelligence influenced the formation of heredity castes. According to Herrnstein, social stratification is due to inborn differences in mental ability. Therefore, one's success in society is influenced by one's mental ability. In 1994, Herrnstein and Charles Murray wrote the controversial book *The Bell Curve*. *The Bell Curve* was an update of Herrnstein's earlier assertion that economic and social hierarchies reflect cognitive and intellectual abilities, as measured by IQ tests.

Studies such as Jensen's, Herrnstein's, and Murray's came under fire because of alleged methodological flaws and were also severely criticized as racist and reflective of the ethnocentric views of European whites toward other cultures. Other critics argued that low intellectual abilities could be associated with the contribution of social class to achievement on IQ tests. This oversight was crucial because critics believe that these tests are biased in favor of those from a middle- and upper-class environment as such people do better on IQ tests than those who are less fortunate. The most obvious criticism was whether IQ tests were a legitimate measure of intelligence at all since IQ tests attempt to measure innate potential, a feat some believe is impossible. For the most part, intelligence tests measure educability. But the problem of such a measure is that achievement in school is also associated with a cluster of other social and motivational factors that IQ tests may not be able to measure (Ryan, 1972).

Contemporary Biological Explanations

Modern biological theories in criminology differ from previous theories in that they examine the entire range of biological characteristics, including those that result from genetic defects (those that are inherited) and those that are environmentally induced. In addition, theories developed since the 1980s do not suggest that biological characteristics directly "cause" crime. Instead, they argue that certain biological conditions increase the likelihood that an individual will engage in some antisocial behavior that can be defined as criminal (Fishbein, 1990). Modern theories increasingly focus on the interaction between biological characteristics and the social environment, rather than looking solely at the effects of biology. Because these explanations stress the interrelationships of nature and nurture, they are more accurately called *biosocial* theories of crime.

Biochemical Conditions and Crime

Biochemical conditions, including those that are genetically predetermined and those acquired through diet and environment, are believed to influence criminal behavior. Biochemical theories received national attention in 1979 after they were used in the criminal trial of Dan White, who was tried and convicted in the murder of the former mayor of San Francisco, Harvey Milk. White was found guilty of a lesser offense and charged with diminished-capacity manslaughter, rather than first-degree murder based upon the now-infamous "Twinkie Defense." The jury accepted his defense attorney's argument that White's behavior was precipitated by his addiction to sugar-laden junk foods (*Time*, 1979). Such explanations have gained cautious acceptance by biocriminologists and are being used to help understand criminal behavior from a different perspective. Biochemical theories see criminal behavior as a function of diet, vitamin intake, hormonal imbalance, environmental contaminants, or food allergies.

Nutrition and Crime.   Biocriminologists maintain that minimum levels of vitamins and minerals are needed for normal brain functioning and growth, especially in the early years of life. If people with normal needs do not receive the appropriate nutrition, they will suffer from vitamin deficiency. People with vitamin deficiency can manifest many physical, mental, and behavioral problems, including lower intelligence test scores (Neisser et al., 1996). Therefore, diet and nutrition play a role in aggression and crime (Schoenthaler and Doraz, 1983).

More recent studies have revealed that an insufficiency of certain chemicals and minerals, including sodium, potassium, calcium, amino acids, and other vitamins or minerals, can lead to depression, mania, cognitive problems, memory loss, and abnormal sexual activity (Krassner, 1986). For example, some studies have examined the relationship between crime and vitamin deficiency and found that antisocial behavior could be caused by insufficient quantities of some B vitamins and vitamin C. Others have discovered that the behavior of schizophrenics and of children with learning and behavior disorders is affected by some B-complex vitamins (B_3 and B_6). It was found that the addition of these vitamins to the diets of children who were deficient in them could control unruly behavior and improve school performance (Hippchen, 1978) .

Hypoglycemia, Hyperglycemia, and Crime.   One of the first studies that focused on chemical imbalances in the body as the cause of crime was published in a British medical journal. This study linked murder to hypoglycemia, or low blood sugar (Hill and Sargent, 1943). Low blood sugar can occur when there is too much insulin in the blood or because of near-starvation diets. It occurs when glucose (sugar) in the blood falls below levels necessary for normal and efficient brain functioning. When deprived of blood sugar, the brain's capacity to properly function is reduced. Symptoms of this chemical imbalance include irritability, anxiety, depression, crying spells, headaches, and confusion.

More recent studies have linked excess consumption of refined white sugar to hyperactivity and aggressiveness. Diets that are high in carbohydrates and sugar have been associated with attention-span deficiencies and students' ability to score on tests measuring reasoning power (Kershner and Hawke, 1979). Another study, however, published in 1994, seemed to contradict the notion that sugar may lead to hyperactivity. S. Schoenthaler and W. Doraz (1983) conducted an experiment on 276 incarcerated youths to determine whether a change in the amount of sugar in their diet would have an influence on their behavior within the institutional setting. They found that after several dietary changes were made, there was a significant reduction in disciplinary actions within the institution. Other studies have failed to produce the same results. One study of 25 preschool children and 23 school-age children who were sensitive to sugar involved following a different diet for three consecutive weeks. The first group of children was placed on a diet high in sugar, the second group on a diet using NutraSweet (aspartame), and the third group used saccharin. The findings revealed little evidence of cognitive or behavioral differences that could be linked to diet. Ironically, the sugar diets seemed to have a calming effect on the children (Wolraich et al., 1994).

Allergies and Crime. Some foods are believed to cause allergic reactions in humans that can lead to violence and even murder. Allergies are defined as unusual or excessive reactions of the body to foreign substances. Cerebral allergies cause an excessive reaction of the brain, whereas neuroallergies affect the nervous system. Both forms of allergic reactions are believed to cause the allergic person to produce enzymes that attack wholesome foods as if they were dangerous to the body (Wunderlich, 1978). Some foods commonly known to produce these allergic reactions are milk, citrus fruit, chocolate, corn, wheat, and eggs, all of which have been found to cause swelling of the brain and the brainstem. Allergic reactions have also been linked to mental, emotional, and behavioral problems, such as hyperactivity in children who may consequently be mislabeled as potential delinquents.

Environmental Contaminants and Crime. Pollution or environmental contaminants are believed to contribute to criminal behavior. Lead, copper, cadmium, mercury, and inorganic gases, such as chlorine and nitrogen dioxide, are sometimes found in dangerous levels. At high levels, these substances can cause severe illness or death; at more moderate levels, they have been linked to emotional and behavioral disorders (Schauss, 1980). Lead poisoning has also been found to contribute to hyperactivity in children and to antisocial behavior (David et al., 1976).

Deborah Denno (1993) investigated the behavior of more than nine hundred African American youths and found that lead poisoning was one of the most significant predictors of male delinquency and persistent adult criminality. Herbert Needleman and his colleagues (Needleman et al., 1996) tracked 300 boys from ages seven to eleven and found that those who had high lead concentrations in their bones were much more likely to report attention problems, delinquency, and aggressiveness. High lead ingestion has also been reported as contributing to lower IQ scores, which is in turn linked to aggressive behavior (Neisser et al., 1996).

Neurophysiological Factors and Crime

Neurophysiology is the study of brain activity. Criminologists began to focus on this area of study after Charles Whitman killed his wife and mother and then barricaded himself in a tower at the University of Texas. While on the tower, he killed 14 people and wounded 24 others with a high-powered rifle before he was shot and killed by police. During his autopsy, the pathologist found a large malignant tumor in his brain. It was believed that this tumor caused his violent behavior. Investigators also found that he had sought psychiatric help. Whitman had kept a diary in which he described his uncontrollable urges to kill and had willed his estate to any mental institution that would study mental problems such as his own (Johnson 1972).

Whitman's fatal ordeal led researchers to theorize that there might be an association between neurological impairment and crime. One such impairment is minimum brain dysfunction, or MBD. MBD can result from a head injury or it can be inherited. In its most serious form, MBD is said to cause an imbalance in the urge-control mechanism, dyslexia, visual perception problems, hyperactivity, poor attention span, and/or explosive behavior. Some studies have found that up to 60 percent of criminal offenders exhibit some brain dysfunction when subject to psychological tests. Others have found some form of dysfunction in the dominant hemisphere of the brain (Bartol, 1999).

Attention deficit/hyperactivity disorder (ADHD) has also been linked to neurological factors. ADHD is most often found in children who exhibit poor school performance, bullying, stubbornness, and lack of response to discipline (Bartol, 1999).

While numerous attempts have tried to link neurophysiological factors with crime, the majority of the theories remain unsubstantiated. However, that does not mean that a link does not exist; it just still needs to be proven.

Hormones and Crime

Some criminologists link criminal behavior to hormonal imbalances in the body, arguing that the male sex hormone, testosterone, accounts for aggressive behavior. Several studies have found that male adolescents and adults with records of violent and other crimes have higher testosterone levels than males without criminal records (Dabbs and Morris, 1990; Udry, Talbert, and Morris, 1988).

D. Olweus (1987) reported that boys aged 15 to 17 showed levels of verbal and physical aggression that correlated with the level of testosterone found in their blood. These boys tended to be habitually impatient and more irritable than the boys with lower levels of testosterone. Olweus concluded that high levels of testosterone contributed to this pattern of behavior.

Alan Booth and D. Wayne Osgood (1993) concluded there was a moderately strong relationship between testosterone and adult deviance. They also believed however, that mediating factors, or an interaction between testosterone and other social factors, increased the chances of juvenile and adult crime. For example, higher testosterone levels were thought to increase the probability of criminal behavior in those persons who were risk-takers and exhibited impulsive behavior. It was also thought to diminish the interpersonal bonds that inhibit persons from committing deviant or criminal acts.

Although most research on hormones and crime has focused on males, some work has examined the role hormones play in female crime, especially in connection with the menstrual cycle. In some women, hormonal changes in the days prior to menstruation appeared to be linked to increased stress, tension, lethargy, and other problems; this condition has been called premenstrual syndrome (PMS). Hormonal changes following ovulation have been linked to irritability and aggression, but research on the strength of this linkage has been inconclusisve (Trurell and Turner, 1988).

Katharina Dalton (1961), a leading researcher, collected data from female prisoners to determine whether there was a link between PMS and female criminality. These prisoners were asked to think back to the time they committed their offense and to remember the dates of their menstruation. From this information, Dalton hoped to determine whether offenses occurred randomly throughout the women's cycles or if the offenses occurred during their premenstrual phase. She found that almost half of the prisoners she studied reported they committed their offenses in the eight-day period immediately preceding and during menstruation.

There are some cases in which women have used PMS as a criminal defense. One 1980 case involved a woman in Britain who was exonerated of murdering her live-in boyfriend. The English defense attorney based the defense on the fact the woman was suffering from premenstrual syndrome at the time of the homicide. The expert witness in this case testified that PMS caused the defendant to be "irritable, aggressive, confused, with a loss of self-control" (Udry, Talbert, and Morris, 1986). In 1991, another case linking PMS to violent or criminal behavior was decided in favor of a woman by a Virginia judge. The judge dismissed drunk driving charges against the woman, who had allegedly kicked and cursed a state trooper, after her gynecologist testified on her behalf. The doctor claimed the woman's behavior was likely to have been due primarily to premenstrual syndrome ("Drunk driving charge," 1991).

The PMS explanation is not without its critics. Some believe the research on this subject is methodologically flawed. For example, critics argue it assumes that women can accurately remember when menstruation occurred, since even a few days' error can place their crime outside their premenstrual phase. Dalton's work has also been criticized because stress and other factors, such as diet, can disrupt women's cycles, so menstruation may occur irregularly. If the stress of committing crime, or the stress leading up to the crime, hastens menstruation, it may appear that the crime was committed in a woman's premenstrual phase only because menstruation occurred sooner than normal (Katz and Chambliss, 1995). These arguments are supported by Diana Fishbein's (1992) study of women incarcerated for crimes of violence. Her findings revealed that for a significant number of women, the crimes were committed during the premenstrual period. Fishbein concluded that these women experienced cyclical hormonal changes that heightened their feelings of anxiety and hostility. However, the fact that the vast majority of women do not commit crimes during PMS appears to make this argument more of a mitigating circumstance than an explanation for criminal behavior.

▨▨▨ SUMMARY ▨▨▨

The link between biology and crime begins with determinism, the view that factors beyond a person's control can determine his or her behavior. Determinism was the basis of the first biological theory of criminality offered by Cesare Lombroso. Lombroso's theories suggested that criminality was linked to physical characteristics. Following in the footsteps of Lombroso were Goring and Hooten, who believed that heredity was linked to criminal behavior and Dugdale and Goddard, who took heredity one step further and looked at family history as a possible factor in criminality. Sheldon examined the effect of body types, which was reinforced by Glueck's research. More recent research has included theories involving twins, chromosomal abnormalities, gender, and intelligence. Contemporary biological research has examined environment, nutrition, allergies, hormones, and neurophysiological factors.

The early biological theories emphasized hard determinism with little regard for the social environment. Later theories stressed soft determinism, in which nature was seen to be the primary influence with nurture having some impact. Modern bio-criminology proposes explanations based on the interaction of nature *and* nurture rather than nature *versus* nurture. Nature is seen as providing the predisposition for behaviors with nurture creating the situations for behaviors to occur.

Biological explanations of crime and criminality have historically been ignored by U.S. criminologists because most received their initial training in sociology. The potential of early and transitional biological theories for racial and class stereotyping has also created opposition both within the social sciences and society at large. However, as we learn more about physiological influences on human behavior, we must consider the interaction of biosocial factors when studying crime and criminality.

DISCUSSION QUESTIONS

1. Describe how the early biological theories exemplified hard determinism.

2. Why did the early studies of physical features and crime receive such strong criticism?

3. How did the transitional theories differ from the early theories? Why did they remain so controversial?

4. How have contemporary theories evolved beyond the limitations of previous theories?

5. Why do you think that even the new biosocial theories do not receive full support or attention?

REFERENCES

Bartol, C. R. (1999). *Criminal behavior: A psychosocial approach,* 5th ed. Englewood Cliffs, NJ: Prentice Hall.

Booth, A., and Osgood, D. W. (1993). The influence of testosterone on deviance in adulthood: Assessing and explaining the relationship. *Criminology* 31(1): 93–117.

Chesney-Lind, M., and Sheldon, R. G. (1992). *Girls, delinquency, and juvenile justice.* Pacific Grove, CA: Brooks/Cole.

Christiansen, K. O. (1974). Seriousness of criminality and concordance among Danish twins. In R. Hood, ed., *Crime, criminology, and public policy.* New York: Free Press.

Dabbs, J., and Morris, R. (1990). Testosterone and antisocial behavior in a sample of 4,462 men. *Psychological Science* 1: 209–11.

Dalgaard, S. O., and Kringlen, E. (1976). A Norwegian twin study of criminality. *British Journal of Criminology* 16(2): 213–32.

Dalton, K. (1961). Menstruation and crime. *British Medical Journal* 2: 1752–53.

David, O., Hoffman, S., Sverd, S., Clark, J., and Voeller, K. (1976). Lead and hyperactivity, behavior response to chelation: A pilot study. *American Journal of Psychiatry,* 133: 1155–58.

Denno, D. (1993). Considering lead poisoning as a criminal defense. *Fordham Urban Law Journal* 20: 377–400.

Driver, E. D. (1972). Introductory essay. In Charles Goring, *The English convict: A statistical study,* 1913 ed. Rpr. Montclair NJ: Patterson-Smith.

Dugdale, R. (1877). *The Jukes: A study in crime, pauperism, disease, and heredity.* New York: Putnam.

Fayetteville (North Carolina) *Observer-Times.* (1991, June 7). Drunk Driving Charge Dismissed: PMS Cited. p. 3A.

Fink, A. E. (1938). *The causes of crime: Biological theories in the United States, 1800–1915.* Philadelphia: University of Pennsylvania Press.

Fishbein, D. H. (1990). Biological perspectives in criminology. *Criminology* 28(1): 27–72.

_____. (1992) The psychobiology of female aggression. *Criminal Justice and Behavior* 19: 99–126.

Glueck, S., and Glueck, E. (1950). *Unraveling juvenile delinquency.* New York: Commonwealth Fund.

_____. (1956). *Physique and delinquency.* Cambridge: Harvard University Press.

Goddard, H. (1912). *The Kallikak family: A study in the heredity of feeblemindedness.* New York: Macmillan.

_____. (1914). *Feeblemindedness: Its causes and consequences.* New York: Macmillan. Rpr. New York: Arno Press, 1972.

Goring, C. (1912). *The English convict: A statistical study.* London: His Majesty's Stationery Office. Rpr. Montclair, NJ: Patterson Smith, 1972.

Gould, S. (1981). *The mismeasure of man.* New York: W. W. Norton.

Hagan, F. E. (1998). *Introduction to criminality,* 4th ed. Chicago: Nelson Hall.

Herrnstein, R. (1973). *I.Q. in the meritocracy.* Boston: Little, Brown.

_____. (1994). *The bell curve: Intelligence and class structure in American life.* New York: Free Press.

Hill, D., and Sargent, W. W. (1943). A case of matricide. *Lancet,* 244: 526–27.

Hippchen, L. (1978). *Ecologic-biochemical approaches to treatment of delinquents and criminals.* New York: Von Nostrand Reinhold.

Hirschi, T., and Hindelang, M. S. (1977). Intelligence and delinquency: A revisionist review. *American Sociological Review* 42: 57–87.

Hooten, E. A. (1939b). *Crime and the man.* Cambridge: Harvard University Press.

Hutchings, B., and Mednick, S. A. (1977). Criminality in adoptees and their adoptive and biological parents: A pilot study. In S. A. Mednick and K. O. Christiansen, eds., *Biological bases in criminal behavior.* New York: Gardner Press.

Jacobs, P. A., Brunton, M., and Melville, M. (1965). Aggressive behavior, mental subnormality, and the XXY male. *Nature* 208: 1351–52.

Jensen, A. R. (1969). How much can we boost IQ and scholastic achievement? *Harvard Educational Review* 39: 1–123.

Johnson. R. (1972). *Aggression in man and animals.* Philadelphia: Saunders.

Jones, D. A. (1986). *History of criminology: A philosophical perspective.* Westport, CT: Greenwood.

Katz, J., and Chambliss, W. J. (1995). Biology and crime. In J. F. Sheley, ed., *Criminology: A contemporary handbook,* pp. 275–303. Belmont: CA: Wadsworth.

Kershner, J., and Hawke, W. (1979). Megavitamins and learning disorders: A controlled double-blind experiment. *Journal of Nutrition* 109: 819–26.

Krassner, M. (1986). Diet and brain functions. *Nutrition Reviews* 44: 12–15.

Lombroso, C. (1920). *The female offender.* New York: Appleton.

Lombroso-Ferrero, G. (1972). *Criminal man according to the classification of Cesare Lombroso.* Montclair, NJ: Patterson Smith.

Lynam, D., Moffitt, T., and Stouthamer-Loeber, M. (1993). Explaining the relation between IQ and delinquency: Class, race, test motivation, school failure, or self control? *Journal of Abnormal Psychology* 102: 187–96.

Mednick, S. A., and Christiansen, K. O. (1971). *Bisocial bases in criminal behavior.* New York: Gardner.

Needleman, H., Reiss, J., Tobin, M., Biesecker, G., and Greenhouse, J. (1996). Bone lead levels and delinquent behavior. *Journal of the American Medical Association* 275: 363–69.

Neisser, U., et al. (1996). Intelligence: Knowns and unknowns. *American Psychologist* 51: 77–101.

Olweus, D. (1987). Testosterone and adrenaline: Aggressive antisocial behavior in normal adolescent males. In S. A. Mednick, T. E. Moffitt, and S. A. Stack, eds., *The causes of crime: New biological approaches.* Cambridge, England: Cambridge University Press.

Rowe, D., and Osgood, D. W. (1984). Hereditary and sociological theories of delinquency: A reconsideration. *American Sociological Review* 49: 526–40.

Ryan, J. (1972). IQ—the illusion of objectivity. In K. Richardson and D. Spears, eds., *Race and intelligence.* Baltimore: Penguin.

Schauss, A. (1980). *Diet, crime and delinquency.* Berkeley: Parker House.

Schoenthaler, S., and Doraz, W. (1983). Types of offenses which can be reduced in an institutional setting using nutritional intervention. *International Journal of Bisocial Research* 4: 74–84.

Shockley, W. (1967). A "try simplest cases" approach to the heredity-poverty-crime problem. *Proceeding of the National Academy of Sciences* 57(6): 1767–74.

Sheldon, W. (1949). *Varieties of delinquent youth.* New York: Harper and Row.

Time Magazine. (1979, May 28). p. 57.

Trunell, E. P., and Turner, C. W. (1988). A comparison of the psychological and hormonal factors in women with and without premenstrual syndrome. *Journal of Abnormal Psychology* 97: 429–36.

Udry, R., Talbert, L., and Morris, N. (1986). Biosocial foundation for adolescent female sexuality. *Demography* 23: 217–27.

Vold, G. B., Bernard, T.J., and Snipes, J. B. (1998). *Theoretical criminology,* 4th ed. New York: Oxford University Press.

Wilson, J. Q., and Herrnstein, R. (1985). *Crime and human nature.* New York: Simon & Schuster.

Wolraich, M., Lindgren, S., Stumbo, P., Stegink, L., Appelbaum, M., and Kiritsy, M. (1994). Effects of diets high in sucrose or aspartame on the behavior and cognitive performance of children. *The New England Journal of Medicine* 330: 303–6.

Wunderlich, R. (1978). Neuroallergy as a contributing factor to social misfits: Diagnosis and treatment. Pp. 229–53 in L. Hippchen, ed., *Ecologic-biochemical approaches to treatment of delinquents and criminals.* New York: Van Nostrand Reinhold.

Zeleny, L. D. (1933). Feeblemindedness and criminal conduct. *American Journal of Sociology* 38: 564–76.

4

Psychological and Psychosocial Theories of Crime Causation

▨ KEY CONCEPTS ▨

behavioral theories

classical conditioning

cognitive scripts model

cognition

cognitive theory

conscious

deindividuation

determinism

ego

eros

Freudian psychology

frustration-induced behavior

expectancy theory

hostile attribution model

id

imitation

mental disorders

mental illness

moral development

Oedipus complex

operant conditioning

personality studies

physiological disorders

preconscious

psychoanalytical

psychodynamic projection

psychometry

pyschopathology

reaction formation

repression

rewards

situational instigators

social learning

social reinforcement

sublimation

superego

unconscious

This chapter was coauthored by Dr. Florence Ferguson of the State University of West Georgia.

▨ LEARNING OBJECTIVES ▨

After reading this chapter, the student should be able to:

1. Discuss the relationship between determinism and psychology.

2. Recognize Freud's psychoanalytic theory.

3. Describe the elements of Freud's theory.

4. Describe the premises of behavioral theory.

5. Contrast moral development, cognitive scripts, and hostile attribution as cognitive explanations of criminal behavior.

6. Contrast expectancy theory, frustration-induced criminality, and situational instigators as cognitive explanations of criminal behavior.

7. Explain personality theory.

8. Discuss psychopathology as it applies to criminal behavior.

9. Describe how the various physiological disorders might affect behavior.

PSYCHOLOGICAL EXPLANATIONS

Chapter 4 introduced biological theories of crime causation. Psychological theories are also viewed as part of the positive school of criminology. As with the biological theories, the psychological theories have a rich background but are often not popular with sociologically trained criminologists. These theories, however, like those in chapter 4 warrant discussion in order to understand the complexities of human (and subsequently criminal) behavior. As with biology, determinism plays a major fundamental role in the psychological theories.

Psychology and Determinism

Psychological and psychiatric theories explain criminal behavior primarily in terms of the personality attributes of the offender. These theories also consider biological and environmental factors in their explanations of criminal behavior. Much of the biological research done by psychologists and psychiatrists considered the impact of the environment on the offender. It also explained behavior by examining the relationship between the offender's biological and psychological characteristics to determine what may have caused the criminal behavior. Psychological theories argue that criminal behavior originates in the personalities of the offenders rather than their biology or their situation (i.e., environmental factors). Psychological theories have been generally classified in one of three areas: psychodynamic or psychoanalytic, behavioral, or cognitive theories. Psychological or *psychodynamic theories* examine unconscious behaviors that are believed to cause criminal behavior; *behavioral theories* examine the learning processes that led to criminal behavior; and cognitive theories look at how thought processes, such as thinking and morals, affect one's behavior. Table 4–1 shows the various psychological theories described within this chapter. Perhaps the best known, and the first of the psychological theories, is found in the works of Sigmund Freud.

Freudian Psychology (Psychodynamic)

Psychodynamic, or psychoanalytic, theory was developed by Sigmund Freud (1856–1939), a Viennese physician who was concerned with the medical treatment of a variety of functional disorders that seemed to be unrelated to any organic causes (Martin, Mutchnick, and Austin, 1990). Freud adopted the idea of the unconscious, an idea used by other psychiatrists, and argued that some behaviors could be explained by traumatic experiences in early childhood. He believed these early childhood experiences left a mark on the individual that was buried in the unconscious. In other words, the individual was not consciously aware of those experiences.

To explain his theory, Freud argued that there were three levels of the mind: conscious, preconscious, and unconscious. The *conscious* mind is the aspect of the mind that people are most aware of, such as their daily thoughts. The *preconscious* mind is said to contain elements of experiences that are outside our awareness but can be brought back to consciousness at any time, such as memories and experiences. The *unconscious* part of the mind contains biological desires and urges that cannot readily be experienced as thoughts. Part of the unconscious contains feelings about sex and hostility, which people keep below the surface of consciousness by a process called "repression" (Martin et al., 1990).

As a way to uncover these unconscious events, Freud developed the technique he called "psychoanalysis." Psychoanalysis was premised on "free association." The patient would be put in a relaxed position and

TABLE 4–1 Psychological Theories

Freudian Psychology	Behavioral Psychology	Social Learning	Cognitive Theory	Mental Disorders
Psychodynamic	Classical conditioning	Imitation	Moral development	Psychometry
Psychoanalytic	Operant conditioning	(See chapter 6)	Cognitive scripts	Psychopathology
			Hostile attribution	Mental illness
			Expectancy	Physiological factors
			Frustration-induced behavior	
			Situational instigators	

allowed to talk freely about whatever came to his or her mind. By exploring the associations among the issues the patient raised, Freud believed the individual would be able to reconstruct the earlier events and bring them to consciousness. Once the patient was conscious of these events, Freud argued that the events would lose their power and the patient would gain conscious control and freedom in his or her life (Vold, Bernard, and Snipes, 1998, p. 91). Freud later categorized his conceptions of the conscious and unconscious into three categories—the id, ego, and superego. The conscious state was called the ego, while the id and superego were the two unconscious states.

The *id* is the great reservoir of biological and psychological drives, the urges and impulses that underlie all behavior. This includes the libido, the full force of sexual energy in the individual. The id is a permanent unconscious state and responds to what Freud called the "pleasure principle," which causes one to seek and maintain his or her own pleasure regardless of the expense to others. The *superego* is the force of self-criticism and conscience. It is the moral aspect of people's personalities and is used to judge one's behavior. The *ego* is the conscious state of the personality, and it operates on the "reality" principle, which orients the person toward the real world in which he or she lives. It attempts to mediate the conflict between the demands of the id and the prohibitions of the superego.

Freud explored how the ego handles the conflict between the id and superego and found that the basic conflict stems around guilt. The individual experiences all sort of drives and urges coming from the id and feels guilty about them because of the prohibitions of the superego. Freud offered some explanations on how the individual might deal with this conflict. One way was through *sublimation,* in which negative drives are diverted to activities approved by the superego. An example would be to work off aggressive feelings in athletic competition. A less positive way is to repress the behavior. In *repression,* the drives are pushed back into the unconscious state in an effort to deny that they exist. Repression can result in *reaction formation,* in which the person acts out in extreme ways regarding certain issues. Prudish behavior by seeking to repress intense sexual desires would be an example of reaction formation (Bartol, 1999). *Projection,* in which individuals with repressed desires attribute those desires or behaviors to others, is also a response to repression according to Freud (1948).

Freud was also interested in the early experiences of childhood. He developed a theory of how children evolve through a series of phases in which the basic human drives become oriented. The most basic human drive at birth is called *eros. Eros* is the instinct to preserve and create life and is expressed sexually. Early in their development, humans experience sexuality, which is expressed in the seeking of pleasure through various parts of the body. According to Freud, the series of phases in which the basic human drives are oriented are the oral stage, the anal stage, and the genital stage. During the oral stage, or first year of the infant's life, the child attains pleasure by sucking and biting. During the second and third years of life, the anal stage, the focus of sexual attention is on the elimination of bodily wastes. In the phallic stage, which occurs around ages four and five, the child focuses attention on his or her genitals. Males begin to have sexual feelings for their mother, a phenomenon Freud called the *Oedipus complex.* Girls develop feelings for their father, and this is called the *Electra complex.* The latency stage occurs at age six, and during this period feelings of sexuality are repressed until the genital stage, which begins at puberty and marks the beginning of adult sexuality. If conflicts are encountered during any of these stages, the child can become fixated at that point and the child, as an adult, will exhibit behavior traits characteristic of those encountered during infantile sexual development. For example, those who are fixated on or who did not receive the attention they needed in the oral stage may become smokers or alcoholics. Freud's contention was that the root of adult behavioral problems could be traced back to the early years of life.

These descriptions have been used to develop psychological explanations for criminal behavior. The psychological perspective on ego development attributes criminal behavior to disturbances or malfunctions in the ego or superego. The id, unlike the other two, is viewed as a constant biological source of drives and urges, and it is similar in all individuals. Freud's theory, although not criminologically based, has been used to explain why some individuals are criminals. Freudians would argue that criminals possess underdeveloped superegos that lead them to have constant feelings of guilt and anxiety (Martin et al., 1990).

Freudians would most likely deal with criminal behaviors in the same manner as they would other psychological disorders, through *transference.* Transference is the healing process in which the analysts attempt to get patients to replay the earlier events in their lives that are thought to generate the problems. Within this process the patients are led to learn to cope with those earlier issues in order to correct current behavioral problems. One of the most common criticisms of this psychoanalytic theory is the claim that it is untestable (Martin et al., 1990). Proponents of psychoanalysis disagree. They argue that Freud's ideas can be expressed in testable hypotheses and that there is sufficient empirical evidence to support the theory. Despite these arguments, Freud's theory is given little weight in current explanations of criminal behavior (Dantzker, 1998).

Behavioral Psychology

Behavioral theories maintain that human behavior is developed through learning experiences. Whereas Freudian theories focus on unconscious behavior or biological factors, behavior theories focus on the actual behaviors people engage in during the course of their daily lives. These theories argue that our behaviors are shaped by other people's reactions to us. Behaviors are constantly being shaped by life experiences and can be reinforced by rewards or eradicated through punishment.

One of the oldest formulations about the nature of learning is that we learn by association (Anderson and Bower, 1973). This reliance on association is a basic tenet of behavioral psychology. Behavioral theories were founded in the work of Ivan Pavlov (1849–1936), a Russian physiologist. Pavlov's work with dogs won him the Nobel Prize in physiology and medicine in 1904. The dogs, who salivated whenever food was presented to them, were always fed in the presence of a ringing bell. Soon Pavlov found the dogs would salivate every time they heard the bell ring, even when no food was present. Pavlov concluded that the dog's salivation was an automatic response to the presence of food, and they could be conditioned to respond to other stimuli. This activity became known as *classical conditioning,* the process by which a learned reaction becomes automatic and internalized. Pavlov's finding was significant because it demonstrated that animal behavior could be modified by manipulating associations with external changes in the environment.

In classical conditioning the subject is passive and learns what to expect from the environment. A more refined version of behavioral conditioning is *operant conditioning.* In operant conditioning, the subject is active and learns how to get what it wants from the environment. Operant conditioning is associated with John B. Watson (1878–1958) and B. F. Skinner (1904–1990) and is now the dominant behavioral theory in psychology. Operant learning uses rewards and punishment to reinforce or curtail certain behaviors. For example, rats may be taught to press a lever by rewarding that behavior with a food pellet or by punishing them with an electric shock for failing to push the lever. The rat learns to influence its environment by associating rewards and punishments with its own behaviors. Thus operant conditioning is another method of learning by association (Vold et al., 1998, p. 182). As to its application to criminal behavior, the argument is that a person may become criminal based on associations with the act. For example, an adolescent who steals something because of prompting by the taunts of friends eventually will steal without the taunting.

Not all behaviorists follow the teaching of Watson and Skinner. Some hold that a person's learning and social experiences, coupled with his or her values and expectations, determine behavior. While classical and operant conditioning are associated with the behaviorist school of learning, a third theory describing how people learn by association attempts to combine them with elements of cognitive psychology.

Social Learning Theory

Social learning theorists believe behavior is learned through a process called *behavior modeling* or *imitation,* and all behavior is thought to be learned, including criminal behavior. In modern Western society, there are three principal models for behavior. The most prominent models are parents. Since children are in close contact with their parents, they model, or imitate, what they see their parents do. If children grow up in a home where violence is a way of life, they may learn to believe that such behavior is acceptable and rewarding. Even if parents tell children not to be violent and punish them if they are, the children will still model the violent behavior of the parents. Rather than altering the child's behavior, the inconsistencies of the parents' actions and statements coupled with seemingly unfair punishment exacerbate the child's frustrations. Albert Bandura described this process as resulting in adolescent aggression resulting from disrupted dependency relations with the parents. Parents who are poor role models, yet hold back affection and nurturing to "teach" their children proper behavior, tend to create frustration and anger within those children (Bandura and Walters, 1959).

Social learning theories are also known as social psychological explanations. Several social learning theories have been proposed by criminologists. Because they are more commonly associated with sociological explanations of crime and criminality, these theories are discussed in chapter 6.

Cognitive Theory

Cognitive theory is another area of psychology that has received increased recognition in recent years. Psychologists with a cognitive perspective focus on the mental process—the way people perceive and mentally represent the world around them and how they solve problems. The pioneers of this perspective were Wilhelm Wundt (1832–1920), Edward Titchener (1867–1927), and William James (1842–1920). The *moral* and *intellectual development* theories are the perspectives that are used to explain the behavior of criminals. Jean Piaget (1896–1980), the founder of this approach, hypothesized that people's reasoning processes develop in an orderly fashion, beginning at birth and continuing until they are 12 or older (Piaget, 1932). At first, during the sensorimotor stage, children respond to the environment in a simple manner, seeking interesting objects and developing their reflexes. By the fourth and final stage, the formal operations stage, they have developed into mature adults who can use logic and abstract thought.

Lawrence Kohlberg (1969) applied the concept of moral development to issues in criminology. He maintained that people travel through stages of moral development during which their decisions and judgments on issues of right and wrong are made for different reasons. It is possible that serious offenders have a moral orientation that differs from that of law-abiding citizens. Kohlberg's stages of development follow:

Stage 1:   Right is obedience to power and avoidance of punishment.

Stage 2:   Right is taking responsibility for oneself, meeting one's own needs, and leaving to others the responsibility for themselves.

Stage 3:   Right is being good in the sense of having good motives, concern for others, and "putting yourself in the other person's shoes."

Stage 4:   Right is maintaining the rules of a society and serving the welfare of the group or society.

Stage 5:   Right is based on recognized individual rights within a society with agreed-upon rules, such as a social contract.

Stage 6:   Right is an assumed obligation to principles applying to all humankind, such as principles of justice, equality, and respect for human personality.

Kohlberg classified people according to the point on this scale at which their moral development ceased to grow. In studies conducted by Kohlberg and his associates, criminals were found to be significantly lower than noncriminals of the same social background in their moral judgment development (Kohlberg, Kauffman, Scharf, and Hickey, 1973). The majority of noncriminals were classified in stages three and four, while a majority of criminals were in stages one and two. Moral development theory, then, suggests that people who obey the law simply to avoid punishment or who have outlooks mainly characterized by self-interest are more likely to commit crimes than those who view the law as something that benefits all of society and who honor the rights of others. Research using delinquent youths has found that a significant number were in the first two moral development categories, while nondelinquents were ranked higher. In addition, higher stages of moral reasoning are associated with such behaviors as honesty, generosity, and nonviolence, which are considered incompatible with delinquency (Henggeler, 1989).

Cognitive Scripts.   Another cognitive theory is the *cognitive scripts model* proposed by L. Rowell Huesmann (1997). In this model, individuals are said to apply cognitive scripts developed from past experiences to deal with new situations. New experiences are interpreted in light of the closest cognitive script that can be applied from memories of past behaviors. Behaviors that have been deemed as most appropriate in previous circumstances are then applied. Sometimes these behaviors are appropriate, sometimes not.

Feedback from the current experience is used to develop new scripts. Whether a script becomes encoded in memory depends upon how others respond and how consistent it is with the individual's other views of him or herself. Like the previously discussed behavioral reinforcement, a variety of competing influences (both internal and external) may determine whether the behaviors selected are criminal or noncriminal.

Hostile Attribution.   Kenneth Dodge (1993) uses a model similar to cognitive scripts to explain how children develop hostile attitudes. According to the *hostile attribution model,* previous influences on mental development cause some people to interpret ambiguous actions as hostile and threatening. The result is that these individuals, because of their flawed perceptions of hostility, respond aggressively to situations that do not warrant aggression. This model not only attempts to explain why some people typically act aggressively, but could also account for other criminal acts that might result from biased personal perceptions of society or specific social situations. This model has the potential to be expanded to social groups as well in that classes of people might develop feelings of hostility toward society or social events or other social groups. For example, hostile attribution could be said to occur among members of ethnic minorities who come to perceive all of society as being biased against them. It might also be applied to working-class whites who may believe that they, rather than ethnic minorities, are the recipients of societal biases.

Expectancy Theory.   Julian Rotter (Bartol, 1999) has done extensive research on the importance of expectations (cognitions) about consequences (outcomes) of behaviors, including the reinforcement that will be gained from them. People think about the consequences or outcome of their actions before they involve themselves in an act. Rotter argues that if an act or specific behavior occurs, it will depend on one's expectations and how much one values the outcome of that act. To predict whether someone will behave a certain way, we must estimate that person's expectancies and the importance he or she places on the rewards gained by the behavior. Often, the person will develop "generalized expectancies" that are stable and consistent across relatively similar situations (Mischel, 1986).

The hypothesis that people enter situations with generalized expectancies about the outcomes of their behavior is an important one for criminologists. Applying Rotter's theory to criminal behavior, one could hypothesize that when people engage in unlawful behavior, they expect to gain something in the form of status, power, security, affection, material goods, or living conditions. The violent person, for example, elects to behave that way in the belief that something will be gained. A serial murderer might be on a mission to kill prostitutes because he or she wants to "cleanse the world" of these women, believing that is "God's will," and that he or she will be rewarded with a "place in heaven for a job well done" (Bartol, 1999, p. 120).

According to *expectancy theory,* to simply label a violent person impulsive, crazy, or lacking in ego control fails to include other essential ingredients in the act. Although self-regulation and moral development are involved, people who act unlawfully interpret situations and select what they consider to be the most effective behavior under the circumstances. When people act violently, they usually do so because that approach has been successful in the past. Less frequently, they may have simply observed someone else gain by employing a violent approach and decide to try it for themselves.

Frustration-Induced Criminality. Leonard Berkowitz (1962) introduced a cognitive model that can be used to explain behaviors that do not appear to reflect previous behaviors as have the earlier cognitive theories discussed. Whereas cognitive scripts or expectations of reward usually reinforce certain behaviors, *frustration-induced criminality* is said to occur when the rewards that individuals or groups have come to accept as normal responses to their behaviors do not occur. According to Berkowitz, the higher the expectation of reward a person has, the more frustrated he or she will become if that reward is not forthcoming. In addition, if the failure of rewards becomes more frequent, the person may become more sensitized to the lack, resulting in increasing levels of frustration.

Unlike the hostile attribution model in which individuals or groups react with hostility due to an ongoing perception of threats or injustice, in frustration-induced criminality the opposite occurs. Individuals or groups react in a criminal manner because their expectations of reward have not been met. This model could be used to explain how a good-looking "ladies man" might react violently toward a woman when his advances are rebuffed. His reaction might be amplified if he felt that the woman rejecting him was somehow inferior to others with whom he had been successful.

Situational Instigators. We conclude our discussion of cognitive theories by examining the influence of situational instigators. Curt Bartol (1999) provides support for the view that behavior may be situational and that the circumstances of the situation may override previously developed prohibitions. Stanley Milgram's (1977) classic study of authority as an instigator of deviant behavior exemplifies this cognitive model. In this experiment, students were led to believe that they were administering electrical shocks to test subjects. The subjects were actually accomplices of the researcher who "reacted to the pain" of being shocked. Milgram found that despite personal concerns for the safety of the subject, the majority of students followed the orders of the "experimenter," even when the voltage applied was thought to be life-threatening. He concluded that for many students the close proximity of an "authority figure" tended to overcome personal inhibitions about causing harm to others. This is actually not a new discovery. Many of the Nazis prosecuted by the Allies after World War II cited the fact that they were following the orders of their superiors as a defense for their behaviors.

Other studies that demonstrated the effects of situational instigators were Philip Zimbardo's deindividuation experiments. In one study, Zimbardo (1970) found that residents of New York City looted an abandoned automobile within 24 hours while residents of Palo Alto, California, left a similarly abandoned vehicle untouched for seven days except, as an act of kindness rather than vandalism, to lower the hood during a rainstorm. He concluded that the anonymity that New Yorkers felt because of population density contributed to their higher potential for criminal behavior.

In a later study, Zimbardo (1973) conducted a prison experiment at Stanford University. College students were payed to assume roles as prisoners or prison guards. The personal identities of both prisoners and guards became secondary to their assigned roles. The situation became so intense with the "guards" becoming abusive and the "prisoners" becoming desperate for release that Zimbardo was forced to complete the experiment early rather than risk causing psychological trauma to his subjects. The deindividuation of the students as they assumed their group personas led Zimbardo to conclude that when placed in "psychologically compelling situations" many people can be made to do almost anything (Zimbardo, 1973, p. 164).

Studies of situational instigators demonstrate that the circumstances in which people find themselves can indeed cause their behaviors to be altered. The loss of individual inhibitions in a mob or riot is all too real for those who have seen it. Likewise, the bad behavior of ordinarily conforming people when they think that their behavior is anonymous has been well documented by the police as well as by a multitude of divorce lawyers. Unfortunately, situational theories do not explain why some individuals are able to resist the pull of group associations while others very easily shed their normal identities.

Psychometry

Psychometry attempts to identify psychological and/or mental differences that might exist between criminals and the law abiding. The feeblemindedness studies of Goddard (1914) and the delinquency studies of the Gluecks (Glueck and Glueck, 1956) discussed in chapter 3 are examples of psychometric research. More recently, Hans Eysenck (1996) has postulated that male hormones in reaction with other chemical imbalances may produce psychosis. However, with the possible exception of the research on the abnormal needs for stimulation on the part of psychopaths, psychometric explanations do not appear to have conclusive support. Perhaps the best known of the psychometric explanations are the *personality studies.*

Personality can be defined as the reasonably stable pattern of behavior, including thoughts and emotions, that distinguishes one person from another (Mischel, 1986). One's personality reflects a characteristic way of adapting to life's demands and problems. The way people behave is a function of how their personality enables them to interpret life events and make appropriate behavioral choices. Some researchers believe personality can be linked to criminal behavior. In their early work, Eleanor and Sheldon Glueck (1956) administered Rorschach (ink blot) tests to 500 delinquents and a control group of 500 nondelinquents. They found greater personality problems in the delinquent group. The Gluecks' findings are suspect because the problems could be the result of delinquent classification as much as distinct personality differences.

Several other research efforts have attempted to identify criminal personality traits. For example, Eysenck (1977) identified two personality traits that he associated with antisocial behavior: extroversion/introversion and stability/instability. Extreme introverts are overaroused and avoid sources of stimulation, while extreme extroverts are unaroused and seek sensation. Introverts are slow to learn and be conditioned; extroverts are impulsive individuals who lack the ability to examine their own motives and behaviors. Those who are unstable, a condition that Eysenck calls "neuroticism," are anxious, tense, and emotionally unstable (Eysenck and Eysenck, 1985). People who are both neurotic and extroverted lack self-insight and are impulsive and emotionally unstable; they are unlikely to have reasoned judgments of life events. While extrovert neurotics may act self-destructively, for example, by abusing drugs, more stable people will be able to reason that such behavior is ultimately harmful and life-threatening. Eysenck believes that the direction of the personality is controlled by genetic factors and heredity. According to Eysenck, these findings do not mean that individuals having these traits will become criminals (in fact, many leaders in business and government exhibit such traits) but that they have a greater potential to do so.

A number of other personality deficits have been identified in the criminal population. A common theme is that criminals are hyperactive, impulsive individuals with short attention spans (attention deficit disorder), conduct disorders, anxiety disorders, and depression (Farrington, 1988). These traits make them prone to problems ranging from psychopathology to drug abuse, sexual promiscuity, and violence (Frost, Moffitt, and McGee, 1989). As a group, people who share these traits are believed to have a character defect referred to as the antisocial, sociopathic, or psychopathic personality. Although these terms are often used interchangeably, some psychologists do distinguish between sociopaths and psychopaths by suggesting that the former are a product of a destructive home environment, while the latter are a product of a defect or aberration within themselves (Lykken, 1996).

Psychopathology

It has been suggested that criminal behavior may result from a personality pattern or syndrome commonly referred to as the *psychopathic* or *sociopathic* personality; these terms are often used interchangeably. Robert Hare (1970) proposed a useful scheme to outline three categories of psychopaths: the primary, the secondary or neurotic, and the dyssocial. Only the primary psychopath is the "true" psychopath. Hare classifies the criminal psychopath in this category. The other two categories meld a heterogeneous group of antisocial individuals who comprise a large segment of the criminal population. Secondary psychopaths commit antisocial or violent acts because of severe emotional problems or inner conflicts. They are sometimes called acting-out neurotics, neurotic delinquents, symptomatic psychopaths, or simply neurotic characters. The third group, dyssocial psychopaths, display aggressive, antisocial behavior they have learned from their subculture, for example, from gangs or families. In both cases, the label "psychopath" is misleading, because the behaviors and backgrounds have little if any similarity to those of primary psychopaths. Yet both secondary and dyssocial psychopaths are often incorrectly called psychopaths because of their high recidivism rates.

In recent years, the term *sociopath* has often been used by criminologists and sociologists to refer to the repetitive offender who does not respond appropriately to treatment, rehabilitation, or incarceration. Psychiatrists use the phrase "antisocial personality disorder" (ASP) and many psychologists refer to those offenders who demonstrate a "failure to conform to social norms with respect to lawful behaviors as indicated by repeatedly performing acts that are grounds for arrest" (American Psychiatric Association, 1993, p. T-4). However, ASP is more narrow than primary psychopathy because it restricts its definition to behavioral indicators. Hare's definition of primary psychopathy includes emotional elements and in the future is likely to include cognitive aspects. However, with each new publication of the *Diagnostic Statistical Manual (DSM)*, the definitions used to describe antisocial personality disorder are increasingly similar to Hare's primary psychopathy.

One respected authority on the behavioral characteristics of the psychopath is Hervey Cleckley. In *The Mask of Sanity,* Cleckley (1976) describes the major behaviors demonstrated by the full-fledged psychopath as distinct from the other psychopathic types referred to previously. Superficial behavior and average to above-average intelligence are two of the psychopath's main features. These characteristics are said to be apparent during initial contacts. Psychopaths usually impress others as friendly, outgoing, likable, and alert. They often appear well educated and knowledgeable and they display many interests. They are verbally skilled and can talk themselves out of trouble. In fact, their vocabulary is often so extensive that they can talk at length about anything (Hare, 1991). Studies show, however, that they often jump "from one topic to another and that much of their speech is empty of real substance, tending to be filled with phrases, repetitions of the same ideas, word approximations,…and half-formed sentences" (Hare, 1991, p. 57).

Psychometric studies indicate that psychopaths usually score higher on intelligence tests than the general population, particularly on individual tests (Hare, 1970). They do not seem to be plagued with mental disorders, either mild or severe, and they lack any symptoms of excessive worry and anxiety, irrational thinking, delusions, severe depressions, or hallucinations.

Even under high pressure, psychopaths can remain cool and calm. Not everyone agrees with the view that psychopaths do not suffer from some mental disorder. Some clinicians argue that psychopathy and schizophrenia are part of the same spectrum of disorders (Hare, 1996). Some forensic clinicians maintain that they occasionally see offenders who qualify as both psychopathic and schizophrenic (Hare, 1996). Some evidence suggests that it is not uncommon to find psychopaths who seem to have mental disorders in maximum security psychiatric units for highly violent or dangerous patients.

Other principal traits of the psychopath are selfishness and an inability to love or give affection to others. According to Cleckley, egocentricity is always present in the psychopath and is essentially unmodifiable. The psychopath's inability to feel genuine, meaningful affection for another is absolute. Psychopaths may be likable, but they are seldom able to keep close friends, and they have difficulty understanding love in others. They may be highly skillful at pretending deep affection, and they may effectively mimic appropriate emotions, but true loyalty, warmth, and compassion are foreign to them. They have a remarkable disregard for truth and are often called "pathological liars." They seem to have no internalized moral or ethical sense and cannot understand the purpose of being honest, especially if dishonesty will bring some personal gain. They are unreliable, irresponsible, and unpredictable, regardless of the importance of the event or the consequences of their impulsive actions. Impulsivity appears to be a central or cardinal feature of psychopathy (Hart and Dempster 1997).

In the 1960s, notorious psychopath or sociopath Charles Manson exhibited an uncanny ability to attract a devout cluster of unresisting followers. Ted Bundy, a charming and physically attractive law student, murdered the women he charmed with his wit and intelligence. Although some psychopaths have little contact with the criminal justice system, many others do because of persistent offending. Many of the murders and serious assaults committed by nonpsychopaths occurred during domestic disputes or extreme emotional arousal. On the other hand, this pattern of violence is rarely observed in criminal psychopaths (Hare et al., 1991). Criminal psychopaths frequently engage in violence as a form of revenge or retribution or during a bout of drinking. Nonpsychopaths tend to attack women they know well, whereas psychopaths attack men who are strangers. Crimes committed by psychopaths are described as cold-blooded, "without the emotions that accompany the violence of nonpsychopaths" (Hare, 1991, p. 395). Hare's research supports the conclusion that psychopaths are not treatable because of their callous attitudes and behaviors (1996, p. 41).

Mental and Physiological Disorders

Mental Illness. *Mental illnesses* range from mild emotional distress to outright insanity. Most of us experience periods of depression and frustration at times in our lives that cause us to think or act irrationally. Such irrational behavior, although notable to friends and family members, may not be severe and may not have lingering consequences. When such behavior does interfere with our ability to function within our work or social situations, some sort of intervention may be necessary. If the behaviors could be harmful to ourselves or others, compulsory intervention may be needed.

There are numerous stories of violent mentally ill people who pose harm to themselves or others. While the police do on occasion have to deal with people who are depressed, schizophrenic, paranoid, or suicidal, these contacts are not frequent. Police contacts with people who are totally out of touch with reality are even less frequent, and rarely will the police officers have to deal with a deranged person who is committing acts of mayhem against others. When such incidents do occur, however, they catch the attention of the media and public alike.

Most acts of violence by mentally ill people are assaults on family members within their home (Monohan, 1996). They are usually the result of mentally disturbed individuals' inability to cope with what is to them an adverse situation. When these situations become explosive and weapons are available, such people can be extremely dangerous. Fortunately, the vast majority of these situations are dealt with through counseling or medical intervention before they escalate to violence.

Physiological Disorders. Physiological disorders would more appropriately be classified as biological influences on human behavior. However, we are discussing them within this chapter because of their psychological impacts on those who suffer from them as well as the responses they evoke from others. There are currently 40 types of muscular diseases affecting more than 1 million Americans (MDA, 1999). Neurological disorders such as multiple sclerosis and cerebral palsy make life difficulty for others. Epilepsy, although not a continuously dehabilitating condition, can also create problems for those who experience periodic seizures. Tourette's syndrome, autism, and Down syndrome are other physiological disorders that can cause serious difficulties for those individuals whose actions are misinterpreted by others.

Attention deficit hyperactivity is another disability that affects many Americans. Inattention difficulties, hyperactivity, and impulsiveness exemplify this disorder. School failure and emotional difficulties are frequent byproducts of this disorder when it is not properly treated. Other physiological disorders include dyslexia, letter reversal that makes reading difficult; dyscalculia, which makes understanding math difficult; and dysgraphia, which is difficulty with written work or handwriting. Last, auditory processing difficulties can make comprehension of auditory information problematic. The effects of physiological disorders may result in truancy and juvenile delinquency resulting from frustration with school failures and may also lead to severe emotional difficulties if left untreated.

SUMMARY

The psychological theories of criminality follow a deterministic path, similar to the biological theories discussed in chapter 3. The early psychological theorists focused on personality development and its link to criminality. Beginning with Freud, this argument was that criminal behavior resulted from arrested development at a particular stage of adolescence.

Behavioral theorists such as Pavlov suggested that conditioning plays a role in criminal behavior. This conditioning may be either classical, which is passive and expectant, or operant, which is active and solicitous. Operant conditioning, associated with John B. Watson and B.F. Skinner, uses rewards and punishment to reinforce certain behaviors. It is probably the dominant learning theory in psychology.

Social learning theories are exemplified by Rotter's expectancy theory, in which expectations about consequences and reinforcement of the behavior play major roles. This is substantiated by social learning theory, which states that learning and social experiences and values and expectations determine behavior.

Cognitive theory focuses on the mental process of perception and problem solving. Cognitive theories combine components of the previous theories. A key cognitive theory is Kohlberg's moral development theory, which offers seven stages of moral development. Other cognitive theories include cognitive scripts, hostile attribution, expectancy theory, frustration-induced criminality, and situational instigators.

Last, we discussed mental disorders, including psychometry which examines personality and how one adapts to life's demands and problems. We also discussed the impacts of psychopathology, physiological disorders, and mental illness on behavior.

Psychological theories have garnered minimal support among criminologists as explanations of criminal behavior. This is due to the sociological training of most U.S. criminologists and the limited application of most psychological explanations to individual offenders. As was the case with biological theories, psychological explanations warrant consideration in an interdisciplinary approach to the problems of crime and criminality.

▓▓▓▓ DISCUSSION QUESTIONS ▓▓▓▓

1. What is the relationship between determinism and psychology? How does it differ from that of biology?

2. Why do you think that Freud's psychoanalytic theory is not a highly recognized or acceptable theory in criminal justice?

3. Compare and contrast psychoanalytic theory with behavioral theory.

4. Does social learning theory address the issue of the formation of gangs and gang behavior? In what way?

5. Which of the cognitive theories do you believe best explains criminal behavior? Justify your selection.

▓▓▓▓ REFERENCES ▓▓▓▓

American Psychiatric Association. (1993). *Draft version of DSM-IV.* Washington, DC: Author.

Anderson, J. R., and Bower, G. H. (1973). *Human associative memory.* Washington, DC: Winston and Sons.

Bandura, A., and Walters, R. (1959). *Adolescent aggression.* New York: Ronald.

Bartol, C. R. (1999). *Criminal behavior: A psychosocial approach,* 5th ed. Upper Saddle River, NJ: Prentice Hall.

Berkowitz, L. (1962). *Aggression: A social-psychological analysis.* New York: McGraw-Hill

Clerkly, H. (1976). *The Mask of Sanity,* 5th ed. St. Louis: Mosby.

Dantzker, M. L. (1998). *Criminology and criminal justice: Comparing, contrasting, and intertwining disciplines.* Newton, MA: Butterworth-Heinemann.

Dodge, K. A. (1993). Social-cognitive mechanisms in the development of conduct disorder and depression. *Annual Review of Psychology* 44: 559–84.

Eysenck, H. J. (1977). *Personality and crime.* London: Routledge and Kegan Paul.

_____, and Eysenck, M. W. (1985). *Personality and individual differences.* New York: Plenum.

_____. (1996). Personality and crime: Where do we stand? *Psychology, Crime and Law* 2: 143–52.

Farrington, D. (1988). Psychobiological Factors in the Explanation and Reduction of Delinquency. *Today's Delinquent*: 37–51

Freud, S. (1948). The ego and the id. In *Complete psychological works of Sigmund Freud* Vol. 19. London: Hogarth.

Frost, L., Moffitt, T., and McGee, R. (1989). Neuropsychological correlates of psychopathology in an unselected cohort of young adolescents. *Journal of Abnormal Psychology* 98: 307–13.

Glueck, S., and Glueck, E. (1956). *Unraveling juvenile delinquency.* New York: Harper & Row.

Goddard, H. (1914). *Feeblemindedness: its causes and consequences.* New York: Macmillan. Rpr. New York: Arno Press, 1972.

Hare, R. D. (1996). Psychopathy: A clinical construct whose time has come. *Criminal Justice and Behavior* 23: 25–54.

_____. (1991). *The Hare psychopathy checklist-revised.* Toronto: Multi-Health Systems.

_____. (1970). *Psychopathy: Theory and research.* New York: Wiley.

_____, Hart, S. D., and Harpur, T. J. (1991). Psychopathy and the DSM-IV criteria for antisocial personality disorder. *Journal of Abnormal Psychology* 100: 391–98.

Hart, S. D., and Dempster, R. J. (1997). Impulsivity and psychopathy. In C. D. Webster and M. A. Jackson, eds., *Impulsivity: Theory, assessment and treatment.* New York: Guilford.

Henggeler, S. (1989). *Delinquency in adolescence.* Newbury Park, CA: Sage.

Huesmann, L. R. (1997). Observational learning of violent behavior: Social and biosocial processes. In A. Raine, P. A. Brennan, D. P. Farrington, and S. A Mednick, eds., *Biosocial bases of violence.* New York: Plenum.

Kohlberg, L. (1969). *Stages in the development of moral thought and action.* New York: Holt, Rinehart, and Winston.

_____, Kauffman, K., Scharf, P., and Hickey, J. (1973). *The just community approach in corrections: A manual.* Niantic, CT: Connecticut Department of Corrections.

Lykken, D. (1996). Psychopathy, sociopathy, and crime. *Society* 34: 30–38.

Martin, R., Mutchnick, R. J., and Austin, W. T. (1990). *Criminological thought: Pioneers past and present.* New York: Macmillan.

Milgram, S. (1963). Behavioral study of obedience. *Journal of Abnormal and Social Psychology* 67: 371–78.

Mischel, W. (1986). *Introduction to personality,* 4th ed. New York: Holt, Rinehart and Winston.

Monohan, J. (1996). Mental illness and violent crime. *NIJ Research Preview.* Washington, DC: National Institute of Justice.

Muscular Dystrophy Association (MDA) Web Page: www.mda.org

Vold, G. B., Bernard, T. J., and Snipes, J. B. (1998). *Theoretical criminology,* 4th ed. New York: Oxford University Press.

Zimbardo, P. G. (1970). The human choice. Individuation, reason, and order versus deindividuation, impulse, and chaos. In W. J. Arnold and D. Levine, eds., *Nebraska symposium on motivation, 1969.* Lincoln: University of Nebraska Press.

_____. (1973). The psychological power and pathology of imprisonment. In E. Aronson and R. Helmereich, eds., *Social psychology.* New York: Van Nostrand.

Social Structure Theories of Crime Causation

▓ KEY CONCEPTS ▓

anomie
conduct norms
concentric zone theory
culture conflict theory
cultural deviance theory
delinquent subcultures
differential opportunity
focal concerns theory
institutional anomie

lower-class culture
middle-class measuring rod theory
relative deprivation theory
social disorganization
social ecology theory
social structure theories
strain theory
structural functionalism

▓ LEARNING OBJECTIVES ▓

After reading this chapter, the student should be able to:

1. Provide an overview of the premises upon which social structure theories are based.

2. Present and discuss the theoretical concepts upon which social disorganization theories are based.

3. Compare and contrast concentric zone theory and social ecology theory.

4. Present and discuss the theoretical concepts upon which strain theories are based.

5. Discuss how Merton's theory of anomie exemplifies strain theory.

6. Contrast institutional anomie theory and relative deprivation theory.

7. Present and discuss the theoretical concepts upon which cultural deviance theories are based.

8. Present and discuss Sellin's culture conflict theory.

9. Present and discuss Cohen's middle-class measuring rod theory.

10. Present and discuss Miller's focal concerns theory.

11. Present and discuss Cloward and Ohlin's differential opportunity theory.

SOCIOLOGICAL THEORIES

In the previous two chapters, you were introduced to theories associated with the human mind and body. Perhaps to many criminologists the next set of theories examined, the social theories, "might best be considered the 'heart and soul' of criminological thought" (Dantzker, 1998, p. 45). It is within the social theories that a majority of the explanations of criminal behavior are found. As Mark L. Dantzker (1998) points out, there are a number of theories or explanations and no common consensus on how they should be divided. In this text, we have opted to divide the social theories into three main categories: social structure, social interaction, and social conflict. This chapter and the next two deal separately with these three social perspectives. This chapter addresses the social structure theories, that is, the theories that examine criminality as a result of social structure.*

Structural Functionalism

To begin, social structure and social interaction theories are considered structural functionalist theories. *Structural functionalism* is based on the view that the overall structure of society is sound (functional), and there is a

---

*Dantzker (1998) makes an excellent argument that several of the theories presented within this chapter could just as accurately be categorized as social process theories because of the social interactions involved in creating deviant and/or criminal behavior. It is a credit to his open-mindedness as a scholar that he has consented to the lead author's request that the more traditional classifications within the social structure theories be included here.

great deal of consensus among members of society as to what is appropriate behavior. However, imbalances may occur that cause individuals or groups to become deviant. These social imbalances may be due to the structure of society or they may be due to social interactions. While the overall social structure does not require drastic overhaul, over time it may require "tweaking" in order to correct inequities or injustices that occasionally arise as social changes take place. The theories to be discussed are shown in Table 5–1.

Social Structure Theories

The primary premise of *social structure theories* is that the lower classes engage in criminal and deviant behavior to a higher degree than does the middle class. A special note of interest is that the majority of the theories to be discussed were built upon the study of youth. Several theories are identified and offered in this section within the broad categories of social disorganization, strain, and cultural deviance.

Social Disorganization

Clifford Shaw and Henry McKay's (1942) ecology of crime theory attempted to explain crime and delinquency as a product of transition or change in the urban environment. They contended that transitional communities manifest social disorganization and maintain conflicting values and social systems. Shaw and McKay determined that environment strongly influenced criminal behavior. It was their belief that delinquency was produced by deteriorated neighborhoods rather than from the individuals who lived there. Their model included evidence of deterioration and disorganization that led to a loss of control over youth and encouraged gangs. The gangs then perpetuated delinquency, leading to higher crime rates (see Figure 5–1).

TABLE 5–1 Social Structure Theories

Social Disorganization	Strain	Cultural Deviance
Concentric zone theory	Strain theory	Culture conflict theory
Social ecology theory	Anomie theory	Middle-class measuring rod theory
	Institutional anomie theory	Focal concerns theory
	Relative deprivation theory	Differential opportunity theory

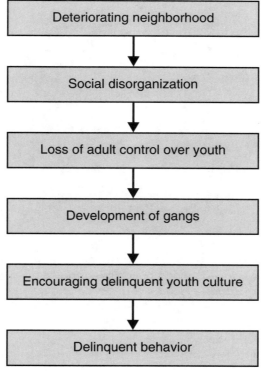

FIGURE 5–1 Shaw and McKay's Social Disorganization Model

Concentric Zone Theory. To support their social disorganization model, Shaw and McKay offered what became recognized as *concentric zone theory*. This model divided the City of Chicago into five zones starting with the innermost circle and moving away (see Figure 5–2). According to Shaw and McKay (1942), the highest crime was in Zone II, the area in transition. Those individuals who lived in this area experienced a lack of community cohesion and severe social disorganization. However, as they became able to afford better housing in Zone III, they left this chaos behind. Unfortunately, those moving into Zone II inherited the same confusion.

All theories have their strengths and weaknesses. The strengths of this theory are that it identifies why crime rates are highest in slum areas and points out factors that produce crime, still a relatively solid explanation for high crime rates in poor neighborhoods today. It is also interesting that it demonstrated that ethnicity's impact on crime was largely due to the areas that certain ethnic groups were forced to reside in rather than any inherent lawlessness.

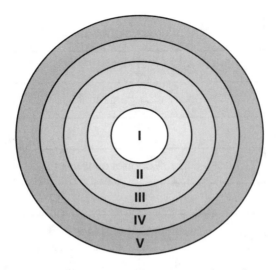

I *Industrial Center* — Heavy industry and manufacturing area
II *Zone in Transition* — Support businesses and some lower-class housing
III *Working-Class Zone* — Homes of unskilled and semiskilled workers
IV *Middle-Class Zone* — Homes of skilled workers and lower management
V *Commuter Zone* — Affluent area of upper-class homes

FIGURE 5–2   Shaw and McKay's Concentric Circles

The weaknesses of Shaw and McKay's theory are that it does not answer the following questions: Why does middle-class crime occur? Why are some youths insulated from a delinquent career? What causes some gang members to forgo criminality as adults? And, why are most lower-class people law abiding? Overall, this theory seemed to create as many questions as it answered. It did, however, become the basis for many of the urban programs used by federal and state governments to deal with urban problems. The effort to eliminate social disorganization continues to receive support from many social scientists, social advocates, and governmental leaders today.

Social Ecology Theory.   *Social ecology theory* is the successor to Shaw and McKay's social disorganization model. While abandoning the concentric zones, later social ecologists focused on the social ills that plagued certain areas of large cities. These "areal studies" emphasized community factors such as community deterioration, high unemployment, concentrated poverty, fear, resentment, and social isolation. Social ecologists argued that the social environments within these depressed urban areas inevitably led to high crime rates.

Bernard Lander's (1954) study of census data in Baltimore led him to conclude that anomic (see p. 92) and socioeconomic factors created social instability that resulted in crime. D.J. Bordua (1958) found support for socioeconomic factors in his areal research in Detroit. Other studies (i.e., Chilton, 1964; Polk, 1957; Quinney, 1964; Shevky and Bell, 1955) also used social area analysis to study the impact of social disorganization on crime. The mixed results from these studies resurrected interest in social disorganization theories but provided limited empirical support.

Today's social ecologists use computer mapping to contrast crime "hot spots" with areas of concentrated poverty, community deterioration, and rapid population changes. These efforts are often used in conjunction with environmental and/or situational crime-prevention strategies.

Strain Theories

The next category of social structure theories are the strain theories. Like social disorganization theories, *strain theory* focuses on the problems of the lower class within society. Strain theories differ from social disorganization theories in that they emphasize an individual's inability to reach higher goals or values because of his or her economic placement in society. When goals are blocked or unattainable, strain occurs that may lead individuals or groups to reject social norms and standards of behavior.

Strain Theory.   The prominent theorist in the development of strain theory was Emile Durkheim, a preeminent sociologist and criminologist. The basic assumptions of Durkheim's (1933) theory are:

1. An explanation of personal behavior must take into account the various social forces surrounding the individual.

2. Social facts, such as customs, obligations, laws, morality, and religious beliefs, are quantifiable and measurable things and may compromise the ingredients of scientific analysis.

3. As societies develop from simple, homogeneous populations to advanced states of division of labor, any explanation of deviance must also change.

4. A most logical and fruitful method for understanding and explaining social features would involve historical and comparative analysis.

5. The application of theory to effect planned change is a justifiable function of social science and specifically of sociology. (Martin, Mutchnick, and Austin, 1990, pp. 50–51)

More simply, Durkheim believed that crime is normal and necessary behavior; is inevitable and linked to the differences within society; can be useful and even, occasionally, considered healthy because the existence of crime implies that there is a way for social change to occur and social structure is therefore not rigid or inflexible; and calls attention to society's ills.

Furthermore, Durkheim is credited with coining the phrase "altruistic criminal" to describe an individual who is offended by society's rules and seeks social change and an improved moral climate through his or her actions. He was also the first to consider that anomie or anomic stress was a cause of strain. *Anomie,* as seen by Durkheim, is a normlessness and apathy experienced by those unable to cope with the rapid social changes that occur around them (Vold, Bernard, and Snipes, 1998). This perspective served as the basis for several subsequent explanations of crime and criminality.

Anomie.   For the average American, it is common to live in some kind of community and to participate in socially acceptable behaviors such as going to school or being employed. Yet numerous individuals drop out of school at an early age, may not have a job, and may not even have a place to live. While many fall into this group as a result of unfortunate circumstances, some live apart, outside the norm, voluntarily. They do not want the responsibility of paying bills or owning property and would rather just be free to do whatever they want. In other words, they actually prefer being in an anomic state. However, while their lifestyles may be considered deviant, many of these people do not engage in criminal activities.

Robert Merton (1968) described anomic stress as the product of cultural values that counterpose a more or less common set of culturally defined goals that can be reached through socially accepted means. Based on this theory, criminal behavior is the result of an individual's inability to reach those goals through the approved means. The key to Merton's theory is adaptation to cultural norms through acceptable means. Merton (1968) supplied a typology of modes for adaptation: conformity, innovation, ritualism, retreatism, and rebellion. For each mode there is either an acceptance or denial of the cultural goals and institutional means of reaching those goals.

The conformist mode, which Merton believes leads to the most stable society, accepts both the cultural goals and the institutional means: a person should own a home and vehicle and get them by working. Criminal behavior is based on the innovation mode whereby the cultural goals are accepted, but the institutional means of reaching them are denied: I want a big house and nice car but not a real job so I sell drugs. The ritualist mode denies the cultural goals but accepts institutional means: I'll work to get what I want, but I don't need a big house or a nice car. The retreatist mode denies the cultural goals and the institutional means. Often these individuals retreat through the use of drugs or alcohol. Others may actually withdraw from society by becoming hermits or joining groups of like-minded people in isolated communities. The final mode is rebellion in which people not only reject the cultural goals and institutional means but seek to change them, often through violence (see Table 5–2).

TABLE 5–2 Merton's Typology of Modes for Adaptation

Mode	Goals	Means	Behavior
Conformity	+	+	stable
Innovation	+	−	criminal activities
Ritualism	−	+	jaded compliance
Retreatism	−	−	drugs, alcohol
Rebellion	+/−	+/−	revolutionary activites

⁺ indicates acceptance of the goals and/or means
⁻ indicates denial of goals and/or means
Source: Adapted from Robert K. Merton (1968), "Social Structure and Anomie," in *Social Theory and Social Structure* (New York: The Free Press).

Anomie aids in explaining the existence of high crime areas and the predominance of delinquent and criminal behavior among particular social and ethnic groups. Yet, while it manages to explain crime rates, it does not help explain particular behaviors. It is also noted that this theory led to advances in subsequent subcultural explanations of delinquency. However, it shares the weakness with its successors of not adequately explaining why many who suffer from anomie do not engage in criminal behavior.

Institutional Anomie. Institutional anomie theory builds upon Merton's earlier work. Steven Messner and Richard Rosenfield (1994) argue that Americans are conditioned by our capitalistic society to accumulate material goods and wealth. We are socialized into devaluing other social institutions, such as family, church, or community, in our quest for financial success. When conflicts emerge between these other institutions and the workplace, they lose out. Ultimately economic norms and standards become dominant even within noneconomic areas.

According to Messner and Rosenfield (1994), the problem with this economic emphasis (other than the obvious neglect of other vital social institutions) is that it weakens informal social controls formerly exercised by families, churches, schools, and other institutions. When success is measured by financial status and social controls are weakened, crime becomes prevalent. This perspective offers an explanation of how, even in good economic times, criminal behavior can occur among those seeking to increase their wealth. It also can account for frustration-induced criminality on the part of those who are unable to do so. In addition, it is not limited to explaining lower-class behaviors but can also be applied to the middle and upper classes.

The weakness of this theory is that despite the emphasis on material success in America, citizens (of all classes) are rejecting lifestyles that are based solely on economic wealth. The American dream is being redefined by many as a comfortable life that may have fewer luxuries but enables them to enjoy their associations with other social institutions. In addition, even among the lower and middle classes, who are hard-pressed to make ends meet financially, anomie usually does not occur.

Relative Deprivation Theory. Another theory that builds on Merton's anomie is *relative deprivation theory.* In his discussion of anomie, Merton (1968) used the concept of relative deprivation to explain why many individuals remained law-abiding despite being in situations that led others to commit crimes. The premise is quite simple: You assess your situation based upon those who are around you. If you determine that others are better off than you are, you may become frustrated and anomic. If you decide that you are as well off or perhaps even better off than your peers, you will not.

Relative deprivation can be used to explain how individuals (even affluent people who believe that they are not as well off as other wealthy people) may experience anomie. It also is useful in explaining how the poor and ethnic minorities can believe that they are victims of income inequality and discrimination. J. Blau and P. Blau (1982) used relative deprivation to explain how the urban poor experience hostility and discontent because of their perceptions of social injustice. The closer their proximity to the affluent, the greater the likelihood that such feelings will develop. Therefore, urban restoration projects that bring the affluent back into inner-city areas are seen as both positive and negative in that they help rejuvenate cities and enhance the tax base for funding social programs while also emphasizing class differences among urban dwellers.

The strength of relative deprivation is that it is useful for understanding individual behaviors as well as group behaviors. In addition to understanding the frustrations of ethnic minorities, it is also useful in understanding the frustrations of lower-class, working-class, and lower-middle-class whites who believe that they are being unjustly penalized by governmental efforts to placate minorities. Therefore, the greatest strength of relative deprivation could also be said to be its greatest weakness in that it can actually be applied to all those, who, for whatever reason, believe that they are not getting their due from society.

Cultural Deviance Theories

The last category of social structure theories that we discuss are the cultural deviance theories. These theories are based upon the general view that criminal behavior is an expression of conformity to lower-class cultural values and traditions. The argument is not that the lower class is less law-abiding than is the middle class, but that it has fundamental differences in its cultural norms and standards that bring it into conflict with laws designed by the middle and upper classes.

Culture Conflict.   Thorsten Sellin's culture conflict theory is the oldest of the cultural deviance theories. This theory was an offshoot of Shaw and McKay's ecology of crime theory. Sellin's (1938) general view was that criminal behavior is an expression of conformity to lower-class cultural values and traditions. The two main assumptions of this theory are

1. Criminal law is an expression of the rules of the dominant culture, therefore a clash may result between middle-class rules and splinter groups, such as ethnic and racial minorities who maintain their own set of conduct norms.

2. Obedience to the norms of their lower-class culture puts people in conflict with the norms of the dominant culture. (Dantzker, 1998, p. 47)

This theory is best summarized through its strengths, which are that it identifies the aspect of lower-class life that produces street crime and adds the idea of culture conflict to Shaw and McKay's social disorganization theory. Its weaknesses are that it ignores middle-class crime completely and does not provide an adequate means of testing its theoretical premises.

Middle-Class Measuring Rod.   Anomie theory led the way to the development of extended theories, the first of which was the delinquent boys or *middle-class measuring rod theory.* This theory was introduced by Alfred K. Cohen in his 1955 text *Delinquent Boys: The Culture of the Gang.* The key points to Cohen's theory were that delinquency is due to status frustration, an inability to achieve success in a legitimate manner, and is a function of the social and economic limitations suffered by less fortunate individuals. Cohen also suggested that the lower-class youth commits crimes because he is unable to meet the standards of the middle class.

Cohen asserts that the lower-class child is constantly being measured by middle-class standards. The result is that the lower-class child, who accepts the middle-class standards but cannot reach them through socially approved means, turns to criminality to meet these goals. Cohen refers to these standards as the middle-class measuring rod.

Cohen identified three types of youth: the corner boy, the college boy, and the delinquent boy. Cohen pays the most attention to the delinquent boy, who adopts norms and principles directly opposite those of middle-class society and joins a gang in which activities are described as follows:

1. Nonutilitarian—delinquents do things because they feel like doing them and because they do not believe they have ties to middle-class values and, therefore, there is no need to conform.

2. Malicious—the delinquent enjoys defying social taboos.

3. Negativistic—the norms of the gang are the opposite of those of adult society.

4. Versatile—a delinquent can do anything as long as it is within the norms of the gang.

5. Short-run hedonistic—the gang is interested in monetary pleasures.

6. Autonomous—the only peer pressure is from within the gang. (Cohen, 1955)

This theory, however, offers little empirical support and assumes that lower-class youths really care what the middle class thinks or really want what the middle class wants. Furthermore, it should be noted that Cohen himself claimed that he was not trying to explain individual behavior, but the development of the delinquent subculture.

Focal Concerns. In line with Cohen's theory was a follow-up by Walter B. Miller, whose theory suggests that delinquency is a product of a united lower-class culture. *Focal concerns theory* claims that the lower class has a separate, identifiable culture distinct from middle-class values. The basis for Miller's theory is that slums are organized by a distinctive lower-class culture that emphasizes membership in one-sex peer groups. The one-sex peer groups, according to Miller (1958), are organized by a unique set of focal concerns that include trouble, smartness, toughness, fate, and autonomy. Ultimately, Miller suggested that the adherence to lower-class focal concerns is what produces delinquency (see Figure 5–3).

The strength of this theory is that it more clearly identifies the aspects of lower-class culture that push people toward criminal behavior. Its weaknesses are that it does not provide empirical support for the existence of a lower-class culture, account for middle-class influence, or explain upper-class crime.

Differential Opportunity. Another extension of anomie theory is *differential opportunity,* a theory introduced by Richard A. Cloward and Lloyd E. Ohlin in their 1960 text *Delinquency and Opportunity.* The aim of this theory is to explain how *delinquent subcultures* arise and persist in the lower-class areas of large urban cities. Their theory is based on the premise that the opportunities for lower-class youths to reach the American dream (education, wealth, status) are blocked, causing them to resort to illegitimate means. Furthermore, they contend that lower-class youths have the same

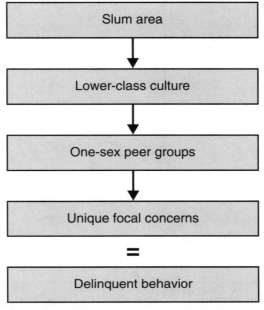

FIGURE 5–3 Miller's Lower-class Culture Model

wishes and needs as middle-class youths, so when legitimate means to success are not available, the lower-class youths resort to criminal means (see Figure 5–4).

Cloward and Ohlin (1960) observed that as an alternative to reaching the American dream, youths gain satisfaction by adapting to one of three subcultures (gangs): the criminal gang, which is the training ground for adult criminal activity; the conflict gang, in which fighting and territorial protection are the norm; and the retreatist gang, which is content to search for kicks through alcohol, drugs, and sex.

Like any theory, differential opportunity theory has its flaws. Major criticisms of the theory include the following:

1. Whether lower-class youths really want the same things their middle-class counterparts do is unknown.

2. The theory is attractive to the middle-class because it reinforces the values they themselves supposedly hold.

3. There is little support that lower-class youths become specialized in one of the three categories offered. (Dantzker, 1998; Martin et al., 1990)

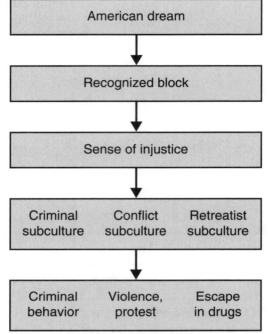

FIGURE 5–4   Cloward and Ohlin's Differential
Opportunity Model

Despite its faults, differential opportunity theory is one of the few theories that actually seems to be more appropriate in its explanation of criminal behaviors among lower-class youths today than it was during the 1950s and 1960s.

To conclude, the social structure theories are relevant to current attempts to understand criminality. Still, one should be aware that these theories all focus on male youths who were drawn to gangs, which places serious limitations on the utility of these theories for other types of criminality.

SUMMARY

The sociological theories are considered by many to be the "heart and soul" of criminological thought. This chapter addressed the social structure theories, that is, the theories that view criminality as a result of social structure. Three theoretical categories were identified: social disorganization, strain, and cultural deviance.

Social disorganization theories focus on the social environment as the cause of crime and criminality. The social disorganization theories discussed were concentric zone theory, and social ecology theory. Concentric zone theory argues that the areas of the city in which people live influences how they are able to live. Social ecology theory abandoned Shaw and McKay's concentric zones but continued to examine the relationships that crime has with overcrowding, concentrated poverty, and social disorganization within urban areas.

Strain theories also examine the effects that the social structure has in producing crime. Strain theories differ from social disorganization theories in that they emphasize an individual's inability to reach higher goals or values because of his or her economic placement in society. When goals for advancement are blocked or unattainable, strain occurs. The strain theories discussed included Durkheim's strain theory, anomie theory, institutional anomie theory, and relative deprivation. Durkheim's strain theory is based on the changes that occur within society and the pressures that are created for those who have difficulty in adjusting to those changes. Merton further developed the theory of anomie by identifying conformity, innovation, ritualism, retreatism, and rebellion as modes of adaptation. Institutional anomie theory argues that because Americans are conditioned by our capitalistic society to accumulate material goods and wealth, those who feel unable to do so are more likely to become deviant. Relative deprivation theory stresses how individuals or groups assess their social situation based upon those around them.

The last theoretical category was cultural deviance theory, which holds that there are distinct differences between the social classes. The lower classes come into conflict with societal norms and laws because of these cultural differences. The theories within this category are culture conflict, middle-class measuring rod, focal concerns, and differential opportunity. Sellin's culture conflict theory views crime as the product of a clash between middle-class rules and lower-class culture. The middle-class measuring rod theory holds that delinquency is due to status frustration of lower-class youths unable to meet the standards of the middle-class. Focal concerns theory claims that the lower class has a separate, identifiable culture distinct from middle-class values. Last, differential opportunity theory is based on the premise that the opportunities for lower-class youths to reach the American dream are blocked, causing them to resort to illegitimate means.

■ DISCUSSION QUESTIONS ■

1. How do the social structure theories apply to today's crime problems, especially among youths? Which one makes the most sense? Why?

2. Explain why social disorganization theory remains so popular today with social activists and governmental leaders.

3. Compare and contrast the strain theories.

4. Compare and contrast the cultural deviance theories.

5. What are the main shortcomings of the social structure theories? Their strongest points?

■ REFERENCES ■

Blau, J., and Blau, P. (1982). The cost of inequality: Metropolitan structure and violent crime. *American Sociological Review* 147: 114–29.

Bordua, D. J. (1958). Juvenile delinquency and "anomie": An attempt at replication. *Social Problems* 6: 230–38.

Chilton, R. (1964). Continuity in delinquency area research: A comparison of studies for Baltimore, Detroit and Indianapolis. *American Sociological Review* 29: 71–83.

Cloward, R. A., and Ohlin, L. E. (1960). *Delinquency and opportunity.* New York: Free Press.

Cohen, A. K. (1955). *Delinquent boys: The culture of the gang.* New York: Free Press.

Dantzker, M. L. (1998). *Criminology and criminal justice: Comparing, contrasting, and intertwining disciplines.* Woburn, MA: Butterworth-Heinemann.

Durkheim, E. (1933). *The division of labor in society.* London: Free Press of Glencoe.

Lander, B. (1954). *Towards an understanding of juvenile delinquency.* New York: Columbia.

Martin, R., Mutchnick, R. J., and Austin, W. T. (1990). *Criminological thought: Pioneers past and present.* New York: Macmillan.

Merton, R. K. (1968). *Social theory and social structure* (revised and enlarged ed.). New York: Free Press.

Messner, S., and Rosenfield, R. (1994). *Crime and the American dream.* Belmont, CA: Wadsworth.

Miller, W. B. (1958). Lower-class culture as a generating milieu of gang delinquency. *Journal of Social Issues* 14: 5–19.

Polk, K. (1957). Urban social areas and delinquency. *Social Problems* 14: 320–25.

Quinney, E. R. (1964). Crime, delinquency, and social areas. *Journal of Research in Crime and Delinquency* 1: 149–54.

Sellin, T. (1938). *Culture conflict and crime.* New York: Social Science Research Council.

Shaw, C. R., and McKay, H. D. (1942). *Juvenile delinquency and urban areas.* Chicago: University of Chicago Press.

Shevky, E., and Bell, W. (1955). *Social area analysis: Theory, illustrative application and computational procedures.* Stanford: Stanford University Press.

Vold, G. B., Bernard, T. J., and Snipes, J. B. (1998). *Theoretical criminology,* 4th ed. New York: Oxford University Press.

6

Social Interaction Theories of Crime Causation

▦ KEY CONCEPTS ▦

commitment to conformity theory
conflict theories
containment theory
differential anticipation
differential association
differential reinforcement
differential social control
functionalist theories
imitation theory
labeling theory
learned behavior
neutralization theory

self-concept
social bonds
social bond theory
social control theory
social ecology
socialization
social learning
social process theory
social reaction theory
social reinforcement
symbolic interaction

▦ LEARNING OBJECTIVES ▦

After reading this chapter, the student should be able to:

1. Provide an overview of the assumptions of social process theories.

2. Provide an overview of the assumptions of social learning theories.

3. Present and describe Sutherland's differential association theory.

4. Present and describe Glaser's differential anticipation theory.

5. Present and describe Akers's differential reinforcement theory.

6. Present and describe Tarde's theory of imitation.

7. Provide an overview of the assumptions of social control theories.

8. Present and describe Reckless's containment theory.

9. Present and describe Hirschi's social bond theory.

10. Provide an overview of the assumptions of social reaction theories.

11. Provide an overview of symbolic interaction theory.

12. Present and describe Matza and Sykes's neutralization (drift) theory.

13. Present and describe commitment to conformity theory.

14. Provide an overview of the assumptions of labeling theory.

15. Describe how the theory of deviant behavior adapts labeling theory.

16. Describe how differential social control theory adapts labeling theory.

SOCIAL INTERACTION THEORIES

In the previous chapter, we discussed the first set of social-oriented theories, those dealing with social structure. Like social structure theories, social interaction theories fall under the umbrella of structural functionalism. Whereas the social structure theories tended to focus more on social conditions and were, therefore, more sociological, social interaction theories may be viewed as being more social-psychological in nature. The social interaction theories present a relatively consistent theme in that social processes and interactions are seen as influencing criminality. Again, there is no consensus as to which theories, probably the majority of existing theories, should be discussed in this arena. Because of the number of theories and the somewhat differing perspectives found among them, we have chosen to divide them into two categories of interaction: social process and social reaction (see Table 6–1).

Social Process Theories

Social process theories examine the social mechanisms by which criminal behaviors are said to develop. Traditionally, social process theories include social learning theories, social control theories, and labeling theory. Because

TABLE 6–1 Social Interaction Theories

Social Process		*Social Reaction*	
Social Learning	*Social Control*	*Symbolic Interactionist*	*Labeling*
Differential association	Containment	Neutralization	Labeling
Differential anticipation	Control	Commitment to conformity	Theory of deviant behavior
Differential reinforcement			Differential social control
Imitation			

labeling theory changes the focus from the individual offender to agents of social control, we have separated it from social process theories and included it, along with symbolic interactionist theories, under social reaction theories. Our discussion of social process theories will begin with social learning theories.

Social Learning

The consistent theme of social process theories is that deviant socialization and intimacy with criminal peers breeds criminality. Social learning theories see this socialization as occurring through a process by which offenders (usually youth) are taught that criminal or deviant behaviors are acceptable and perhaps even more desirable than legitimate behaviors. This chapter presents four social learning theories. Each emphasizes a different way individuals learn to engage in criminal behavior. Our discussion begins with the oldest of the social learning theories, the theory of imitation.

Imitation Theory. The first social learning theory that we discuss is Gabriel Tarde's theory of imitation. This is the oldest of the social learning theories and influenced subsequent learning theories in both sociology and psychology. Tarde (1912) noted that

1. Individuals in close and intimate contact with one another imitate one another's behaviors.

2. Imitation spreads from the top down.

3. New acts and behaviors are superimposed on old ones and subsequently act to reinforce or to discourage previous customs (what Tarde referred to as the law of insertion).

Tarde's theory is built upon by Bandura's social learning theory, which claims that people learn to be aggressive and violent through life experiences. According to Bandura (1977), aggressive acts are often the result of modeling. He identified three principle sources or models: family members (i.e., if a parent is an alcoholic or abuser, chances are good the child will be), environmental experiences (i.e., getting "stoned" at a party with friends on cocaine), and the mass media (i.e., constant publicity of volatile events leading to violent actions). Bandura's theory concludes by looking at the four factors he attributes to producing violent and aggressive behavior: an event that heightens arousal, aggressive skills, expected outcomes, and consistency of behavior with values.

Differential Association.   Edwin Sutherland's theory of *differential association* is based on the laws of learning and includes the concept of symbolic interactionism. The basic focus is on social relations—the frequency, duration, intensity, and meaningfulness of association—rather than on the individual's qualities or traits or on the external world of concrete and visible events. Sutherland's major premise was that people learn to commit crime from their exposure to antisocial definitions, in particular individuals will respond to the cultural standards of their associates, especially the intimate ones. In his textbook, *Principles of Criminology,* which was first published in 1924, Sutherland offered the nine propositions that are the foundation of his theory:

1. Criminal behavior is learned.

2. Criminal behavior is learned in interaction with other persons in a process of communication.

3. The principal part of the learning of the criminal behavior occurs within intimate personal groups.

4. When criminal behavior is learned, the learning includes techniques of committing the crime, which are sometimes very complicated, sometimes very simple.

5. The specific directions of the motives and drives is learned from definitions of the legal codes as favorable or unfavorable. In some societies, an individual is surrounded by persons who invariably define the legal codes as rules to be observed, while in others he [or she] is surrounded by persons whose definitions are favorable to the violation of the legal codes.

6. *A person becomes delinquent because of an excess of definitions favorable to violation of law over definitions unfavorable to violation of law. This is the principle of differential association (emphasis added).*

7. Differential associations may vary in frequency, duration, priority, and intensity. This means that associations with criminal behavior and also associations with anticriminal behavior vary in those respects.

8. The process of learning criminal behavior by association with criminal and anticriminal patterns involves all of the mechanisms that are involved in any other learning.

9. While criminal behavior is an expression of general needs and values, it is not explained by those general needs and values, since noncriminal behavior is an expression of the same needs and values. Thieves generally steal in order to secure money, but likewise honest laborers work in order to secure money. The attempts by scholars to explain criminal behavior by general drives and values, such as the happiness principle, striving for social status, the money motive, or frustration, have been, and must continue to be, futile, since they explain lawful behavior as completely as they explain criminal behavior. They are similar to respiration, which is necessary for any behavior, but which does not differentiate criminal from noncriminal. (Sutherland and Cressey, 1978, pp. 80–82)

Sutherland's theory has its strengths and weaknesses. Its strengths include explaining the onset of criminality, the presence of crime in all elements of social structure, and why some people in high-crime areas refrain from criminality. An additional strength is that it can apply to both juveniles and adults.

On the other hand, the theory provides no answers to these questions: Where do antisocial definitions originate? How can we measure antisocial definitions or prove that someone has been exposed to an excess of them? The theory also fails to explain illogical acts of violence and destruction and offers no discussion as to how to adequately test the theory. Despite these concerns, differential association continues to be one of the more popular sociological theories. It may be seen as the foundation for later social learning theories.

Differential Anticipation. In light of Sutherland's differential association theory comes the theory of *differential anticipation.* The main contributor of this theory was Donald Glaser, whose major premise was that people commit crimes whenever and wherever expectations of gain from the criminal act exceed the expected losses with respect to social bonds (Glaser, 1956). The strength of this theory is that it combines principles of social bond, differential association, and classical thought. However, its weaknesses are that it has not been subjected to extensive empirical testing and it does not explain why expectations and crime rates vary.

Differential Reinforcement. A third social learning theory is *differential reinforcement theory.* By adapting the views of B. F. Skinner and other psychologists on operant conditioning and integrating them with Sutherland's differential association concept, R.L. Burgess and R.L. Akers (1966) argued that criminal behavior and attitudes are more likely to be learned when they are reinforced or rewarded by friends and/or family. When the rewards for criminal behavior outweigh the rewards for alternative behaviors, differential reinforcement occurs and the criminal behavior is learned. According to Burgess and Akers, people decide whether to commit crime after calculating whether the potential rewards will outweigh the potential risks. As Akers (1994, p. 98) noted, "whether individuals will refrain from or commit a crime at any given time (and whether they will continue or desist from doing so in the future) depends on the past, present, and anticipated future rewards and punishments for their actions." Although much learning of criminal behavior occurs within the intimate personal groups emphasized by Sutherland, Burgess and Akers observed it can also result from the influence of school authorities, police, the mass media, and other nonprimary group sources. These sources all provide rewards and punishments that influence the learning of behavior (Akers, 2000).

While Burgess and Akers stressed the social context of differential reinforcement, they also recognized that criminal behavior can provide its own rewards, such as excitement and increased wealth. Akers accepts the validity of Albert Bandura's modeling (see chapter 4) as a necessary factor in the initial acquisition of deviant behavior. But its continuation will depend greatly on the frequency and personal significance of *social reinforcement,* which comes from association with others.

The strengths of this theory are that it adds learning theory principles to differential association, and it links sociological and psychological principles. The weaknesses of this theory are that it fails to explain why those rewarded for conventional behavior will commit crimes and why some delinquent youths do not become adult criminals despite their having been rewarded for criminal behavior. In addition, some scholars consider it tautological, or circular, in that behavior is said to occur because it is reinforced, but it is reinforced because it occurs. R. Kornhauser (1978) points out that there is no empirical support for this theory. Still, the theory remains a very popular one within both psychological and sociological criminology. We should also note that with its blend of psychological, sociological, and classical features, it would also qualify as an integrated theory of criminality.

Social Control

The second group of theories in the social process typology are the *social control theories*. These theories start with an assumption that human nature is the motivator for criminal behavior, and that if some type of outside controls did not exist, individuals would naturally commit crimes. The first of the social control theorists, Albert Reiss, argued that the failure of personal controls (the inability to refrain from meeting personal needs in ways that conflict with society's norms and rules) leads to criminality (Reiss, 1951). However, he failed to consider the effect of family, environment, and community controls on an individual's behavior. Despite the obvious flaws in his argument, Reiss's assumptions paved the way for two social control theories: containment and social bond.

Containment Theory. Another of the social control theories is referred to as the *containment theory.* The main theorist, Walter Reckless (1967), claimed that each person has inner and outer controls that push him or her toward conformity or pull him or her toward criminality. He further contended that society produces these pushes and pulls and that they can be counteracted by internal and external containments:

1. Inner containment—the individual's personality

2. Outer containment—the constraints that society and social groups use

3. Internal pushes—personal factors such as restlessness, discontent, and boredom

4. External pressures—such as adverse living conditions

5. External pulls—such as deviant associates

The strengths of containment theory are that it brings together psychological and sociological principles and can explain why some people are able to resist the strongest social pressures to commit crime. For example, despite situational influences that might predispose other youths toward criminality, the "good boys" studied by Reckless and his associates (1957) were able to resist temptation because of their positive self-images. These self-images were seen as the product of encouragement and support from significant adults.

The findings from containment theory studies have been criticized over the methodology used (Shoemaker, 1996). In particular, one might argue that the labeling and subsequent treatment of "good" and "bad" youths by adult authority figures may have more influence on their self-images and actions than do "inner containments."

Social Bond. Finally, the last of the social control theories is T. Hirschi's *social bond (or control) theory,* whose main assumption was that it is the person's bond to society that prevents him or her from participating in criminal behavior. Should the bond weaken, the individual feels free to commit crime. Hirschi (1969) identified four elements of a bond to conventional society: attachment, commitment, involvement, and belief.

Attachment, which Hirschi claimed is the strongest bond, refers to how an individual attaches him- or herself to others. It takes into account the internalization of norms, conscience, and superego. The bond of commitment involves how an individual invests his or her time and energy in certain activities. The individual also considers the costs of being involved in delinquent behavior. Perhaps the most pragmatic bond is involvement in which an individual is just so busy participating in conventional activities that there is no time to engage in criminal acts. Last, the belief bond relates to an individual's acceptance of the moral validity of society's rules.

From a positive perspective, social bond theory explains the onset of criminality, applies to both middle- and lower-class crime, and explains its theoretical constructs in a manner that can be measured and empirically tested. From a negative perspective, it fails to explain the differences in crime rates, show whether a weak bond can be strengthened, and distinguish the importance of different elements of the social bond (which is more important, attachment or commitment, commitment or involvement, etc.?).

On the whole, social process theories have led to many discussions as to how criminal behavior is either learned or suppressed. Yet, there are those who would argue that it is how one reacts or responds to society that leads to criminality. We shall examine those arguments in the next section.

Social Reaction Theories

The second typology of social interaction theories, social reaction, includes two categories: labeling and symbolic interactionist. Social reaction theorists have postulated that it is impossible to understand criminality merely through the study of criminals but insist that crime must be viewed in its entire social context. Therefore, social reaction theorists argue that criminal behavior can be understood only in the context of how others react to it. This includes official reactions in which individuals and events are legally defined as criminal. It has been argued that criminal behavior is defined solely by the reactions that others have to it, creating what can be referred to as a "reactive" definition of crime.

Social reaction theories can best be summarized as attempts to explain the initial occurrence of criminal behavior in light of societal reaction to individuals or groups that are different from the norm. Additional occurrences of criminal behavior after the societal reaction are seen as the result of socialization caused by the social reaction. This leads to the question, "Is it the reaction of an individual, a group, or society as a whole that influences the behavior?" The following theories assist in responding to this question.

Symbolic Interactionist Theories

Symbolic interactionist theories focus on how human behavior is influenced by how situations are perceived and interpreted. Individuals tend to alter their behavior based on how they think that others perceive them. Therefore, behavior is a function of self. The roles that we think others have assigned to us determine our own self-image (Mead, 1934). We see ourselves in a mental looking glass that may or may not accurately depict how we are viewed by others. If these roles are positive, we adopt behaviors that we believe are compatible with them. Unfortunately, if those roles are believed to be negative, we are very likely to adopt negative behaviors.

Symbolic interactionism is an important theory in explaining all human behavior. It is particularly useful in explaining crime and criminality. The remaining theories all qualify as symbolic interactionist explanations. However, because of its importance in the evolvement of criminology as a discipline, we have separated labeling theory and its direct descendants from the other symbolic interactionist theories. The first symbolic interactionist theory to be examined is neutralization or drift theory.

Neutralization or Drift Theory. *Neutralization theory* (sometimes called drift theory) was proposed by David Matza and Gresham Sykes. Their main assumption was that youths learn ways to neutralize society's moral constraints and will periodically drift in and out of criminal behavior. They contended that delinquency is essentially an unrecognized extension of "defenses to crimes" in a form of justifications (Matza, 1964). In other words, criminal behavior can be rationalized by the offender but not by the legal system or society. These rationalizations can precede or follow criminal behavior and are said to serve to protect the individual from self-blame and the blame of others after the act.

Matza and Sykes (1961) identified five ways that delinquents rationalize or neutralize their actions:

1. Denial of responsibility—implies that the deviant act resulted from forces beyond the individual's control

2. Denial of injury—despite the fact that it was unlawful, the individual does not believe that the behavior really harmed anyone

3. Denial of victim—again, despite its unlawfulness, the belief is that the victim deserved the action taken against him or her and that the act was actually a form of punishment

4. Condemnation of the condemners—focuses attention from the deviant act to those who have condemned it

5. Appeal to higher loyalties—legal norms are replaced by a loyalty to other norms

The strengths of neutralization theory include explanations as to why many delinquents do not become adult criminals and why youthful law violators can participate in conventional behavior. However, the theory fails to show whether neutralization occurs before or after the criminal behavior, to explain why some youths drift and others do not, and to explain self-destructive acts such as alcohol and drug use.

Commitment to Conform. To complement the theory of drift, there is Scot Briar and Irving Piliavin's *commitment to conform theory.* This theory's main assumption is that short-term stimuli that influence behavior are controlled by the individual's commitment to conventional society (Briar and Piliavin, 1965). This commitment is believed to help the individual resist temptations. The positive aspects of this theory are that it helps explain both middle- and lower-class criminality and shows how control is maintained in the middle-class, keeping members from committing crimes. The negative side of this theory is that it fails to explain variations in crime and crime rates and why some children develop commitments and others do not.

Labeling Theory

Edwin Lemert's *labeling theory* has been recognized as the leading social reaction theory. The main assumptions of this theory are that

1. Two types of deviance exist: primary, in which crimes are situationally induced, and secondary, which is the result of labels and sanctions resulting from primary deviance.

2. Individuals will enter into a career of law violations when they are labeled for their personalities, especially if the labeling isdone by people important to the individual.

3. Labeling creates a stigma and affects self-image.

4. Labeled individuals view themselves as deviant and will increasingly commit criminal behavior. (Lemert, 1951)

Furthermore, labeling theory emphasizes the process and does not see deviance as a state of being but as an outcome of social interaction. It also argues that one problem with labeling someone deviant is that standards and norms used to define transgressions are not universal in character. Ultimately, the assumptions of labeling theory provide two models (see Figure 6–1). In Model One, the individual who has committed a deviant act receives the label of deviant and, accepting that label, continues to commit deviant acts. In Model Two, socially created rules automatically label a violator as deviant, stigmatizing the individual and allowing society to maintain stability.

The strengths of labeling theory include explanations of the role that society has in creating deviance and why some juvenile delinquents do not become adult criminals. It also helps develop the concept of the career criminal. The weaknesses are that it does not explain the reason the crime was originally committed, and it places too much emphasis on society's role. The two theories that follow attempt to address the weaknesses of labeling theory by incorporating other social interaction theories into labeling theory.

Theory of Deviant Behavior. One effort to strengthen labeling theory involves using social control theory to explain how negative self-images can lead to criminal and/or deviant behavior. Individuals who lack desirable social traits may become isolated from others. This isolation leads to feelings of self-hate and low self-image. The product of this self-hate is that commitment to conventional values is lessened. These social outcasts then associate with others like themselves, creating a deviant subculture that defies conventional values. Criminal acts are then committed as acts of defiance and/or acceptance of unlawful behaviors as appropriate responses to societal rejection (Kaplan and Fukurai, 1992; Kaplan and Johnson, 1991). The advantage of this theory over conventional labeling theory is that it explains how noncriminal deviance can actually lead to criminal behavior rather than emphasizing society's responses after criminal activity has occurred.

Model One

Primary deviance

↓

Dramatization of evil

↓

Deviant self-image

↓

Secondary deviance

Model Two

Creation of rules

↓

Labeling of selected individuals

↓

Stigmatization of the offender

↓

Societal stability

FIGURE 6–1   Models of Labeling Theory

Differential Social Control Theory. The last of the social reaction theories incorporates symbolic interactionist concepts into labeling theory to explain how youths' self-perceptions lead to deviance. Both formal and informal social controls are seen as causing young people to engage in reflective role taking (Heimer and Matsueda, 1994). Parental labels are seen as having a particularly great impact upon the young person's self-perception (Matsueda, 1992). If the youth's self-image is damaged by labeling, young people assume the deviant identity that they believe they have been labeled with. With this new identity, the likelihood of criminal behavior is heightened. This theory enhances labeling theory by explaining how an individual who is "different" can come to accept the label that they believe has been forced upon them prior to actual involvement in criminal behavior.

Before leaving the social reaction theories, we wish to note that these theories are of particular importance because they serve as the bridge between structural functionalist and social conflict theories. The previous sociological theories focus on how limitations imposed by the social structure or flawed social interactions might lead individuals to become criminal. The conflict theories that are discussed in the next chapter focus on how power and economic conflicts within society create criminality. The social reaction theories link these two perspectives by addressing how the actions of agents of social control might influence individuals or groups to engage in criminal behavior.

▬ SUMMARY ▬

Social interaction theories present a relatively consistent theme in their claim that culture and intimacy with criminal peers breeds criminality. Because of the number of theories and the somewhat differing perspectives found among them, we chose to divide them into two levels of interaction: social process and social reaction. The social process theories were further subdivided into social learning and social control theories. The consistent theme of social learning theory is that intimacy with criminal peers breeds criminality. Four social learning theories were examined starting with imitation.

The first social learning theory examined was Tarde's theory of imitation. Tarde's theory suggests that individuals in close and intimate contact with one another imitate one another's behaviors. This theory was further developed through Bandura's social learning theory, which claims that people learn to be aggressive and violent through life experiences.

The next social learning theory to be discussed was differential association theory, which is based on the laws of learning. The basic focus is on social relations rather than on the individual's qualities or traits or on the external world of concrete and visible events. Differential association theory led to the development of several learning theories that sought to better explain how the process of association influenced criminality. Differential anticipation was the first such theory discussed. The main premise of this theory is that people commit crimes whenever and wherever expectations of gain from the criminal act exceed the expected losses with respect to social bonds. Yet another social learning theory is Akers's differential reinforcement. The major assumption of this theory is that criminal behavior depends on the person's experiences with rewards for conventional behaviors and punishments for deviant ones.

The second group of social process theories was the social control theories. These theories start with an assumption that human nature is the motivator for criminal behavior. It is believed that if some type of controls did not exist, individuals would naturally commit crimes. Two social control theories evolved from Reiss's assumptions of social control. Reckless's containment theory argues that each person has inner and outer controls that push him or her toward conformity or pull him or her toward criminality. Society produces these pushes and pulls, which can be counteracted by internal and external containments. The second control theory was Hirschi's social bond theory. Its main assumption is that it is the person's bond to society that prevents him or her from participating in criminal behavior.

The second overall category of social interaction theories discussed was referred to as social reaction theories, which can best be summarized as attempts to explain the initial occurrence of criminal behavior in light of societal reactions to individuals or groups that are different from the norm. Additional occurrences of criminal behavior are seen as the result of socialization caused by the social reaction.

Symbolic interactionist theories focus on how human behavior is influenced by how situations are perceived and interpreted. Neutralization theory proposed that youths learn ways to neutralize society's moral constraints and will periodically drift in and out of criminal behavior. Criminal behavior can be rationalized by the offender. These rationalizations can precede or follow criminal behavior and are said to serve to protect the individual from self-blame and blame of others after the act. Complementing neutralization theory was commitment to conform theory. This theory's main assumption was that short-term stimuli that influence behavior are controlled by the individual's commitment to conventional society. This commitment is believed to help resist temptations to engage in criminal behavior.

The final grouping of social reaction theories was Lemert's labeling theory and its derivatives, the theory of deviant behavior and differential social control. These labeling theories assume that two types of deviance exist, primary and secondary. Primary deviance is the offender's first involvement with criminal behavior resulting from situational factors. Secondary deviance is the offender's subsequent involvement in criminal activities after having been sanctioned or labeled for primary deviance. Individuals are thought to enter into a career of law violations when they are labeled as deviant, especially if done so by "significant others." The labeling theories were seen by the authors as having particular importance because they serve as the bridge between structural functionalist theories and social control theories.

▰▰▰ DISCUSSION QUESTIONS ▰▰▰

1. What is the underlying theme of the social process theories? How would you apply these theories to current criminality?

2. What is the underlying theme of the social reaction theories? How would you apply these theories to current criminality?

3. What is the underlying theme of the social control theories? How would you apply these theories to current criminality?

4. Compare and contrast the three sets of social interaction theories. Which set appears to be the most useful in explaining today's criminal behavior?

▰▰▰ REFERENCES ▰▰▰

Akers, R. L. (2000). *Criminological theories: Introduction, evaluation and application,* 3rd ed. Los Angeles: Roxbury.

_____. (1984). *Criminological theories: Introduction, evaluation and application.* Los Angeles: Roxbury.

_____. (1977). *Deviant behavior: A social learning approach,* 2nd ed. Belmont, CA: Wadsworth.

Bandura, A. (1977). *Social learning theory.* Englewood Cliffs, NJ: Prentice Hall.

Briar, S., and Piliavin, I. (1965). Delinquency, situational inducements, and commitment to conformity. *Social Problems* 13: 35–45.

Burgess R. L., and Akers, R. L. (1966). A differential association-reinforcement theory of criminal behavior. *Social Problems* 14: 128–47.

Dantzker, M. L. (1998). *Criminology and criminal justice: Comparing, contrasting, and intertwining disciplines.* Woburn, MA: Butterworth-Heinemann.

Glaser, D. (1956). Criminality theories and behavioral images. *American Journal of Sociology* 61: 433–44.

Heimer, K., and Matsueda, R. L. (1994). Role-taking, role-commitment and delinquency: A theory of differential social control. *American Sociological Review* 59: 400–37.

Hirschi, T. (1969). *Causes of delinquency.* Berkeley: University of California Press.

Kaplan, H. B., and Fukurai, H. (1992). Negative social sanctions, self-rejection and drug use. *Youth and Society* 23: 275–98.

Kaplan, H. B., and Johnson, R. J. (1991). Negative social sanctions and juvenile delinquency: Effects of labeling in a model of deviant behavior. *Social Science Quarterly* 72: 98–122.

Kornhauser, R. (1978). *Social sources of delinquency.* Chicago: University of Chicago Press.

Lemert, E. (1951). *Social pathology.* New York: McGraw-Hill.

Matsueda, R. L. (1992). Reflected appraisals, parental labeling, and delinquency: Specifying a symbolic interactionist theory. *American Journal of Sociology* 97: 1577–1611.

Matza, D. (1964). *Delinquency and drift.* New York: Wiley.

_____, and Sikes, G. M. (1961). Juvenile delinquency and subterranean values. *American Sociological Review* 26: 712–19.

Mead, G. H. (1934). *Mind, self and society.* Chicago: University of Chicago Press.

Reckless, W. (1967). *The crime problem.* New York: Appleton-Century-Crofts.

_____, Dinitz, S., and Murray E. (1957). The "good boy" in a high delinquency area. *Journal of Criminal Law, Criminology and Police Science,* 48: 18–25.

Reiss, A. (1951). Delinquency as the failure of personal and social controls. *American Sociological Review* 16: 196–207.

Shoemaker, D. J. (1996). *Theories of delinquency,* 3rd ed. New York: Oxford University Press.

Sutherland, E. H., and Cressey, D. R. (1978). *Criminology,* 10th ed. Philadelphia: Lippincott.

Tarde, G. (1912). *Penal philosophy.* Boston: Little, Brown.

7

Social Conflict Theories of Crime Causation

■ KEY CONCEPTS ■

capitalism

class conflict theory

communism

conflict theory

criminalization theory

critical theory

economic explanations

elites

elitist theory

feminist theory

group conflict theory

haves

have nots

instrumental Marxism

interest group competition

left realism

Marxist theory

non-Marxist conflict

neo-conflict theory

neo-critical theory

neo-Marxist theory

peacemaking theory

pluralism

postmodernism

power struggles

social reality theory

radical theory

socialism

status theory

structural Marxism

■ LEARNING OBJECTIVES ■

After reading this chapter, the student should be able to:

1. Distinguish between non-Marxist and Marxist theories of social conflict.

2. Contrast the social conflict perspectives of Dahrendorf and Vold.

3. Contrast the social conflict perspectives of Weber, Turk, and Quinney.

4. Discuss the relevance of non-Marxist conflict theory in modern American society.

5. Provide an overview of Marxist criminology.

6. Compare and contrast structural Marxism and instrumental Marxism.

7. Compare and contrast the premises of critical criminology with those of radical criminology.

8. Discuss how left realism differs from traditional Marxist theory.

9. Present and discuss the feminist perspectives on crime and justice.

10. Present and discuss the views of postmodernism.

11. Present and discuss the principles of peacemaking.

12. Provide an overview of elitist theory.

SOCIAL CONFLICT AND STRUCTURAL FUNCTIONALISM

In the preceding coverage of sociological theories, there has been an assumption that the social structure is functional and that despite the ills that lead to crime and criminality, there is a consensus among the majority of citizens within society in regard to how the overall system is administered. The focus of both social structure and social interaction theories is to determine why individuals or groups deviate from societal norms. As we noted in chapter 6, the social reaction theories, most notably labeling theory, see society as functional but change their emphasis to explain how agents of social control can lead to criminality.

Social conflict theories expand this analysis of social institutions. However, they do not start from a view of structural functionalism but from continuous competition and conflict within a society that is politically, economically, and socially divided. Unlike previously discussed positivist theories that take into account biological, psychological, and individual sociological factors as the basis for explaining criminal behavior, conflict theorists focus on society as the major influence on criminal behavior. Their position is that imposition of law and justice is determined by those who are in power (i.e., those in control of government and/or business). The foundation of the conflict perspectives are power struggles between those who are in power and those who are not. Non-Marxist theories focus on interest group competition and power relationships. Marxist theorists focus on the effects of capitalism and social class. Contemporary theorists examine social conflicts from a variety of perspectives that may or may not include class struggle.

The Social Conflict Perspective

Conflict theories attempt to identify society's power relations and draw attention to their role in promoting criminal behavior. Although conflict is viewed as an essential social process upon which society depends (Durkheim, 1964), group interests and their influence on legislation that arises from these conflicts are linked to criminal behavior. The conflict model espouses three themes:

1. *The relativity of criminal definitions*—conflict theory says that every act defined as immoral, deviant, or criminal must be viewed as tentative, at best, and that it is always subject to redefinition (depending on the group with the most power).

2. *Control of institutions*—conflict theorists debate that there are three basic means to maintaining and enhancing society's interests: force, compromise, and the dominance of social institutions, such as law, church, schools, and government.

3. *Law as an instrument of power*—conflict theory views the law as an extremely potent weapon of social conflict, whoever has control over the laws retains powers. (Dantzker, 1998, p. 59)

Conflict theory believes that the power of those with control over the laws to protect themselves and their interests leads those not in power toward criminal behavior. In this chapter four categories of conflict theories are offered: traditional conflict (pluralist or group explanations), neo-conflict (elitist or power and authority explanations), Marxist (including critical, radical, structural, and instrumental), and contemporary (left realism, feminism, and peacemaking). While myriads of other theories qualify as social conflict theories, we limit our discussion to these better known subjects (see Table 7–1). Our examination begins with the non-Marxist conflict theories.

Non-Marxist Conflict Theories

Non-Marxist conflict theories can be traced to the writings of George Vold and Rolf Dahrendorf during the 1950s. Their arguments that competition and conflict, rather than consensus and stability, governed the social order

TABLE 7–1   Social Conflict Theories

Non-Marxist Theories	Marxist Theories	Contemporary
Group conflict	Instrumental	Feminist
Status	Structural	Postmodernist
Class conflict	Critical	Peacemaking
Criminalization	Radical	Elitist
Social reality	Left realist	

challenged the basic premise of structural functionalism. In their works, and in the works of criminologists who succeeded these pioneers, the focus of research moved from individual offenders who were somehow "out of step" with society to society and its institutions. The result of this approach is seen not only in the non-Marxist theories but in the application of all conflict theories (both Marxist and non-Marxist) that followed.

Group Conflict Theory.   George Vold (1958) incorporated the premises of political pluralism and Thorsten Sellin's (1938) culture conflict into his theory of group conflict. Vold's *group conflict theory* postulates that conflict between groups should be viewed as one of the principal and essential social processes upon which the continuance of society depends. Like Emile Durkheim (1964), Vold saw social conflict as normal and beneficial. *Interest group competition* serves to hold all groups in check to keep any one from becoming too powerful. Both the making of laws and the breaking of laws were seen as products of this competition. Unlike Marxist theorists, Vold saw capitalism as but one of many political interests that led to interest group competition.

Status Theory.   Max Weber (1953), like Vold, believed that the Marxist theories (see pp. 121–124) and a capitalist economy were only part of the many issues involved within social conflict. However, Weber did emphasize social class within his perspective. In *status theory*, power and prestige are seen to be key issues within the conflict that exists in society. According to Weber, "criminality exists in all societies and is the result of the political struggle among different groups attempting to promote or enhance their life chances" (Bartollas, 2000, p. 181).

Class Conflict Theory.   Dahrendorf (1959) expanded Weber's perspective on power and authority. Like Weber he rejected the Marxist emphasis on property ownership as the sole determinant of political and social power. However, he did see *class conflict* as integral to social conflict. Class was seen as determining the allocation of power and authority within society, and struggles between the classes were seen as being regulated by legal sanctions, to the advantage of the upper classes.

Criminalization Theory. Austin Turk (1966, 1977) incorporated Dahrendorf's views into his own extension of Weber's perspective on power and authority. The conflicts that Turk described were seen as covering a wide range of social and cultural issues. Those holding power were seen as using their abilities to make, interpret, and enforce legal standards to maintain control. Those out of power were seen as resisting those legal standards that they perceived to be contrary to their own interests.

Turk's (1966, 1977) *criminalization theory* centers on (1) the conditions under which cultural and social differences between authorities and subjects will probably result in conflict; (2) the conditions under which criminalization will probably occur in the course of conflict; and (3) the conditions under which the degree of deprivation associated with becoming a criminal will probably be greater or lesser.

Social Reality Theory. Another theory that advocates power and authority relationships as the basis of social conflict was presented by Richard Quinney. Quinney's (1970) *social reality theory* argues that conflict is intertwined with power and that differential distribution of power produces conflict, which is rooted in the competition for power. Quinney offered six postulates for explaining conflict as social reality: (1) the *definition of crime*—authorized government agents define criminal conduct; (2) the *formulation of criminal definition*—criminal definitions are interpreted by those who have the power to shape public policy; (3) the *application of criminal definition*—those in power enforce their definitions of criminal behaviors; (4) the *development of behavioral patterns in relation to criminal behaviors*—behavioral patterns within society are structured by how criminal behaviors are defined and enforced; (5) the *construction of criminal conceptions*—the conceptions of crime are constructed and diffused within the different segments of society through various means of communication; (6) the *social reality of crime*—crime is the product of the previous propositions, meaning that those in power attempt to use criminal definitions to impose their will on the rest of society (adapted from Quinney, 1970, pp. 15–23).

These conflict theories not only influenced non-Marxist criminological research but also served to expedite the development of Marxist perspectives on crime and criminality, which are presented in the following section.

Marxist Theories

The economic and social philosophies of Karl Marx are the foundation for several conflict theories. Marx's view was that class biases resulting from class division in a capitalist society made up of two classes—elite (bourgeoisie) and subordinates (proletariat)—and inevitably lead to conflict. His solution was a classless society that would be created by overthrowing capitalistic society and adopting a socialistic system (Marx, Engels, and Malia, 1998).

The explanation of critical and radical theories of criminality begins with Marxist theory. *Marxist theory* includes the following:

1. A struggle exists between the proletariat (working class) and the bourgeoisie (owners and controllers of production).

2. The political and economic philosophies of the dominant class influence all aspects of life.

3. Society's structure(s) are unstable and can be changed through slow and evolving violence. (Dantzker, 1998, p. 59)

The Marxist view of law and behavior is that individuals are not naturally inclined to be either criminal or noncriminal, but that the inclination toward criminal behavior is a result of social laws designed to maintain control of the powerless by the powerful. Willem Bonger (1969), the individual credited with first applying Marxist theory to the study of criminology, noted that

1. The abnormal element of crime is of social and biological origin.

2. The response to crime is punishment—the application of penalties considered more severe than spontaneous moral condemnation.

3. No act is naturally immoral or criminal.

4. Crimes are antisocial acts harmful to those who have the power at their command to control society.

5. In every society divided into ruling class and an inferior class, penal law serves the will of the former.

6. Crime is a function of poverty.

The views of Marx and Bonger are the starting point for the various Marxist perspectives currently found within criminology. Bruce Arrigo (1999) identifies several theories derived from Marxist perspectives (instrumental Marxists, structural Marxists, anarchists, structural interpellationists, left realists, socialist feminists, postmodernists, critical race theorists, and peacemaking criminologists are but a few) within modern criminology. Our overview discusses the following: instrumental Marxism, structural Marxism, critical theory, and radical theory.

Instrumental Theory. Instrumental Marxists see capitalism as the root of social conflict within society. Property ownership and perpetuation of social injustices by the owners of production against the poor and the powerless are the basis for crime and criminality. The owners of production control the economy. They also determine how laws are enacted, how crimes are constructed, and how deviance is defined. These powerful elites are seen by instrumental Marxists as being the true criminals because they use their power to impose poverty and powerlessness on the poor in order to maintain their own power. Poverty is seen as the cause of crime. Ordinary criminals are viewed as victims who have reacted to the social injustices perpetrated against them (Arrigo, 1999; Bohm, 1982).

Structural Theory. *Structural Marxists* share the view of instrumental Marxists that capitalist society produces social inequities that lead to crime. Like instrumental Marxists, they see the rich as abusing the criminal justice system to impose their will on the poor. They also see poverty and hopelessness as the root causes of criminality. They believe, however, that other autonomous forces within society also influence crime and criminal behavior. While capitalism is evil, all capitalists need not be. Nor are all criminals revolutionaries railing at social injustice (Arrigo, 1999; Bohm, 1982). However, they do agree with the instrumental Marxists in their belief that class struggle is the basis of social conflict.

Critical Theory. Critical theory is based to a large degree on structural Marxism. The emphasis of *critical theory* is that the social order is dominated by class interests and that crime is the product of social inequality (Quinney, 1974). Critical criminologists study the impact of capitalism on government and society. They call for governmental actions to redistribute the wealth, regulate business, and protect the poor from elites (Bohm, 2001). While the basis of their critique may be seen as Marxist (although one might argue that liberal criminology now shares many of these criticisms), they do not necessarily call for the total restructuring of society, but instead they call for increased governmental interventions on behalf of the poor and the powerless. Their proposed solutions would be appropriately labeled as socialistic.

Radical Theory. Radical criminologists also study the effects of capitalism. Their views are more in line with those of instrumental Marxists. Big business is seen as acting in its own behalf. Government is seen as being corrupted by economic interests. Capitalistic society is seen as promoting greed and self-interest, which lead directly to poverty and crime (Quinney, 1980). Unlike critical theorists, *radical theorists* see society as needing a total overhaul in which capitalism is replaced by a communist society. Only through the creation of such a society can the twin evils of poverty and crime be eliminated.

Left Realism. Criticisms of Marxist theory have flourished. Generally these critiques focus on the lack of quantitative support for Marxist interpretations and its ideological interpretation of social events. Karl Klockars (1980) has provided one of the stronger criticisms of Marxist theory in which he lists several issues in which it is found lacking. His argument is that Marxists set themselves up as being morally superior and then examine issues through their own ideologically biased prism in order to justify their views. By doing so they fail to consider their own theoretical weaknesses or the existence of criminality in socialistic societies.

In an effort to address the issues raised by Klockars as well as common assertions of methodological weaknesses, a new generation of Marxists has emerged. These *neo-Marxists* are more pragmatic and tend to provide empirical rather than subjective support for their arguments. Proponents of this neo-Marxist approach are recognized as left realists.

Left realism has its roots in the works of Ian Taylor, Paul Walton, and Jock Young. The approach used by Taylor, Walton, and Young (1973) acknowledges that criminals may be found in all levels of the social strata. Instead of railing about the injustices of capitalistic society, *left realists* demonstrate how social inequities produce criminal activities at all levels. While acknowledging that socialism would be a preferred solution to easing the burdens of crime and poverty, left realists advocate providing solutions within the existing capitalistic social order. Because of these views, left realists are often criticized by other Marxists as having sold out to pressures from mainstream criminology (Bohm, 2001).

Contemporary Criminology

Contemporary criminology covers a variety of modern conflict theories that may or may not include Marxist interpretations. Of the theories that we discuss, all but elitist theory have been categorized as being critical or even radical perspectives (Arrigo, 1999; Bohm, 2001). Left realism could also be categorized as a contemporary theory. The contemporary theories presented here include feminism, postmodernism, peacemaking, and elitist theory. Contemporary theories may also be called *neo-critical theories.*

Feminist Theory.   *Feminist theory* covers a spectrum of arguments related to the effects of gender and the inequitable treatment of women within society. While these perspectives vary considerably in their orientation, they share a feminist emphasis not generally found in the criminology literature. As a whole, feminist theories hold that society has traditionally been dominated by males who have sought to subjugate women. Despite considerable advances within contemporary society, women are still seen as being constricted by the chauvinism and paternalism by society's male-oriented power bases (Daly and Chesney-Lind, 1988). The purpose of feminist theory is to provide insight from the female perspective on social inequality and crime.

Liberal feminists argue for more equitable treatment of women within social institutions and recognition of the feminist perspective in dealing with social issues such as the administration of justice. Governmental intervention is seen as necessary to create opportunities for female empowerment and equality. Education of both males and females is viewed as an important mechanism to achieve these results.

Marxist feminists call for the elimination of capitalism as the means of achieving equity for women, the poor, and ethnic minorities (Bohm, 2001). Radical feminists see "male aggression and control of female sexuality as the basis for patriarchy and female subjugation" (Hagan, 1999, p. 165). Socialist feminists see capitalistic society as reinforcing male dominance in both the work force and the home. Rather than seeking to rectify inequitable treatment through education and governmental intervention, socialist feminists stress the need to promote socialism as the cure for the injustices of capitalism (Messerschmidt, 1986).

N. Jane McCandless argues that despite differences within the feminist perspectives, four common principles should be considered in addressing the social inequality of women:

1. *Education*—the necessity of producing and disseminating information so that women can make informed choices

2. *Egalitarianism*—the need for women to be treated as equals within society

3. *Empowerment*—enacting changes in the fundamental structure of society that will provide women with the ability to meet their own needs and solve their own problems by taking control of their lives

4. *Inclusion*—providing women access to career opportunities and equity in pay and earnings potential. (McCandless and Conner, 1999)

Postmodernism.   Postmodernism is a response to the pressures of contemporary society. *Postmodernism* argues that the modern emphasis on scientific rationality has reduced the importance of humanistic thinking, causing a multitude of social ills. Proponents of postmodernism desire a return to a simpler, more caring social order that stresses cooperation rather than competition. Branches of postmodernism include poststructuralism, which calls for a simplification of the complex social processes found within modern society; semiotics, which calls for reducing the myriad of signs, symbolism, and complex wordings that have complicated social interactions; and deconstruction, which calls for the realignment of the social hierarchy into a simpler, more understandable and therefore less stressful social order based on social harmony and cooperation (Bohm, 2001; Hagan, 1999). Thus far postmodernism has received only limited support within criminology.

Peacemaking.   The reader may have noticed that the work of Richard Quinney has been cited several times. The reason is quite simple. Quinney has been actively involved in the development of several social conflict perspectives. He has, at different stages of his career, advocated social reality theory (Quinney, 1970), critical theory (Quinney, 1974), and radical theory (Quinney, 1980). More recently he has been instrumental in developing peacemaking criminology theory (Quinney, 1991). While one might wonder at his changes in ideological orientation, he has remained consistent in his zeal for social justice and equity, which are important components of peacemaking criminology.

Peacemaking includes a variety of issues within its overall philosophy. These issues are built around the concepts of dispute resolution, restorative justice, and nonviolence. John Fuller (1998) presents the primary tenets of peacemaking criminology within his Peacemaking Paradigm Pyramid (see Figure 7–1). The foundation of peacemaking is nonviolence. Peacemakers stress that the criminal justice system should not condone violence in the application of justice. Coercion, excessive force, and the imposition of the death penalty are seen as contradictory to the goals of justice.

According to Fuller (1998), the following components build on the nonviolence foundation:

- *Social justice*—social injustices such as sexism, racism, and ageism must be dealt with to provide equity and harmony within society.

- *Inclusion*—attempts must be made to involve both the victim and the offender in the dispute resolution process rather than just imposing governmental edicts upon them. Deterrence and punishment goals should be subverted to the mutual needs of victims and offenders.

- *Correct means*—the process by which justice is attained must be addressed, and the legal safeguards of due process must be accorded to offenders.

- *Ascertainable criteria*—the justice process must be conducted in a manner that all participants understand and have confidence in.

- *Categorical imperative*—the decisions and outcomes of the justice process must be based on moral precepts (reasoning) that are universally applicable to all situations and all persons. (Fuller, 1998, pp. 54–57)

These principles are not all inclusive, but they serve as a model of how the peacemaking perspective is applied. The current strategies for administering justice are believed to actually promote crime and social conflict. By using

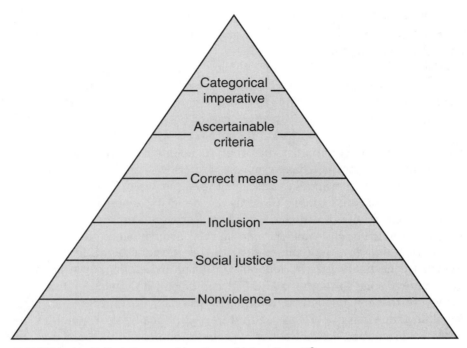

FIGURE 7–1　Fuller's Peacemaking Pyramid Paradigm (P³)

Source: Adapted from J. R. Fuller (1998). *Criminal Justice: A Peacemaking Perspective* (Boston: Allyn & Bacon), p. 55.

the peacemaking approach throughout the justice system, peacemakers hope to rectify the shortcomings of a system that is seen as perpetuating its own failure.

Elitist Theory.　The last neo-critical theory that we present is our own *elitist theory.* Our view is that all of the social conflict explanations have merit in their critiques of society and the administration of justice. In particular, theories that consider class and wealth but focus on power struggles between competing interest groups as universal rather than as uniquely the product of capitalism have special appeal. However, the previous theories have looked on the use of power and group conflicts as means by which the powerful maintain control over the powerless. Instead we see power brokers on all points on the political spectrum (conservative, liberal, socialist, communist) conspiring with one another to maintain control over the poor, the working class, and the middle class.

The elitist perspective holds that every society is ruled by an elite oligarchy. These elites may preside over totalitarian governments or they may permit their citizens to enjoy considerable freedom in allegedly democratic societies.

Regardless of the nature of the government, the elites conspire to maintain their political control. However, we argue that the behavior of elites may actually benefit the lower classes.

Using precepts espoused by G. William Domhoff (1998), Thomas R. Dye and L. Harman Zeigler (1999), C. Wright Mills(2000), and Thornstein Veblen, (1998), we view power relations as being defined through a conflict in which the middle class is exploited by advocates of both the haves and have-nots. Class struggle is seen as normal and continuous whether the society is capitalist, socialist, or communist. In order to maintain control, the powerful make concessions to the "dangerous classes." However, the concessions are at the expense of the middle class, not the upper class. Through a process known as symbolic reassurance (described in detail in chapter 13), elites co-opt those who would oppose them. In addition, threats to power are diminished by pitting the lower class and the middle class against each other.

Political and economic elites, despite the considerable differences they present to the public, are in general consensus. Whether they espouse the conservative policies of the traditional capitalistic bourgeois or the liberal policies of the new "bohemian bourgeois" (Brooks, 2001), their actions are based on their own upper-class self-interests. Ironically, they maintain their power by promoting conflict within society. By appealing to class, race, and gender divisions, they are able to impose their collective will on the populace. Only when there is such considerable discontent within society that their position of authority is threatened will they respond to pressures from the middle class. However, the response is measured only to the extent necessary to diffuse the perceived threats.

Posturing on issues such as "making the rich pay their fair share," and "tax cuts only benefit the affluent," and alleging that "certain programs would hurt women, minorities, and the poor" enables liberal elites in government to generate support for their programs. Posturing on issues such as "eliminating welfare" and "eliminating affirmative action" and arguing that "big government is causing economic harm to the working and middle classes" by conservative elites obtains support for their programs. These are actually only tokens provided to ensure that their control is continued. For the most part, there are few differences in how elites actually govern. An example of elitism in action is the operation of the social security system as a pyramid scheme that would be unlawful in the private sector. Likewise, the theft of social security funds to create an alleged budget surplus was a result of agreement between Democrats and Republicans in Washington, D.C.

Elite theory holds that seeking to dramatically overhaul the current system of government (through either revolution or the ballot) would only replace one group of elites with another. Therefore the key to reducing conflict and crime within society lies in educating the middle class about how they are being used to provide the resources to placate the lower class. These efforts would not result in change in the political structure but would obtain more concessions on behalf of the middle class, whose conformity is the source of stability for the continuance of society.

▓▓▓ SUMMARY ▓▓▓

Conflict theories attempt to identify society's power relations and draw attention to their role in promoting criminal behavior. Basically, conflict theory views crime as the ability of those groups in power to protect themselves and their interests, thus leading those not in power toward criminal behavior. Three categories of conflict theories were examined: non-Marxist, Marxist, and contemporary.

Non-Marxist conflict theories stress that social conflict is prevalent within society. Interest group competition and power and authority relationships create power struggles within society. Class and economic issues are only a part of the myriad political causes contested within these struggles. Vold's group conflict theory postulates that conflict between groups should be viewed as one of the principal and essential social processes upon which the continuance of society depends. Weber's status theory presents power and prestige as key issues within social conflict. Dahrendorf saw class conflict as integral to social conflict. Quinney's social reality theory advocates that conflict is intertwined with power and that differential distribution of power produces conflict, which is rooted in the competition for power. Turk's criminalization theory examines the conditions under which cultural and social differences between authorities and subjects will probably result in conflict.

The two main individuals credited with the development of Marxist criminology are Marx and Bonger. Marx was the social philosopher who developed the economic concepts upon which Marxism is based. Bonger was the social scientist who first applied Marxist concepts to criminology. There are many Marxist views. Those discussed within this chapter included instrumental Marxism, which sees capitalism as the root of social conflict and crime; structural Marxism, which also views capitalism as evil but considers other social influences; critical theory, which is comparable to structural Marxism; and radical theory, which is comparable to instrumental Marxism. Left realism is a more pragmatic approach that uses empirical techniques in the study of social conflict.

Contemporary theories may also be called neo-critical theories. The contemporary theories discussed included feminist theory, postmodernism, peacemaking, and elitist theory. Feminist theories range from liberal, Marxist, socialist, to radical. However, they share a common concern for education, egalitarianism, empowerment, and inclusion of women. Postmodernism seeks to return to a kinder, gentler society by reducing the complexities of modern life. Peacemaking offers the precepts of nonviolence, social justice, inclusion, correct means, ascertainable criteria, and categorical imperative to create a fair and equitable justice system. Last, elitist theory sees society's elites as forcing concessions from the middle class to placate the lower class.

▬ DISCUSSION QUESTIONS ▬

1. Conflict theory says the definition of any as immoral, deviant, or criminal must be viewed as tentative, at best, and that it is always subject to redefinition. Do you agree? Who should do this redefining?

2. Conflict theorists debate that there are three basic means to maintaining and enhancing society's interests: force, compromise, and the dominance of social institutions such as law, church, schools, and government. Which means do you believe are the best for the United States? Are there other means?

3. Law is viewed as an instrument of power, that is, as an extremely potent weapon of social conflict in that whoever has control over the laws retains power. If this is true, how will any other class but the elite ever have power? Isn't there power in numbers regardless of social status?

4. On what should contemporary criminologists focus their energy? Does female criminality really differ so much from that of males that it requires a separate set of theories?

▬ REFERENCES ▬

Arrigo, B. A. (1999). *Social justice/criminal justice: The maturation of critical theory in law, crime and deviance.* Belmont, CA: West/Wadsworth.

Bartollas, C. (2000). *Juvenile Delinquency,* 5th ed. Needham, MA: Allyn & Bacon.

Bohm, R. M. (1982). Radical criminology: An explication. *Criminology* 19: 565–89.

_____. (2001). *A primer on crime and delinquency,* 2nd ed. Belmont, CA: Wadsworth.

Bonger, W. (1969). *Criminality and economic conditions.* Introduction by A. T. Turk. Bloomington: Indiana University Press.

Brooks, D. (2001). *Bobos in paradise: The new upper class and how they got there.* Upper Saddle River, NJ: Prentice Hall.

Dahrendorf, R. (1959). *Class and class conflict in industrial society.* Palo Alto: Stanford University Press.

Daly, K., and Chesney-Lind, M. (1988). Feminism and criminology. *Justice Quarterly* 5: 497–538.

Dantzker, M. L. (1998). *Criminology and criminal justice: Contrasting and intertwining disciplines.* Boston: Butterworth-Heinemann.

Domhoff, G. W. (1998). *Who rules America?: Power and politics in the year 2000,* 3rd ed. Mountain View, CA: Mayfield.

Durkheim, E. (1964). *The division of labor in society.* New York: Free Press.

Dye, T. R., and Zeigler, H. (1999). *The irony of democracy,* 11th ed. Fort Worth: HAJ College and School Division.

Fuller, J. R. (1998). *Criminal justice: A peacemaking perspective.* Boston: Allyn & Bacon.

Hagan, F. E. (1999). *Introduction to criminology* 4th ed. Chicago: Nelson-Hall.

Klockars, C. (1980). The contemporary crisis of Marxist criminology. In J. Inciardi, ed. *Radical criminology: The coming crisis.* Beverly Hills: Sage, pp. 92–123.

Marx, K., Engels, F., and Malia, E. (1998). *The Communist manifesto.* New York: Signet Classic.

McCandless, N. J., and Conner, F. P. (1999). Working with terminally ill older women: Can a feminist perspective add new insight and direction? *Journal of Women and Aging* 11 (2&3): 101–14.

Messerschmidt, J. W. (1986). *Capitalism, patriarchy and crime: Toward a socialist feminist criminology.* Totowa, NJ: Rowman and Littlefield.

Mills, C. W., and Mills, W. C. (2000). *The power elite,* 2nd ed. Los Angeles: Getty Trust.

Quinney, R. (1970). *The social reality of crime.* Boston: Little, Brown.

_____. (1974). *Criminal justice in America: A critical understanding.* Boston: Little, Brown.

_____. (1980). *Class, state and crime,* 2nd ed. New York: Longman.

_____. (1991). The way of peace: on crime, suffering, and service. In H. E. Pepinsky, ed., *Criminology as peacemaking.* Bloomington: Indiana University Press.

Sellin, T. (1938). *Culture conflict and crime.* New York: Social Science Research Council.

Taylor, I., Walton, P., and Young, J. (1973). *The new criminology: For a social theory of deviance.* London: Routledge and Kegan Paul.

Turk, A. T. (1966). Conflict and criminality. *American Sociological Review* 31: 338–52.

_____. (1977). Class, conflict and criminalization. *Sociological Focus* 10: 209–20.

Veblen, T. B. (1998). *The theory of the leisure class* (Great Minds series ed. rpr.). Amherst, NY: Prometheus.

Vold, G. (1958). *Theoretical criminology.* New York: Oxford University Press.

Weber, M. (1953). Class, status, party. In R. Bendix and S. M. Lipset, eds., *Class, status and power.* New York: Macmillan.

CHAPTER

Integrated Theories of Crime Causation

■ **KEY CONCEPTS** ■

age-graded theory
bio-conditioning theory
control balance theory
criminal personality theory
delinquency development theory
general strain theory
human nature theory
integrated biological theory
integrated classical theory
integrated conflict theory
integrated control theory
integrated learning theory
integrated psychological theory
integrated sociological theory

integrated strain theory
integrated structural Marxist theory
integrated theory
integrative delinquency
interactional theory
interdisciplinary criminology
network analysis theory
power control theory
rational choice theory
reintegrative shaming theory
routine activities theory
self-derogation theory
social development theory

■ **LEARNING OBJECTIVES** ■

After reading this chapter, the student should be able to:

1. Present and discuss the integrated classical theories.

2. Present and discuss the integrated biological theories.

133

3. Present and discuss the integrated psychological theories.

4. Present and discuss the integrated learning theories.

5. Present and discuss the integrated control theories.

6. Present and discuss the integrated strain theories.

7. Present and discuss the integrated conflict theories.

CRIMINOLOGY AS AN INTERDISCIPLINARY SCIENCE

As noted in chapter 2, criminology does not draw its theoretical basis from any one discipline. In the previous chapters, you were exposed to a variety of legal, psychological, biological, and sociological explanations of crime, ranging from individual offender orientations to societal interpretations. Just as no one medicine cures all illnesses, no one theory explains all crime. Therefore, criminologists approach the study of crime and criminality from a number of perspectives.

While an individual criminologist may prefer a particular discipline's perspective (i.e., biological or psychological), another may use a very different technique (i.e., sociological or legal) in his or her studies. Indeed, there is often a great deal of disagreement among criminologists who share similar views as to the fundamental causes of crime (e.g., variation is readily apparent among critical criminologists). It is for these reasons that better criminology programs tend to hire faculty from divergent disciplines or those whose training was interdisciplinary.

INTEGRATED THEORIES

An interdisciplinary approach to the study of criminology produces explanations that use two or more of the "standard criminological theories" within their theoretical perspectives. These are known as integrated theories. This chapter examines the better known integrated theories: integrated classical theories, integrated biological theories, integrated psychological theories, and integrated sociological theories. The integrated theories to be discussed are shown in Table 8–1.

TABLE 8–1 Integrated Theories

Integrated Classical Theories	Integrated Biological Theories	Integrated Psychological Theories	Integrated Sociological Theories
Routine activities	Bio-conditioning	Delinquency development	Integrated learning
	Human nature		Integrated control
Rational choice		Age-graded	Integrated strain
		Self-derogation	
Criminal personality			Integrated conflict

Integrated Classical Theories

Integrated classical theories merge classical and positivist approaches to crime prevention based on the individual's rationality and freedom of choice as expressed within classical theory. This ability to choose is merged with positive theory's use of empiricism to understand how choices are influenced by situational factors. Situational influences are then altered or adjusted to deter or prevent crime from occurring. While a number of integrated classical theories exist, we present the three that are most commonly discussed within the criminological literature.

Routine Activities Theory

The concept of *routine activities theory* was developed by Lawrence E. Cohen and Marcus Felson (1979), who believe that changes in the routine activities of everyday life can lead to criminality. Cohen and Felson contend that the disruption of daily activities influences criminal opportunity and therefore affects trends in a class of crimes, which they label as direct-contact predatory violations: illegal acts in which an individual definitively and intentionally takes or damages the person or property of another. Their argument rests on the belief that structural changes in routine activity patterns can influence crime rates by affecting the convergence in space and time of the three minimal elements of direct-contact predatory violations: motivated offenders, suitable targets, and the absence of capable guardians against a violation (Cohen and Felson, 1979).

Cohen and Felson's ultimate conclusion is that criminality is a given. For whatever reason (social learning, social conflict, etc.), there will always be motivated offenders. Rather than worrying about the nature of criminality, they focus on preventing or deterring crime. For classical theory's use of punishment as deterrence to work, strategies that reduce the opportunity for crime to succeed must be employed. Rather than relying on punishment, the attractiveness of and/or accessibility to the target needs to be reduced. While some crimes will be displaced to other areas, times, or targets, many will be prevented from occurring.

Rational Choice Theory

Another integrated classical theory that emphasizes situational aspects was proposed by Derek B. Cornish and Ronald V. Clarke (1986). *Rational choice theory* (also known as choice theory and situational theory) argues that crime prevention can be accomplished by focusing on those situational aspects that influence the commission of particular types of crimes. Criminals do not randomly select their targets. Instead they rationally choose both the crime that they will commit and the target of that crime. This assumption of rationality and choice led many criminologists (e.g., Akers, 2000; Schmalleger, 1999; Shoemaker, 1996; Siegel, 2000) to categorize rational choice as a neoclassical theory. However, its focus on empirical techniques to assess and reduce vulnerability to crime rather than on the process of dispensing justice places it solidly within the domain of positive theory.

Rational choice theory, like routine activities theory, focuses on opportunity. The social control aspect of deterrence is left to others. Situational factors are emphasized. Clarke (1997, pp. 17–27) identifies sixteen factors that influence vulnerability to crime. These situational factors or crime prevention techniques are presented in Table 8–2.

Criminal Personality Theory

The third integrated classical theory is Samuel Yochelson and Stanten E. Samenow's (1976) *criminal personality theory.* This theory is based on the belief that the social environment has little impact on the development of criminal behavior. Instead, criminals are said to freely choose their actions. Sociological, psychological, and economic theories are seen as mere excuses offenders use to rationalize their behavior. In a return to early biological theories, offenders are seen as being born with criminal personalities. These individuals are innately selfish, untrusting, and untrustworthy. Instead of

TABLE 8–2 Clarke's Situational Factors

A. *Increasing Perceived Effort*
  1. Target hardening
  2. Access control
  3. Deflecting offenders
  4. Controlling facilitators
B. *Increasing Perceived Risks*
  5. Entry/exit screening
  6. Formal surveillance
  7. Surveillance by employees
  8. Natural surveillance
C. *Reducing Anticipated Awards*
  9. Target removal
  10. Identifying property
  11. Reducing temptation
  12. Denying benefits
D. *Inducing Guilt or Shame*
  13. Rule setting
  14. Strengthening moral condemnation
  15. Controlling disinhibitors
  16. Facilitating compliance

Source: Adapted from Clarke, R.V. (1997). *Situational Crime Prevention*, 2nd ed. New York: Harrow and Heston, chap. 1.

being victims of society, they are victimizers of society. Therefore, in order to change their behavior patterns, criminals must be forced to accept their own responsibility for their actions.

Critiques of this theory (e.g., Hagan, 1998) argue that it is not a true theory but a rehashing of old biological precepts of born criminals. However, the argument that criminals are self-serving antisocials who knowingly refuse to conform to societal standards is appealing to "get tough on crime" advocates.

Integrated Biological Theories

Integrated biological theories stress the importance of physiological factors on an individual's behaviors. Yet, they seek to explain how these natural features are influenced by psychological and/or sociological factors. A number of integrated biological explanations were discussed as biosocial theories in chapter 4. In this section, we limit our discussion to Hans Eysenck's bio-conditioning theory and James Q. Wilson and Richard Herrnstein's human nature theory.

Bio-conditioning Theory

Bio-conditioning theory (Eysenck and Gudjonsson, 1989) merges biology, behavioral psychology, and classical criminology. The premise of bio-conditioning theory is that guilt and conscience are conditioned responses to pleasure and pain. How well behavior is conditioned is due to biological influences. Extroverts are seen as being more outgoing and needing more external stimulation than are introverts. As a result of these stimulation needs, extroverts are less likely to accept pleasure/pain conditioning. Therefore, they are more likely to engage in behaviors that are delinquent or criminal. This theory was discussed briefly in chapter 5.

Although biological factors are said to contribute to crime and delinquency, social factors are seen as providing the conditioning that leads to crime. Eysenck argues that permissive child-rearing practices result in underdeveloped consciences. To remedy this problem, he contends that behavioral psychology should be applied to modify deviant behaviors (Eysenck and Gudjonsson, 1989).

Human Nature Theory

Wilson and Herrnstein (1985) proposed another integrated biological theory, *human nature theory*. They contend that genetic makeup, intelligence, and body type have considerable impact on human behavior. Individuals' personalities are influenced by these physical features that shape how they see themselves as well as how others see them. Like Eysenck, Wilson and Herrnstein stress the importance of biological and psychological factors in the behavioral choices that humans make. They differ from Eysenck in their recommendations for influencing those choices.

According to Wilson and Herrnstein (1985), human decision making is a product of the interactions of biological, psychological, and sociological influences. To overcome predispositions that may lead to crime choices, they call for programs to aid families and schools in teaching children moral standards. Personal responsibility is an integral component of these moral teachings. These precrime interventions are seen as preferable to imposing harsh punishments after criminal behaviors have occurred.

Integrated Psychological Theories

Integrated psychological theories explain how social factors can influence individual self-perceptions. These may also be called psychosocial theories or social psychological theories. Some of the theories discussed in chapter 5 could just as readily have been located here; conversely, these theories could also have been discussed within chapter 5. We selected them for inclusion here because they are good examples of the integration of psychological and sociological approaches, not exclusive examples of such. The theories included here are David Farrington's delinquency development theory, Robert Sampson and John Laub's age-graded theory, and Howard Kaplan's self-derogation theory.

Delinquency Development Theory

Farrington (1988) used his analyses of longitudinal studies of delinquent boys to theorize that delinquent behavior patterns emerge early in life and that these behaviors become more developed as the child matures. According to Farrington's *delinquency development theory,* there is a continuity in criminal behavior that reaches from early childhood into the adult years. Social and economic conditions are seen influencing children and their parents, and the actions of parents and older siblings in response to these conditions serve as models for the children. Children raised in poverty who have role models who are criminal are likely to adopt criminogenic tendencies.

The development of a deviant personality is the likely product of poor child rearing, economic deprivation, and resentment of social responses to prior deviance. After the deviant personality has emerged, it is reinforced by continued criminal activities. Life experiences influence future behavior choices. Some individuals will abandon deviant behaviors in adulthood. However, the personality is often so well established that behavior change is not possible. The cycle of criminality continues as the children of these deviant-personality adults are subjected to the same bonding and social learning influences that shaped their parents' personalities.

Age-Graded Theory

Sampson and Laub (1993) used a delinquent maturation approach similar to Farrington's. Social structure factors (e.g., poverty) and social control processes (e.g., family and peer deviance) interact with individual factors (e.g., temperament, learning difficulties) to create delinquent behaviors.

Outcomes from social responses to delinquent behaviors then interact with the prior influences to reduce or reinforce future behaviors. Unlike Farrington's delinquency development theory, Sampson and Laub's *age-graded theory* does not see the deviant personality as necessarily being developed at an early age. Therefore, positive life events as the delinquent matures may well lead to a cessation in delinquent activity. The building of social capital (i.e., obtaining work, school success, marriage) enables the previously delinquent person to reject future criminal behaviors.

Self-Derogation Theory

Kaplan (1975) proposed the *self-derogation theory* of delinquency, which emphasizes self-esteem as integral to the occurrence of delinquent behavior. According to Kaplan, each person has a "self-esteem motive" that causes him or her to try to maximize positive perceptions of self and minimize negative perceptions of self. In a process that uses strain, social control, labeling, social learning, and cognitive concepts, youths are seen as turning to deviant groups and activities if they are unable to construct positive self-perceptions within conventional groups or activities.

If young people are unsuccessful in school, in their family, or in peer activities, they are less likely to accept social controls imposed by those groups. Conventional behaviors are seen as contributing to self-derogation. Delinquent alternatives are seen as means of enhancing self-esteem and countering self-derogation. The importance of peer groups is stressed within this perspective. Subsequent involvement in conventional or deviant activities is influenced by the individual's self-perceptions. If conventional opportunities emerge (such as participating in extracurricular activities) that enhance self-perceptions, the youth may return to conventional behaviors. If conventional opportunities are not available, or do not enhance perceptions, deviant activities and associations will continue.

Integrated Sociological Theories

Perhaps the best known integrated theory is Robert Burgess and Ronald Aker's (1966) differential reinforcement theory. Because we have discussed it in chapter 6, we will not do so again, but we do use it as an example of how criminologists may disagree on the nature of a theory and where it should be classified. For the most part, the theories discussed in this section combine two or more sociological explanations of crime and criminality. Integrated sociological theories include integrated learning theories, integrated control theories, integrated strain theories, and integrated conflict theories.

Integrated Learning Theories

Integrated learning theories emphasize social learning theory as the foundation for their explanations of criminal behavior. The theories reviewed here are Marvin Krohn's network analysis and Terence Thornberry's interactional theory.

Network Analysis Theory. Krohn (1986) merges aspects of social learning theory with social bonding theory in his *network analysis approach.* The nature and extent of social learning and social bonding are said to be based upon social and personal networks. These networks include friends, family, peers, teachers, and other people and institutions with whom the young person interacts. How these networks influence the youth is said to depend on multiplexity and density. *Multiplexity* refers to the number of activities that specific individuals have in common with one another in their daily activities; *density* refers to total number of contacts that an individual might have with others in the community.

According to Krohn, the learning that occurs and the bonding that takes place within a community may be either conventional or deviant. If contacts with deviant individuals are frequent due to multiplexity (several common activities) and significant due to a lack of density (few interactions with others), then deviant behaviors are reinforced. Conversely, if conventional contacts dominate, conventional behaviors are reinforced.

Interactional Theory. In *interactional theory,* Thornberry (1987) incorporates social learning theory, social bonding, cognitive theory, and social structure theories of criminal behavior to explain delinquency. As in the maturation theories discussed earlier, Thornberry sees delinquency activities as changing over time. As youths enter adolescence, their bonds to their parents and social institutions are said to weaken. Peer groups become more important to them. If these young people reside in socially disorganized environments, they are at high risk to have weak social bonds and peers who engage in deviance. Adolescents who are from more stable environments may engage in deviancy (they are, after all, adolescents), but their actions are better controlled by stronger social bonds and associations with peers who engage in more conventional behaviors.

Thornberry sees delinquent behaviors as influenced by age. As young people enter their late teens, the influence of peers gives way to perceptions of their roles in society (i.e., work activities, involvement in social institutions, and domestic relationships). As commitment to these conventional influences increase, deviant activities decrease. Therefore, Thornberry argues that involvement in delinquency is a dynamic social process that changes over time.

Integrated Control Theories

Integrated control theories use the social control perspective as the foundation of their integrated approaches. The social control emphasis may be easily observed in Charles Tittle's control balance theory, Joseph Weis's social development theory, and John Braithwaite's reintegrative shaming.

Control Balance Theory. *Control balance theory* merges concepts from social control, social learning, rational choice, and anomie. Tittle (1995, p. 142) proposes that "the amount of control to which people are subject relative to the amount of control that they exercise affects the general probability that they will commit specific types of deviance." In other words, you do not always have control over your behavior, but are subject to the control of others. Even in those situations in which you do have control over your behavior, it is not certain that you will exercise that control. Whether or not you choose to exercise behavioral control is dependent upon four factors: predisposition, provocation, opportunity, and constraint.

Predisposition is defined by Tittle as deviant motivations. For any number of reasons, a potential offender may be inclined to engage in criminal behavior. Provocation refers to the positive or negative stimulation that will be derived from the behavior. Opportunity is the actual chance to commit an act of deviance. And, constraint is the actual or perceived likelihood of being subject to restraints imposed by others.

According to Tittle, the probability of deviance is higher when the control ratio (likelihood of control to actual ability to control) is not in balance. When the control ratio is balanced, the probability of deviance is lower. The rationale for these actions is that people who have control surpluses (a great deal of actual control over their actions, with little restraint from others) are likely to engage in exploitative or decadent behaviors. People with control deficits (little actual control over their behaviors) are likely to engage in predatory, defiant, or submissive behaviors. People who have a balance of control are not as likely to engage in deviance. This view of deviance as responding to control opportunities is useful in explaining not only juvenile delinquency but adult behaviors as well.

Social Development Theory. Another integrated control theory has been presented by Weis and his associates at the Seattle Social Development Project (Weis and Hawkins, 1981; Weis and Sederstrom, 1981). *Social development theory* is based on social control theory augmented by social learning and structural modeling. According to social development theory, young children are socialized through family interactions. The opportunities for interactions, the degree of involvement in interactions, the skills to participate in interactions, and reinforcement for participation are all thought to affect the family bonds that develop. In strong supportive families, children develop prosocial bonds that will aid them in resisting antisocial behaviors as they mature. If the family bonds are lacking or the family's commitment to conventional behaviors are weak, the child will be more susceptible to developing antisocial behaviors.

Even in supportive, law-abiding families, as the child matures, interactions with peers and other adults outside the family may result in the development of antisocial bonds that facilitate antisocial behaviors. Young people's position within the social structure, their interaction skills, the strength of their family interactions, and their perceptions of the rewards of engaging in deviance all factor into whether they will participate in antisocial behaviors. They also influence whether they will develop antisocial values from having done so.

The strength of family commitments provides a foundation for the development of commitments to school and other social institutions but does not guarantee that interactions with deviant others and/or social influences will not overcome these commitments by providing rewards for antisocial behaviors. Subsequent attachments to deviant peers and antisocial activities may then result in the adoption of antisocial beliefs and values.

Despite the impact of antisocial influences and deviant peers, Weis and his associates see strong bonds to family and school as integral in young people's ability to resist delinquent behaviors.

Reintegrative Shaming Theory.   Braithwaite (1989) integrates the theories of control, labeling, social learning, and strain in his *reintegrative shaming theory*. Shaming, as seen by Braithwaite (1989, p. 100), includes "all social processes of expressing disapproval which have the intention or effect of invoking remorse in the person being shamed and/or condemnation by others who become aware of the shaming." Shaming is divided into two categories: stigmatization and reintegration. Stigmatization occurs when the labeling of the offender causes that person to feel deviant; reintegration occurs when, despite the shaming, the condemners ensure that they maintain bonds with the offender. Stigmatization is seen as causing additional criminality, stemming from the acquired sense of deviance. Reintegration is seen as allowing the offender to acknowledge his or her wrongful behavior and then gain reentry into the conforming group.

According to Braithwaite, offenders who have stronger social bonds are more likely to reject deviance and return to conformity. The cohesiveness of the social structure and opportunities for legitimate behaviors affect the strengths of the social bonds. In turn, the strengths of the bonds affect the nature and extent of the shaming as well as how the offender responds to it.

Integrated Strain Theories

Integrated strain theories include Delbert Elliot's integrated theory and Robert Agnew's general strain theory. These theories stress their integrated aspects but are solidly built upon the concepts of strain theory.

Integrated Theory.   Elliott, David Huizinga, and Suzanne Agerton (1985) developed an integrated strain theory that draws heavily from social learning and control theories. In *integrated theory,* strain within family and school results in weakened bonds to conventional society and promotes stronger bonds with delinquent peers. Association with these delinquent peers increases the likelihood of delinquent behavior. This view differs from traditional social bonding theories in which socialization is seen as promoting conventional behaviors and reducing the risk of deviant behaviors. Instead, socialization is similar to Edwin Sutherland's differential association theory (see chapter 6) in that deviant behaviors may be learned and reinforced within the bonding process.

This theory is similar to Weis's social development theory, discussed in the previous section. However, it goes further to explain how the bonds within the family and school are weakened by strain from various social factors. Living in disorganized communities, believing that legitimate opportunities for success are unavailable, and involvement in petty crimes lead to feelings of hopelessness. Strain occurs, which then causes deviant groups and activities to appear as acceptable substitutes. Experimentation with drugs and engaging in delinquent behaviors result in the development of a deviant life style.

General Strain Theory.   Agnew's (1985) *general strain theory* enhances traditional strain theory by using psychological concepts to explain how strain occurs within individuals. Whereas traditional strain theories focus on the effects of the social structure on lower-class youth in general, Agnew describes how internal stresses and strains can affect individuals regardless of social class. The negative affective states—anger, frustration, and hopelessness—are caused by failure to achieve goals, the removal of positive or desired stimuli, and the confrontation with negative stimuli.

Since the stressors that influence individuals' perceptions of themselves within the social order can occur to anyone, general strain theory is not limited to a racial or social category. Anyone affected by the strains described by Agnew may come to see him- or herself as isolated and rejected by society. Ultimately, Agnew sees social factors as being influential but concludes that personal temperament and the ability to positively cope with stress are more important.

Integrated Conflict Theories

Integrated conflict theories are premised on the conflictive nature of society. John Hagan's power control theory, and Mark Colvin and John Pauly's integrated structural Marxist theory are innovative mergers of different conflict perspectives.

Power Control Theory. As the reader will have noted, many of the integrated sociological theories focused on the influence of families on youthful deviance. Hagan, John Simpson, and A. R. Gillis (1987) continue this focus with an innovative description of relations within the family setting to explain why female delinquency is less frequent than male delinquency. In *power control theory*, females are seen as less likely to engage in risk taking because of the socialization that occurs within the home. Male dominance within the home is thought to impose submissive behaviors on young women. Since young men are given more "freedom to deviate" within this chauvinistic environment, they are more likely to engage in deviance.

Hagan and his associates argue that larger gender differences in delinquent activities will be seen in patriarchal families. Conversely, egalitarian families will have smaller gender differences in delinquency. Female-headed households produce higher levels of females delinquency than other types of households. Using this knowledge, Hagan, Simpson, and Gillis postulate that as female equality within the workplace creates a more equitable home environment, female delinquency will increase. Conversely, it will also eventually have the positive effect of lowering levels of female victimization in domestic situations.

Integrated Structural Marxist Theory. Colvin and Pauly (1983) also explore domestic relations in their *integrated structural Marxist theory*, wherein the coercive workplace environment of capitalism contributes to coercive family environments. Negative relations in the workplace are said to create strain and alienation in the domestic setting. Frustrations that the parents bring home from their jobs are displaced onto family members. In particular, parents are likely to excessively exercise the controls that they have over their children as compensation for their powerlessness at work and in a capitalistic society.

This repressive home environment causes strain in the family. Consequently, the normal bonds of family are drastically weakened. Coercive school situations further aggravate the frustrations that young people feel. They may, in expressing their frustration and hopelessness, act out in a violent manner and/or they may engage in deviant behaviors as a means of seeking positive rewards that are otherwise unattainable. This theory is thought to be a significant contribution to the Marxist literature in that it clearly demonstrates how capitalism can promote delinquency.

▨▨ SUMMARY ▨▨

Criminology is an interdisciplinary science. This interdisciplinary nature has been both a blessing and a hindrance in understanding crime and criminality. Integrated theories attempt to address the shortcomings of individual theories by merging two or more theoretical explanations into a more complete explanation. The current field of integrated theories can be classified as integrated classical theories, integrated biological theories, integrated psychological theories, and integrated sociological theories.

Integrated classical theories merge classical and positivist approaches to crime causation. Integrated classical theories include routine activities theory, rational choice theory, and criminal personality theory. Integrated biological theories stress the importance of biological factors on human behavior. The biological theories include bio-conditioning theory and human nature theory. Integrated psychological theories explain how social factors can influence self-perception. Integrated psychological theories include delinquency development theory, age-graded theory, and self-derogation theory.

Integrated sociological theories combine two or more sociological explanations of crime and criminality with other sociological, biological, or psychological explanations. Integrated sociological explanations include integrated learning, integrated control, integrated strain, and integrated conflict theories. Integrated learning theories include network analysis and interactional theory. Integrated control theories are control balance theory, social development theory, and reintegrative shaming theory. Integrated strain theories include integrated theory and general strain theory. Integrated conflict theories include power control theory and integrated structural Marxist theory.

Integrated theories must emphasize both the physical and social environments. Otherwise they offer little more than do single-factor explanations. However, integrated crime explanations cannot just provide a broad framework; they must be adaptable and explain specific behaviors. Some of the theories discussed in previous chapters accomplish this task; most do not.

▨▨ DISCUSSION QUESTIONS ▨▨

1. Debate the pros and cons of integrated approaches in explaining crime and criminality.

2. Select the integrated theory that you think best explains crime and criminality. Justify your selection.

3. Using at least one biological, one psychological, and two sociological concepts from the explanations offered, create your own integrated theory of crime causation.

▓▓▓ REFERENCES ▓▓▓

Akers, R. L. (2000). *Criminological theories: Introduction and evaluation,* 3rd ed. Los Angeles: Roxbury.

Agnew, R. (1985). A revised strain theory of delinquency. *Social Forces* 30: 47–87.

Braithwaite, J. (1989). *Crime, shame and reintegration.* Cambridge: Cambridge University Press.

Burgess, R. L., and Akers, R. L. (1966). A differential association-reinforcement theory of criminal behavior. *Social Problems* 14: 128–47.

Clarke, R. V. (1997). *Situational crime prevention,* 2nd ed. New York: Harrow and Heston.

Cohen, L. E., and Felson, M. (1979). Social change and crime rate trends: A routine activities theory. *American Sociological Review* 44: 588–608.

Colvin, M., and Pauly, J. (1983). A critique of criminology: Toward an integrated structural-Marxist theory of gender and delinquency. *American Journal of Sociology* 89: 513–51.

Cornish, D. B., and Clarke, R. V. (1986). *The reasoning criminal: Rational choice perspectives on offending.* New York: Springer.

Elliott, D. S., Huizinga, D., and Agerton, S. S. (1985). *Explaining delinquency and drug use.* Beverly Hills: Sage.

Eysenck, H. J., and Gudjonsson, G. H. (1989). *The causes and cures of criminality.* New York: Plenum.

Farrington, D. P. (1988). Psychobiological factors in the explanation and reduction of delinquency. *Today's Delinquent* 7: 44–46.

Hagan, J., Simpson, J. H., and Gillis, A. R. (1987). Class in the household: A power-control theory of gender and delinquency. *American Journal of Sociology* 92: 788–816.

Kaplan, H. B. (1975). *Self-attitudes and deviant behavior.* Pacific Palisades, CA: Goodyear.

Krohn, M. D. (1986). The web of conformity: A network approach to the explanation of delinquent behavior. *Social Problems* 33: 581–93.

Sampson, R. J., and Laub, J. H.(1993). *Crime in the making: Pathways and turning points through life.* Cambridge: Harvard University Press.

Schmalleger, F. (1999). *Criminology today,* 2nd ed. Upper Saddle River, NJ: Prentice Hall.

Shoemaker, D. J. (1996). *Theories of delinquency: An examination of explanations of delinquent behavior,* 3rd ed. New York: Oxford University Press.

Siegel, L. J. (2000). *Criminology,* 7th ed. Belmont, CA: Wadsworth/Thomson Learning.

Thornberry, T. P. (1987). Towards an interactional theory of delinquency. *Criminology* 25: 863–91.

Tittle, C. R. (1995). *Control balances: Toward a general theory of deviance.* Boulder, CO: Westview Press.

Weis, J., and Hawkins, J. D. (1981). *Reports of the national juvenile justice assessment centers, preventing delinquency.* Washington, D.C.: U.S. Department of Justice.

_____, and Sederstrom, (1981). *Reports of the National Juvenile Justice Assessment Centers, the prevention of serious delinquency.* Washington, D.C.: U.S. Department of Justice.

Wilson, J. Q., and Herrnstein, R. J. (1985). *Crime and human nature.* New York: Simon & Schuster.

Yochelson, S., and Samenow, S. E. (1976). *The criminal personality* (vol.1). New York: Jason Aronson.

Holistic Theories
of Crime Causation

■ KEY CONCEPTS ■

bioenvironmental theory
conceptual absorption theory
conceptual integration theory
general theory
general paradigm theory
holistic incorporation theories
identity theory
individual difference theory

integrative delinquency theory
interdisciplinary criminology
multifactor approach
self-control theory
self-derogation
self-esteem
structure process theory

■ LEARNING OBJECTIVES ■

After reading this chapter, the student should be able to:

1. Discuss the benefits of an interdisciplinary approach to criminology.

2. Contrast the four holistic interpretations of criminological theory and explain their limitations.

3. Present and discuss the general theories.

4. Present and discuss identity theory.

5. Contrast the benefits and weaknesses of holistic theories of crime causation.

Chapter 8 discussed several categories of integrated theories. This chapter discusses efforts to go beyond the simple integration of two or more theories in order to create general explanations of crime and criminal behavior. The theories discussed in this chapter are shown in Table 9–1.

THE HOLISTIC APPROACH TO CRIME

The benefit of criminology taking an interdisciplinary science approach rather than adhering to a single discipline is that it enables scholars to view a specific type of crime or criminal offender from several perspectives (Jeffery, 1977a, 1977b, 1990). Rather than seeing a one-dimensional picture, multiple disciplinary approaches allow criminologists to see the entire panorama. Unfortunately, such an approach can be so general in nature that it is difficult to test and even more difficult to apply (Hagan, 1998). Because of these difficulties, most contemporary theories of crime and criminality emphasize a single disciplinary approach to a specific crime or criminal type. As we noted in chapter 8, however, one should not become so fixed on one perspective that the benefits of other methods are overlooked.

Despite the problems inherent in using an integrated theoretical perspective, a number of efforts have combined multifactor perspectives regarding crime and criminality into more holistic (general) explanations. Four of the better known efforts at holistic incorporation of criminological theories are

TABLE 9–1   Holistic Theories

Holistic Incorporation Theories	General Theories
Bioenvironmental theory	Self-control theory
Conceptual absorption theory	Integrative delinquency theory
Conceptual integration theory	Identity theory
General paradigm theory	

C. Ray Jeffery's bioenvironmental theory, Ronald Aker's conceptual absorption, Frank Pearson and Nerl Weiner's conceptual integration, and Bryan Vila's general paradigm.

Jeffery's Bioenvironmental Theory

Jeffery's (1977a, 1977b, 1990) *bioenvironmental theory* argues that human behavior is the product of complex and constantly changing interactions between the physical environment and the social environment. Nature creates a predisposition for certain behaviors. Nurture creates opportunities for the behaviors to occur and also provides reinforcement for subsequent occurrences.

According to Jeffery, the physical environment includes biochemical activities within the brain, the effects of air and water pollution, ingestion of chemical substances, physiological defects that impact the brain and central nervous system, and damage from physical trauma. The social environment includes all social interactions at all levels (individual to societal) that might influence an individual's perceptions of him- or herself and others. Because of the enormity of investigating all social and physical interactions, Jeffery has focused his efforts on exploring how biological deficiencies can cause maladaptive behaviors.

Akers's Conceptual Absorption Theory

Akers (2000) argues that we already have theory integration in criminology because of *conceptual absorption.* He posits that the concepts used to explain the behaviors of criminal offenders are compatible and in some cases the same as concepts used by other theories. Akers compares social learning theory and other sociological theories to demonstrate that they are explaining the same behavioral processes. Therefore, integration is said to have already occurred to a considerable degree. The difference is one of terminology.

In short, Akers (2000) argues that all criminal behavior can be said to be based on social learning because every other theory uses social learning components. However, Akers is the first to acknowledge that such a broad interpretation provides little insight into criminal behavior other than noting that learning is involved in all the social theories.

Pearson and Weiner's Conceptual Integration

Yet another holistic interpretation is provided by Pearson and Weiner (1985). Like the previous two explanations, *conceptual integration* does not provide an integrated theory as much as a framework that demonstrates how other theories complement one another. The basis for the theoretical framework is that eight concepts can be identified in all criminological theories. The concepts that determine behavior are

1. Utility

2. Behavior skill

3. Signs of opportunities to commit crimes

4. Behavioral resources

5. Rules of expedience

6. Rules of morality

Consequences of the behavior are interpreted by

7. Utility receptions

8. Information acquisition

Like Akers's theory, the Pearson and Weiner framework is predominately an effort to incorporate all other theories into a social learning explanation. While it has received some support, most notably from Akers (2000), it has limited application as a theoretical model.

Vila's General Paradigm

The fourth holistic approach to criminological explanation is Vila's paradigm for understanding criminal behavior. According to Vila (1994), a theory must include ecological, integrative, developmental, and both macro- and microlevel explanations if it is to explain all types of criminal behavior. Theories that include only one component or explain only one type of crime are seen as being only partial theories. *General theories*, in Vila's view, must incorporate biological, sociocultural, and developmental factors into complex and constantly changing ecological interactions.

A primary assumption in Vila's paradigm is that all crimes are the product of human desire to acquire "resources." The type of resource desired (material, hedonistic, or political) and ecological factors determine the type of crimes committed (or not committed). How these interactions occur is demonstrated within a complex "mathematical chaos model" that incorporates all factors rather than using a traditional linear model of analysis. Like the previous explanations, Vila's paradigm has great appeal in its general explanation. However, it shares the same weakness as the others in that the broadness of the approach limits its applicability. The complex methodology required for assessing this paradigm is also an impediment to its application.

THE NEED FOR GENERAL THEORIES

Single-factor approaches to crime causation do not adequately explain the myriad of criminal offenders and criminal behaviors studied within criminology. However, multifactor approaches (such as the integrated theories presented in chapter 7 and holistic incorporation efforts presented thus far in this chapter attempt to apply a particular theoretical framework to other explanations as seen in the Akers and Pearson and Weiner models or like Jeffery's bioenvironmental approach) are so broad as to require single-factor assessments in order to be applied to criminal behavior. What is needed is a theoretical explanation that can be applied to a number of crimes and offenders without being so broad as to be useless in its practical application. The following section reviews two attempts at theoretical integration that accomplish this goal with varying degrees of success. We refer to these efforts as general theories of crime and criminality.

GENERAL THEORIES OF CRIME AND CRIMINALITY

The integrated theories discussed in chapter 8 seemed to have the most impact. Here, we have identified two theories as *general theories* that we believe come nearest to providing integrated explanations of crime and criminality. These theories are Michael Gottfredson and Travis Hirschi's self-control theory and Donald Shoemaker's integrative delinquency theory.

Self-Control Theory

Gottfredson and Hirschi's (1990) *self-control theory* merges concepts of control theory with rational choice, routine activities, and biological and psychological explanations. Integral to their explanation is that crime and criminal behavior are different concepts. People who engage in criminal acts are seen as having low self-control. They engage in many conventional behaviors, but due to low self-control, they are predisposed to committing crimes if opportunities arise. This explanation explains all types of crimes and criminal behaviors.

According to Gottfredson and Hirschi, the causes of crime are impulsive personalities, low self-control, weakened social bonds, and criminal opportunities. An impulsive personality is developed by certain biological and psychological factors. Low self-control is a product of impulsive personality combined with social factors such as deviant parents and poor supervision. Weakened social bonds are the product of low self-control and the subsequent development of alternative attachments, involvements, commitments, and beliefs. If criminal opportunities should come about, the combination of low self-control and weakened social bonds will very likely result in crime.

While self-control theory has been criticized as too general as well as tautological, it is perhaps the clearest and most understandable theory to date incorporating biological, psychological, and sociological influences (Akers, 2000).

Integrative Delinquency Theory

Gottfredson and Hirschi explain how low self-control can influence criminality; in his theory of *integrative delinquency,* Shoemaker emphasizes self-esteem as integral to understanding juvenile delinquency. According to Shoemaker, a juvenile's self-esteem is determined by interactions with conforming adults and these interactions may result in a positive or negative self-concept. The linkage of self-concept to criminal behavior may be direct but is more often an indirect influence that interacts with other influences. Influences on behavior are said to be structural (relating to social conditions), individual (biological and psychological), and social psychological (social controls, self-esteem, and peer associations).

In this model, individual and structural conditions indirectly influence delinquency first through social controls and later through self-esteem and peer associations. Weakened social bonds created by structural and/or individual situations lead to lowered self-concept and increased association with deviants. As attachments to deviant associates are strengthened, conventional attachments are weakened. The combination of weakened social bonds, lowered self-concept, and negative peer influences directly and powerfully influence delinquency.

Like self-control theory, integrative delinquency theory provides a rational explanation of how biological, psychological, and sociological factors can be incorporated into a general explanation of criminality. Unfortunately, it may also be seen by critics of multifactor approaches as being too general and as having restricted applicability.

A SYNOPSIS OF INTEGRATED AND HOLISTIC THEORIES

Integrated theories must emphasize both the physical and social environments. Otherwise they offer little more than do single-factor explanations. Integrated crime explanations cannot just provide a broad framework, however; they must be adaptable to explain specific behaviors. Some of the theories discussed in the previous chapters accomplish this task but most do not. The complexities of holistic incorporation theories limit their application in explaining specific criminal behaviors. The two general theories that we have just discussed are more readily adapted to explaining specific criminal behaviors, though Shoemaker's integrative delinquency theory is limited in that its focus is to explain how delinquent behavior develops. Of the theories that we have discussed, it is our opinion that Gottfredson and Hirschi's self-control theory best explains crime and criminality. Nevertheless, we believe a need for improvement remains.

IDENTITY THEORY

The final holistic theory that we discuss is our own *identify theory*, which might also be called enviro-classical conflict in that it draws from a variety of approaches that might ordinarily be seen as being incompatible. It is our view that rather than being incompatible, these seemingly contradictory perspectives actually complement one another in creating a general theory of crime and criminality. Our premise is quite simple: criminal behavior is the product of nature and nurture. The determination of whether behavior will be criminal depends on how the individual and society interrelate. These interrelationships are influenced by complex and constantly changing biological, psychological, and social factors.

The biological factors that influence human behavior include physiological, (physical attractiveness, physical size, and gender), genetic (gender, ethnicity, and intelligence), and environmental (effects of pollution and diet) influences. These influences interact with psychological factors, including problem-solving abilities, emotional stability, personality, and belief systems. These combined influences interact with sociological factors, such as social structure, economic systems, culture, family, religion, class, ethnicity, gender, and sexual orientation. These complex interrelationships are constant and frequently conflictive. Compared to this complex approach, single-factor theories, though useful to describe group activities, can be seen as inadequate to explain the actions of individual offenders.

In order to understand crime and criminality at the individual level, the combined effects of the previously discussed factors must be considered. However, this does not mean that criminologists must evaluate a lengthy checklist of environmental factors for each criminal offender. Instead, it means that we must locate an indicator of those influences that will then enable us to assess criminality. Previous considerations of self-concept and self-esteem have proven valuable in explaining the development of criminal and deviant behaviors. It is our belief that these concepts should be expanded into a theory of human behavior based on personal identity.

Human beings have an innate need to feel worthy. It is important that people significant to us feel that we are worthwhile, but it is even more important that we feel self-worth. Every action that we take in dealing with others and in dealing with ourselves is a product of our desire for positive self-worth. All human behavior, no matter how compassionate or selfless, is driven by the desire to feel good about ourselves. Thorstein Veblen (1998) saw greed as motivation not only for seemingly selfish acts but for altruistic acts as well. The basis of this view is that we will do whatever is necessary to have positive feelings.

As human beings we have many desires. Food, shelter, and material comforts are fundamental concerns. But ego needs ultimately determine behavior. It is our argument that ego gratification is necessary for mental and emotional well-being. Without this gratification, we cannot maintain a positive self-image, and without a positive self-image, we have no identity. Therefore, in order to develop and maintain our personal identity, we do what we think is necessary to enhance our self-worth.

If our ecological makeup has disposed us to being gregarious and outgoing, our self-identity is influenced by what others think of us. If we have suffered rejection, frustration, and loneliness, we may come to rely solely upon our own self-image. Social bonds and controls are important but only if they contribute to a positive identity. If such social influences should happen to lead to identity conflict, we will do what is necessary to remove negative stimuli so as to reestablish our positive identity. The means by which we remove negative stimuli may be to conform to social pressures or it may be to reject the sources of those pressures. These actions may range from internal responses (cognitive acceptance or denial) to efforts on a societal level (attempting to change the social and economic order). Whether these individual responses are criminal or lawful may be due more to the opinions of others than to the personal ideology of the respondent. The choice of lawful or criminal behavior is determined by whether compliance or deviance best serves our identity needs.

While ecological concerns have substantial impact, broad social factors are also influential. As indicated earlier, we choose our actions based on what aids us in maintaining our identity. If we have been socialized into the view that work status is important, we shall seek to enhance our work status. If we are unable to do so, maintaining our positive identity requires that we reject such status labels. This rejection may not be deviant and may seek to lawfully alter the system or circumstances that created the threat to our identity.

Identity theory is compatible with all other explanations of criminal behavior. Classical theory stresses the need for individual responsibility; so does identity theory. But whether that responsibility is socially acceptable is not as important as whether it promotes a positive identity. Fortunately, because of early socialization efforts, most of us comply with classical mandates not out of fear of punishment but because it makes us feel good about ourselves. We support the punishment of others because that also makes us feel good about ourselves. We may support positive theories for similar identity support. Likewise, we may advocate Marxist ideologies because our perceived involvement in the struggle for equality enables us to maintain (or further develop) our positive identity.

Identity theory can explain both legal and illegal behaviors committed by all classes of people and all categories of crime. For example, racism can be explained as the product of socialization that leads to hostility and contempt for other races. This hostility may result in any number of behaviors, but ultimately those behaviors will be selected based on what is deemed most beneficial to the individual's personal identity. Whether that selection be cool indifference, nonviolent protest, or violent action is determined by personal identity. What seems to be an irrational act to others may be a deliberate (and personally rewarding) act of martyrdom to another. All actions, even on the part of those thought to be deranged or mentally incompetent are rational—to them—efforts to enhance their personal identity.

ASSESSMENT OF HOLISTIC THEORIES

Like the computers we have come to rely upon, human beings are affected by hardware issues (nature) and software issues (nurture) that determine the ability to process information and provide adequate responses. To ignore biological or physiological influences on human behavior is akin to ignoring hardware aspects of our computers; to ignore psychological and sociological influences is the same as trying to use a computer without having software installed. Like the computer *we must understand what issue is relevant when a particular problem emerges*. The question then arises, is it important that we debate a plethora of competing and/or complementary theories or that we understand the variables that are found to influence criminal behavior?

The holistic approaches discussed earlier in this chapter tend to use multifactor orientations while emphasizing specific approaches (i.e., biology with Jeffery, social learning with Akers). Thomas Bernard and Jeffrey Snipes (Vold, Bernard, and Snipes, 1998) take the stance that these efforts are self-defeating. They argue that all of the criminology theories can be integrated into two categories. The bases for their categories are not theoretical orientations but crime variables used within those orientations.

According to Bernard and Snipes, theories that emphasize individual-level data should be classified as *individual difference theories*. Theories that emphasize aggregate-level data should be classified as *structure/process theories*. Most of the single and multifactor approaches that we discussed previously can be located within these categories. For example, conflict theorists can study those issues they believe to be important while biosocial theorists can study issues they believe to be important. Acceptance of a theory does not mean that others cannot also be supported.

For the most part, aggregate-level and individual-level data should not be combined (this leads to a dilemma referred to in methods texts as the ecological fallacy). Following this logic, the primary concern of criminological research is not adhering to artificial theoretical delineations, but to use the correct level of analysis in evaluating the individual or societal variables that influence criminality.

We accept Bernard and Snipes's argument. However, we note, as they did, that their theoretical categories are not mutually exclusive (meaning that some variables may be appropriate for either type of analysis). Bernard and Snipes (Vold, Bernard, and Snipes, 1998, p. 314) address this by stating that "while competitive testing of theories within and without categories is almost always inappropriate...integration of theories both within and between categories is almost always possible." In our opinion, it is in those common areas, where cautious explanation of how individual factors and societal factors are interrelated, that multifactor (holistic/general) criminological theories are not only proper, but necessary.

▬▬ SUMMARY ▬▬

Despite the problems inherent in using an integrated theoretical perspective, there have been a number of efforts to combine different perspectives regarding crime and criminality into more holistic explanations. Four of the better known efforts at holistic incorporation of criminological theories are Jeffery's bioenvironmental theory, Akers's conceptual absorption theory, Pearson and Weiner's conceptual integration theory, and Vila's general paradigm.

Jeffery argues that human behavior is the product of complex and constantly changing interactions between the physical environment and the social environment. Akers argues that we already have theory integration in criminology because of conceptual absorption. He posits that the concepts used to explain the behaviors of criminal offenders are compatible and in some cases the same as concepts used by other theories. Pearson and Weiner provide a framework demonstrating how other theories complement one another. The basis for their theoretical framework is that eight common concepts can be identified in all criminological theories. Vila's paradigm for understanding criminal behavior assumes that all crimes are the product of human desire to acquire resources. The type of resource desired (material, hedonistic, or political) and ecological factors determine the type of crimes committed (or not committed).

Each of the four holistic explanations has great appeal in its general explanation. However, they all share the same weakness in that the broadness of the approach limits applicability. Two theories thought to better represent holistic theoretical integration are categorized here as general theories.

Gottfredson and Hirschi merge concepts of control theory with rational choice, routine activities, and biological and psychological explanations within their general theory of crime. People who engage in criminal acts are seen as having low self-control. Although they may engage in many conventional behaviors, due to low self-control, they are predisposed to committing crimes if opportunities arise.

In his theory of integrative delinquency, Shoemaker emphasizes self-esteem as integral to understanding juvenile delinquency. Influences on behavior are said to be structural (relating to social conditions), individual (biological and psychological), and social psychological (social controls, self-esteem, and peer associations). In this model, individual and structural conditions indirectly influence delinquency first through social controls and later through self-esteem and peer associations.

Our identity theory provides a general explanation that can be applied to all crimes and criminal typologies. Criminal behavior is seen as the product of nature and nurture. The determination of whether behavior will be criminal depends on how the individual and society interrelate. These inter-relationships are influenced by complex and constantly changing influences of biological factors, psychological factors, and social factors. Personal identity was identified as the best indicator how of those influences may create crime and criminality.

Last, integrated and holistic theories were assessed on the basis of their strengths and weaknesses. It was concluded that a holistic approach is both proper and necessary in explaining crime and criminality.

▓▓▓ DISCUSSION QUESTIONS ▓▓▓

1. Debate the pros and cons of multifactor approaches in explaining crime and criminality.

2. Select the integrated theory that you think best explains crime and criminality. Justify your selection.

3. Using at least one biological, one psychological, and two sociological concepts from the explanations offered, create your own integrated theory of crime causation.

▨ **REFERENCES** ▨

Akers, R. L. (2000). *Criminological theories: Introduction and evaluation* 3rd ed. Los Angeles: Roxbury.

Gottfredson, M., and Hirschi, T. (1990). *A general theory of crime.* Palo Alto: Stanford University Press.

Hagan, F. E. (1998). *Introduction to criminology: Theories, methods and criminal behavior,* 4th ed. Chicago: Nelson-Hall.

Jeffery, C. R. (1990). *Criminology: An interdisciplinary approach.* Englewood Cliffs, NJ: Prentice Hall.

_____. (1977a). *Crime prevention through environmental design,* 2nd ed. Beverly Hills: Sage.

_____. (1977b). Criminology as an interdisciplinary behavioral science. *Criminology* 16: 153–56.

Pearson, F. S., and Weiner, N. A. (1985). Toward an integration of criminological theories. *Journal of Criminal Law and Criminology* 76: 116—50.

Shoemaker, D. J. (1996). *Theories of delinquency: An examination of explanations of delinquent behavior,* 3rd ed. New York: Oxford University Press.

Veblen. T. (1998). *The theory of the leisure class* (Great Minds Series ed.). Amherst, NY: Prometheus.

Vila, B. (1994). A general paradigm for understanding criminal behavior: Extending evolutionary ecological theory. *Criminology* 32: 311–60.

Vold, G. B., Bernard, T. J., and Snipes, J. B. (1998). *Theoretical criminology*, 4th ed. New York: Oxford University Press.

CHAPTER 10

Victimization Theories

▦ KEY CONCEPTS ▦

active precipitation
compatible victimology theory
crime event theory
critical victimology theory
deviant place hypothesis
equivalent group hypothesis
functional responsibility theory
general victimology theory
lifestyle theory
passive precipitation
personal factors theory
primary victimization

proximity hypothesis
routine activities theory
secondary victimization
situational factors theory
tertiary victimization
victim precipitation
victim precipitation theory
victim typology
victimization
victimizer
victimology

▦ LEARNING OBJECTIVES ▦

After reading this chapter, the student should be able to:

1. Define victimology and discuss its historical developments.

2. Contrast von Hentig's personal factors theory with Mendelsohn's situational factor's theory.

3. Contrast Schafer's personal responsibility theory with Sellin and Wolfgang's situational theory.

4. Define victim precipitation and discuss its strengths and weaknesses.

5. Contrast general victimology theory, critical victimology theory and Karmen's victimology theory.

6. Describe the premise of lifestyle theory and explain how the equivalent group hypothesis and the proximity hypothesis address lifestyle influences.

7. Contrast deviant places hypothesis with routine activities theory.

VICTIMOLOGY

Discussions in previous chapters focused on the causes of crime and on criminal offenders. This chapter discusses the victims of crime and the causes of victimization. The study of crime victims and issues related to victimization is known as *victimology*.

Victimology is seen by some scholars as a separate discipline (Wallace, 1998). Others see victimology as an important subfield within criminology (Doerner and Lab, 1998). Regardless of one's viewpoint as to victimology's disciplinary status, the study of crime and its consequences would not be complete without examining the issues leading to victimization, the subsequent effects of crime on victims, and society's responses to victims' needs.

Concern for victims is not a new phenomenon. Offenders in early tribal societies were held accountable to victims for the harm they had caused to them. Social customs such as the blood feud placed responsibility on the victim's family to exact vengeance. Offenders could often avoid retribution by paying restitution to the victim or the victim's families in compensation for the harm caused (Territo, Halstead, and Bromley, 1998). This arrangement prevented future violence, reinforced societal prohibitions against specific crimes, and also aided victims.

As tribal societies evolved into nation states, the need of the state to collect revenues took precedence over concern for victims. Compensation paid to victims gave way to fines paid to the government for the harm crime caused to society. Victims gradually became witnesses in the governmental efforts to promote justice, and criminal offenders became the focus of these enforcement efforts (Doerner and Lab, 1998). This emphasis on offenders would continue as modern nations developed, and it remains the focal concern of criminal justice administration to this day.

Only within the last fifty years have victims become a subject of study for social scientists. Furthermore, justice system concerns for the welfare of victims did not gain impetus until the mid-1970s when victim-assistance programs and crime-compensation efforts began to emerge. In recent years, victimology has become an important area of study within sociology, criminology, and criminal justice programs. More important perhaps, criminal justice practitioners have become more aware and responsive to the needs of crime victims.

Early Victimization Theories

Chapters 3 through 9 presented numerous theories of crime causation. This chapter discusses several different theories of victimization. Whereas the earlier theories of crime focused on the motivations and actions of criminal offenders, these theories concentrate on the behaviors of victims. The victimization theories discussed in this chapter are shown in Table 10–1.

Personal Factors Theory

Hans von Hentig's research was instrumental in drawing the attention of other social scientists to the victim's role in the commission of crime. After much research on criminal offenders, von Hentig began focusing on the events that caused certain types of individuals to become victims. He was among the first to claim that the victim could be a contributing factor to his or her successive victimization (von Hentig, 1941); this is known as *victim precipitation*. Von Hentig's later research developed the premise that victims could actually be provocateurs of the crime committed against them (von Hentig, 1948).

TABLE 10–1   Victimization Theories

Early Theories	*Contemporary Theories*
Personal factors theory	General victimology theory
Situational factors theory	Critical victimology theory
Functional responsibility theory	Compatible victimology
Crime event theory	Lifestyle theories
Victim precipitation theory	*Equivalent group hypothesis*
	Proximity hypothesis
	Deviant place hypothesis
	Routine activities theory

In examining victims' roles in their own victimization, von Hentig developed a typology of potential victims (see Table 10–2). These characteristics were based on physical, social, and psychological disadvantages that made victims less able to resist criminals' efforts (Doerner and Lab, 1998). While von Hentig did not blame victims for their misfortunes, he was the first to argue that studying a victim's *personal factors* might provide understanding to their susceptibility to criminal victimization.

Situational Factors Theory

Benjamin Mendelsohn is credited by some as being the father of victimology. As a practicing attorney, Mendelsohn investigated the situational factors that led to the criminal event. His research resulted in the belief that a relationship often existed between offenders and victims that set up the victimization episode (Wallace, 1998). Like von Hentig, he believed that victims could be categorized within a victim precipitation typology. However, Mendelsohn focused on factors within the social relationship rather than on features of the victims.

While Mendelsohn did not argue that victims warranted the crime that occurred against them, he did believe that they should be assigned some of the blame for having placed themselves at risk. Mendelsohn's

TABLE 10–2 Von Hentig's Victim Typology

1. The Young—children
2. The Female—women
3. The Old—the elderly
4. The Mentally Defective—the feebleminded, mentally ill
5. Immigrants—newly arrived and naive about the culture
6. Minorities—disadvantaged due to racial bias
7. Dull Normals—the slow or ignorant
8. The Depressed—the dejected and emotionally drained
9. The Acquisitive—greedy people seeking to gain
10. The Wanton—promiscuous individuals
11. The Lonesome/Heartbroken—suffering from emotional loss
12. The Tormentor—the abuser who provokes violence
13. The Blocked, Exempted, or Fighting—those whose actions have placed themselves in losing situations
14. The Activating Sufferer—victim as perpetrator

Source: Hans von Hentig, *The Criminal and His Victim: Studies in the Socio-Biology of Crime* (New Haven: Yale University Press, 1948), pp. 404–438.

situational factors typology is displayed in Table 10–3. One can see that Mendelsohn was more than willing to hold victims partially, if not fully, accountable for their having become victims. This perspective developed the concept of victim precipitation beyond that initially discussed by von Hentig.

Functional Responsibility Theory

Stephen Schafer examined the earlier works of both von Hentig and Mendelsohn before developing his own classification of victims. Rather than categorizing victims based on risk factors, as had been done by von Hentig and Mendelsohn, Schafer (1968) used responsibility as his rationale for categorization. He believed that examining the relationship between criminals and victims would enable the criminal justice system to better deal with the problem of crime.

The key to Schafer's *functional responsibility theory* is that everyone within society has a responsibility to conduct him- or herself appropriately. Crime is a social phenomenon that is in most cases the product of inappropriate behavior on the part of both victims and offenders. Therefore, in order to deal with the problem of crime, victim responsibility must be acknowledged. Schafer's victim precipitation typology is shown in Table 10–4.

TABLE 10–3   Mendelsohn's Victim Precipitation Typology

1. *The completely innocent victim.* Individuals who did nothing to precipitate the act against them.
2. *The victim with minor guilt.* Persons whose ignorance or inadvertent actions placed them in jeopardy.
3. *The victim who is as guilty as the offender.* Those whose voluntary actions helped create the situation.
4. *The victim more guilty than the offender.* People who provoke others to commit a crime against them.
5. *The most guilty victim.* Perpetrators who initiate a crime against another and end up being killed or harmed by their would-be victim.
6. *The imaginary victim.* Individuals who are delusional and believe that they have been victimized or who deliberately fabricate a crime to cover up their own responsibility for their misfortune.

Source: Adapted from H. Wallace, *Victimology: Legal, Psychological and Social Perspectives* (Boston: Allyn & Bacon, 1998), p. 6.

TABLE 10–4 Schafer's Victim Precipitation Typology

1. *Unrelated Victims*	No criminal responsibility. Victim is unfortunate target.
2. *Provocative Victims*	Victim shares responsibility due to provocative actions.
3. *Precipitative Victims*	Some degree of victim responsibility due to careless or inappropriate actions.
4. *Biologically Weak Victims*	No victim responsibility due to physical conditions that led to being targeted.
5. *Socially Weak Victims*	Immigrants, minorities, and others who are seen as easy targets.
6. *Self-Victimizing*	Total victim responsibility due to individual's own criminal activity.
7. *Political Victims*	No victim responsibility due to abuses by those in power.

Source: Adapted from W.G. Doerner and S. Lab, *Victimology*, 2nd ed. (Cincinnati: Anderson, 1998), p. 6.

Crime Event Theory

In 1964, yet another typology of crime victims was offered by Thorston Sellin and Marvin Wolfgang. Instead of concentrating on the relationship between victims and offenders, they focused on crime situations in a manner similar to Mendelsohn's earlier work. However, they emphasized the actual crime event more than Mendelsohn did. As a result of their research, Sellin and Wolfgang (1964) offered five categories of victimization.

- *Primary victimization* refers to personalized or individualized victimization in which the victims were selected for victimization based on personal attributes. This would be exemplified by an attack on an individual because of knowledge about that person or because that individual fit the offender's victim profile.

- *Secondary victimization* occurs when the victim is an impersonal but available target of the offender. The victim in this situation may merely be in the wrong place at the wrong time.

- *Tertiary victimization* occurs when the public or society as a whole is considered to be the victim of criminal activity, for example, when public officials engage in unlawful or corrupt behavior that is detrimental to the welfare of their constituents.

- *Mutual victimization* occurs when one offender is victimized by an associate or accomplice. For example, a falling-out among gang members might result in a shooting incident.

- *No victimization* occurs when willing participants engage in allegedly victimless crimes, such as gambling or prostitution.

Victim Precipitation Theory

Most of the early victimization theories classify victims in order to better understand the offender-victim relationship or the situational factors leading to victimization. The theories themselves received very little empirical support. However, the idea that the victim's actions could possibly influence or actually cause their victimization received a great deal of attention from scholars and criminal justice practitioners.

One study that did provide support for the idea that victims' actions could lead to their victimization was conducted by Marvin Wolfgang. In a study of homicide victims in Philadelphia, Wolfgang (1958) found that the victims often had prior interpersonal relationships with the offender, that the act of homicide was the product of a disagreement that escalated in violence, and that alcohol consumption often exacerbated the situation. This led Wolfgang to conclude that many homicides resulted from victim precipitation. Individuals who engaged in behavior that was provocative or instrumental in causing their victimization are said to have engaged in *active precipitation*. When victims unwittingly contribute to their victimization though actions (or inaction) that make them more vulnerable, *passive precipitation* occurs.

Another study that provided further support for the concept of victim precipitation was conducted by Menachim Amir (1971), who analyzed rape data from Philadelphia police records. Amir concluded that 19 percent of all forcible rapes were victim-precipitated. When this controversial study was publicized, the negative reactions to not only Amir's conclusion but to the concept of victim precipitation were immediate and strong.

The study of victimology was actually disrupted because of disagreements about victim precipitation among scholars, criminal justice practitioners, the media, and the public. Proponents argued that the victim's involvement in crime must be understood in order to prevent future victimization. Critics argued that victim precipitation was nothing more than blaming the victim for what the offender had done. Ultimately, a compromise was reached (Doerner and Lab, 1998) as victimologists established a middle ground that recognized that in some situations victims had some responsibility, but that in many other situations victim behavior had little or no bearing on their victimization.

Contemporary Victimization Theories

As the study of victimology has developed, several other theories have emerged to either supplement or complement the earlier postulations. This section presents three theoretical perspectives that allow for broad differentiation on the part of victimologists. We then discuss two theories that revisit the issue of victim behavior in preventing or precipitating victimization.

General Victimology Theory

In an effort to promote stability within the discipline, Mendelsohn (1976, p. 59) called for victimology to "investigate the causes of victimization in search of effective remedies." To emphasize the concern for victims, Mendelsohn offered five new definitions of victims:

1. *Victim of a criminal*—covers all acts initiated by other individuals or groups of individuals

2. *Victim of one's self*—involves acts of self-abuse or injury such as suicide

3. *Victim of the social environment*—refers to incidents such as discrimination based on race or class, as well as governmental abuses of power

4. *Victim of technology*–alludes to people who fall prey to technological advances and their impacts

5. *Victims of the natural environment*—those affected by natural disasters such as floods, earthquakes, and tornados. (Doerner and Lab, 1998, pp. 13–14)

While the reader may object that such a typology of victims makes everyone a potential victim, it does manage to allow victimologists to pursue different perspectives within victimology without splintering the field of study.

Critical Victimology Theory

The general victimology described previously allows for many diverse views on what victimhood is and what causes it. Earlier we saw that many critical criminologists define crime based on social conflict and the actions of those in power against those deemed to be powerless. R. I. Mawby and S. Walklate (1994) exemplify the perspective of critical victimologists who seek to examine the wider social context of power and control within society that results in different definitions of and responses to victimization. *Critical victimology theory* tends to focus more on social conditions that are thought to influence the incidence of crime and victimization than does contemporary victimology. Indeed, to a critical victimologist the offender-victim relationship as defined by a contemporary victimologist or criminologist may be the reverse of that which he or she sees.

Compatible Victimology Theory

A theory that perhaps best describes the multidisciplinary nature of victimology and the divergent views that are held within this emerging discipline (or criminological subfield if the reader prefers) was provided by Andrew Karmen. Like Mendelsohn's general theory, *compatible victimology theory* provides for divergent perspectives in the study of victimization. Karmen (2001) noted three compatible areas of concentration for victimologists:

1. Victimologists study the reasons (if any) why and how the victim entered a dangerous situation. This approach does not attempt to fix the blame on the victim, rather it examines the dynamics that resulted in the victim's being in a dangerous situation.

2. Victimology evaluates how police, prosecutors, courts, and related agencies interact with the victim, and how the victim was treated at each stage in the criminal justice system.

3. Victimologists evaluate the effectiveness of efforts to reimburse victims for their losses and meet the victims' personal and emotional needs.

Lifestyle Theory

Lifestyle theory holds that people may increase or decrease their potential to become victims of crime based on their lifestyles. Some individuals have lifestyles that are very high risk, whereas others tend to live more sedate or conventional existences, which are much lower in risk. The premise is actually quite simple: The more you place yourself in harm's way, the more likely you are to be harmed. Therefore, proponents of lifestyle theory seek to educate potential victims as to their propensity for victimization. The three distinct hypotheses that may be found among lifestyle advocates are equivalent group hypothesis, proximity hypothesis, and deviant place hypothesis.

Equivalent Group Hypothesis. Individuals who become victims of crime often exhibit the same lifestyle characteristics as do their offenders. People who engage in criminal activities are frequently victimized by their associates. Indeed, for law enforcement officials, it may sometimes be difficult to determine who is the offender and who is the victim when investigating an act of violence. It is within this equivalent group that we frequently see repeat victimization or victim recidivism (Doerner and Lab, 1998), in which victims tend be victimized on a continual basis.

Proximity Hypothesis. *Proximity hypothesis* is similar to equivalent group hypothesis in that it considers the influence of the victim's lifestyle on his or her vulnerability to crime, but it emphasizes where victims live rather than their individual characteristics. Often there is no victim precipitation other than the misfortune of being in close proximity to would-be offenders. For example, urban dwellers may have no choice but to reside and conduct their daily activities near those who are predisposed to victimize them (Meadows, 1998). The more people compressed within an area, the greater the potential for victims and offenders to come into contact.

Deviant Place Hypothesis. *Deviant place hypothesis* takes the concept of proximity further by focusing on those areas in which social disorganization and crime tend to flourish. The supposition is that the proximity to offenders is increased among those who live in areas in which crime flourishes. Despite precautions taken by potential victims, they are still at high risk for victimization (Stark, 1987). Many areas within American society are more dangerous than others and those who are forced to live within these areas will most certainly experience higher incidences of victimization.

Routine Activities Theory

The *routine activities theory* was discussed in chapter 8. The basic premise of the theory is that there are always individuals who are motivated to commit crimes. If these motivated offenders either consciously or unconsciously note suitable targets (either for property or personal offenses) and capable guardians (police, vigilant homeowners, etc.) are absent, they commit crimes (Cohen and Felson, 1979). When motivated offenders and suitable targets come into contact in the same place and time in the absence of any deterrent, crime will occur. The routine activities approach goes beyond the lifestyle theories in that it encourages potential victims to reduce their potential for victimization by reducing their attractiveness as victims and by using various crime prevention strategies.

▦ SUMMARY ▦

The study of crime victims and issues related to victimization is known as victimology. Victimology is seen by some scholars as a separate discipline in itself. Others see it as an important subfield within criminology. Victimology has its origins in early societies where concerns for the victim outweighed concerns for exacting societal punishment upon the offender. It has only been within the last thirty years that concerns for the welfare of the victim have reemerged.

As scholars, politicians, criminal justice practitioners, and the public as a whole have become more knowledgeable about victimization, strategies for determining the nature and extent of victimization have changed dramatically. Similarly, theories of victimology have developed from simple typologies that classified victim characteristics to diverse explanations of victimization. As the study of victimology developed, it was both helped and hindered by the concept of victim precipitation. While victim precipitation was seen by many scholars as an important means of understanding both victim-offender relationships and situational factors, critics believed that it unfairly blamed victims for the offenses committed against them.

More recent theories of victimology allow for scholars from diverse perspectives such as critical criminology and routine activities theory to pursue their particular interests in understanding, and it is hoped remedying, the problem of criminal victimization. Victim precipitation is no longer believed to be as divisive a topic within victimology. Indeed, situational and personal factors originally discussed in the early victim precipitation discussions are dealt with within contemporary lifestyle theories.

DISCUSSION QUESTIONS

1. Discuss how early societies dealt with the problems of victims. How has this changed over time? What do you think could be done to make our current criminal justice system more victim-friendly?

2. Describe how victimology came to be a field of study. Decide whether you believe that victimology should be seen as a subfield of criminology or as a separate discipline. Justify your decision.

3. Which theory of victimology best explains victimization? Justify your selection.

4. Discuss how the concept of victim precipitation has been both a useful tool and an impediment to the study of victimology. What is your personal view of victim precipitation?

REFERENCES

Amir, M. (1971). *Patterns in forcible rape*. Chicago: University of Chicago Press.
Cohen, L., and Felson, M. (1979). Social change and crime rate trends: A routine activities approach. *American Sociological Review* 44: 588–608.

Doerner, W. G., and Lab, S. (1998), *Victimology*, 2nd ed. Cincinnati: Anderson.

Karmen, A. (2001). *Crime victims: An introduction to victimology* , 4th ed. Belmont, CA: Wadsworth/Thomson Learning.

Mawby R. I., and Walklate, S. (1994). *Critical victimology*. Thousand Oaks, CA: Sage.

Meadows, R. J. (1998). *Understanding violence and victimization*. Upper Saddle River, NJ: Prentice Hall.

Mendelsohn, B. (1976). Victimology and contemporary society's trends. *Victimology* 1: 8–28.

Schafer, S. (1968). *The victim and his criminal*. New York: Random House.

Sellin, T., and Wolfgang, M. E. (1964). *The measurement of delinquency*. New York: Wiley.

Siegal, L. J. (2000). *Criminology,* 7th ed. Belmont, CA: Wadsworth/Thomson Learning.

Stark, R. (1987). Deviant places: A theory of the ecology of crime. *Criminology* 25: 893–911.

Territo, L., Halstead, J. B., and Bromley, M. L. (1998). *Criminal justice in America: A human perspective*, 5th ed. Woburn, MA: Butterworth-Heinemann.

von Hentig, H. (1941). Remarks on the integration of perpetrator and victim. *Journal of Criminal Law, Criminology and Police Science* 31: 303–9.

_____. (1948). *The criminal and his victim: Studies in the socio-biology of crime*. New Haven: Yale University Press.

Wallace, H. (1998). *Victimology: Legal, psychological, and social perspectives*. Boston: Allyn & Bacon.

Wolfgang, M. E. (1958). *Patterns of criminal homicide*. Philadelphia: University of Pennsylvania Press.

CHAPTER 11

Dealing with Lawbreakers

▥ KEY CONCEPTS ▥

adjudication

alibi

atonement

classical school

certainty

coercion

community correction

community service

decriminalization

determinate sentencing

deterrence

diversion programs

due process

duress

entrapment

equity

fines

incapacitation

incarceration

insanity

mandatory sentencing

overcriminalization

parole

positive school

prevention

probable cause

probation

punishment

reasonable doubt

recidivism

rehabilitation

reintegration

restitution

restorative justice

retribution

self-defense

severity

swiftness

youth

▓ LEARNING OBJECTIVES ▓

After reading this chapter, the student should be able to:

1. Describe ancient rationales for punishment and discuss how they were applied.

2. Describe the rationales for punishment provided by the classical school.

3. Discuss the interrelationships of the classical concepts of swiftness, severity, certainty, and equity.

4. Describe the rationales for treatment provided by the positive school.

5. Contrast the positive concepts of rehabilitation, incapacitation, and prevention.

6. Explain how the concepts of overcriminalization and decriminalization relate to the making and enforcement of criminal laws.

7. Explain what is meant by due process of law and how this relates to arrest and prosecution.

8. Present and discuss the various legal defenses for behaviors that might otherwise be considered criminal.

9. Present and discuss the various standards used to determine insanity.

10. Describe issues involved in adjudication.

11. Discuss the constitutionality of the death penalty.

12. Present and discuss the various sentencing options that are available to judges.

DEALING WITH LAWBREAKERS

Since the beginning of time, society's wrongdoers have been punished in some form or fashion. For many centuries, punishment was primarily physically oriented—from whippings, brandings, and mutilations to hangings and beheadings. However, as society matured, the emphasis of punishment has changed from the physical to more humane approaches: incarceration, community service, fines, and so on. Unfortunately, today's results may not be as beneficial as society would like. Therefore, we continue to be faced with the dilemma of how to deal with lawbreakers. This chapter discusses the rationales for imposing sanctions on lawbreakers and the means by which these sanctions are applied.

The Rationales for Imposing Sanctions

The imposition of criminal sanctions has historically been tied to a particular society's views of human nature. In ancient societies, lawbreakers were considered to be inherently evil and deserving of the direst of punishments for their alleged sins against society, God, or the gods. The Enlightenment, which took place from the late 1600s through the 1700s, brought about new perspectives on human nature that ultimately led to the precepts of the classical school of criminological thought. In Western societies, draconian measures such as torture and mutilation were replaced by efforts to match the punishments with the seriousness of the crime in order to benefit both the offender and society. Later, the positive school of criminological thought would call for treatment based on the needs of the offender in order to address factors that caused the offender to engage in unlawful behaviors. As these philosophies have developed, the responses to criminal behavior have changed (Albanese, 2000).

Historical Responses to Crime

The earliest historical accounts of response to crime date from the ancient civilizations of biblical Israel, the Greeks, and the Romans (Johnson and Wolfe, 1996). It is within these societies that we find the foundation for punishment; all three cultures established strict laws and delivered swift, harsh punishment. The form of punishments varied depending on the type of crime. For example, someone who intentionally killed another might suffer the punishment of banishment or execution. Similar punishments were given for crimes of a sexual nature and theft.

Delivering punishment (e.g., mutilation, banishment, flogging, torture, and execution) was the main method of serving justice in many early societies, including early America, until the transition from harsh and often arbitrary punishment to the provision of strong constitutional rights, rehabilitation, and more appropriately applied punishments would prevail. This transition included the development of more acceptable jails and prisons, separation of juveniles from adults, more lenient sentencing and punishments, and enforcement of constitutional guarantees.

The Classical Response to Crime

The main focus of the classical response to crime was that crime could be controlled by punishing identified offenders. Instead of imposing harsh punishments that often had no relationship to the severity of the offense, punishment was to be applied fairly and equitably based on the severity of the offense committed. This punishment should be carried out in a way that would make potential offenders fearful of the consequences of committing crime. The foundation for this approach is found in the tenets of the *classical school of criminology* (see chapter 2), which stressed that individuals

1. Were bound to society only by their own consent and the society was responsible to them, creating the "social contract"

2. Chose to act as they do, using their "free will"

3. Sought pleasure and avoided pain

4. Should be punished and the punishment used as a means of deterring criminal behavior

5. Who commit identical crimes should receive identical punishments (Vold, Bernard, and Snipes, 1998)

Ultimately, the classical response is to punish individuals for their criminal behaviors with the belief that the punishment serves also as a means of deterrence. This has lead to the acknowledgment of two types of deterrence: general and specific (see chapter 2). Punishment as a general deterrent refers to the belief that based on the type of punishment issued, others will be deterred from committing the same act. Punishment as a specific deterrent is meant to deter the individuals from committing additional criminal acts by teaching them that the crime was not worth the pain it caused. In order for deterrence to work, the imposition of punishment must be equitable, swift, severe, and certain. In this context, *equity* means that all similar crimes should be punished in a similar manner (allowing for legal considerations such as mitigating and aggravating circumstances, see chapter 5). *Swiftness* means that the time between the commission of the crime and the imposition of punishment should be reasonably short so that both the offender and the public will be able to note the connection between the two. *Severity* means that the punishment should exceed the benefits of the crime so that it dissuades future criminality but not so much so as to be unreasonable or unduly harsh. Finally, *certainty* means that the likelihood of being caught, adjudicated, and punished is perceived as high enough to discourage both the offender and similar-minded individuals.

Under the classical model, prison became the primary form of punishment used in the United States. Since 1990, the number of individuals incarcerated has continued to rise (see Table 11–1). As of June 30, 1998, more than 1.8 million people were incarcerated in jails or prisons (*Sourcebook of Criminal Justice Statistics, 1999*). However, the high rates of recidivism in this country suggest that punishment does not have the specific deterring effect desired. This may be seen as the failure of the criminal justice system to accomplish the goals of equity, swiftness, and certainty.

Differences in sentencing have led to charges that the poor and ethnic minorities receive harsher penalties and lengthy waits and/or delays before the implementation of sanctions contradicts swiftness. Estimates that only one-half to one-third of serious crimes committed in the United States are reported to the police (Schmalleger, 1999) preclude certainty. This leaves us emphasizing severity as the means of dealing with criminal behavior. Unfortunately, while we have seen declines in the overall crime rates during recent years, the general deterrent effect of punishment is considered to be minimal (Albanese, 2000). Advocates of the positive

TABLE 11–1   Number of Incarcerated Persons, 1990–1998

Year	Total in Custody	Federal Prisoners	State Prisoners	Jail Prisoners
1990	1,148,702	58,838	684,544	405,320
1991	1,219,014	63,930	728,605	426,479
1992	1,295,150	72,071	774,495	444,584
1993	1,369,185	80,815	828,566	459,804
1994	1,476,621	85,500	904,647	486,474
1995	1,585,586	89,538	989,004	507,044
1996	1,646,020	95,088	1,032,440	518,492
1997	1,743,886	101,755	1,075,052	—
As of June 1998	1,802,496	107,381	1,102,653	592,462

Source: Adapted from the *Sourcebook of Criminal Justice Statistics 1998* (Washington, D.C.: Department of Justice, 1999).

school of criminology argue that strategies that deal with the root causes of crime and criminal behavior are more appropriate and effective than punishment models.

The Positive Response to Crime

During the 1930s, there was a major shift from the classical school to the *positive school* of criminology. Here the emphasis was placed on treatment based on offender needs as opposed to punishment based on the crime. The positive school's (see chapter 2) tenets include

1. Denial of the concepts of the social contract and free will

2. Suggestions that there are multiple causes of criminal behavior, including biological and environmental factors

3. Belief that actions toward the criminal should be to correct the behavior, not punish it (Vold, Bernard, and Snipes, 1998)

The efforts of the positive response have led to three means of dealing with criminal behavior: rehabilitation, incapacitation, and prevention.

Rehabilitation

The main concept of the positive approach to criminal behavior is the concept of *rehabilitation*. The underlying basis of rehabilitation is that criminal behavior results from sociological, psychological, or physical imperfections. These imperfections require correction through treatment or training. This concept of "fixing the offender's problems" is the mainstay of rehabilitation. Today, rehabilitation includes medical treatment, individual counseling, group therapy, education, job training, and reintegration (Barlow, 2000).

Physiological problems such as chemical imbalances are treated with medication, surgery, or other medical solutions. Individual counseling is a psychological strategy that strives to deal with the mental and emotional ailments thought to have precipitated the criminal behavior. Group therapy is a social-psychological technique of teaching offenders how to deal with the circumstances that may have led to their illegal actions. Educational programs and job training seek to provide offenders with the educational or vocational credentials necessary to obtain adequate employment when they reenter society. In many cases, such as the rehabilitation of drug offenders, several strategies (e.g., medication, individual therapy, group counseling, and job training) may be used.

The success of rehabilitation has been questioned since its beginning. Conservatives have challenged rehabilitation as being unsuccessful and as coddling criminals instead of punishing them. Liberals have criticized treatment efforts for "experimenting" on criminals, and for often being more punitive than therapeutic. Much is still left to be learned about whom to target and which rehabilitative efforts to practice in dealing with those who commit crime.

Reintegration is a newer strategy advocated by positivists. This strategy calls for offenders to either remain within the community or be placed within the community prior to their release from correctional custody. The object is to retain or restore offenders' ties to the community (family, social network, job, etc.) so that they have a support network established to help them remain crime free (Barlow, 2000). We talk more about this technique later in the chapter.

Incapacitation

In the classical sense, *incapacitation* generally refers to incarceration: locking someone away for a specific period of time based on the seriousness of the crime committed. The logic is that past behavior is the best predictor of future behavior and that, while incarcerated, offenders will not be preying on society (a belief that may no longer be true because of technological advancements in communication). The positive approach to incapacitation is oriented toward enabling the offender to return to society by delivering needed treatment. Under this approach, to incapacitate is to make unable to perform or act. Mandatory drug testing, required medications, chemical castration of sex offenders, and interlocking devices for convicted drunk drivers are but a few examples of the positive approach to incapacitation.

Prevention

The final aspect of the positive response to crime is *prevention*. Whereas the classical approach uses the threat of punishment to prevent crime, the positive approach uses education. These efforts may be applied to society as a whole or specifically to offenders. Teaching pre-delinquent adolescents (youths who have not been charged with crimes but appear to be headed for trouble) the difference between what is acceptable and unacceptable behavior and emphasizing what may happen if criminal behavior is chosen is such a strategy. Warnings about the detrimental effects of drug use is another. Working to address social ills thought to create criminogenic environments is yet another aspect of prevention.

Applying Criminal Sanctions

Whether one prefers the classical approach to crime or the positive approach, the first consideration in administering justice is deciding what is criminal. This section discusses the making of laws, arresting of alleged offenders, adjudication, and correctional techniques.

Making Law

Perhaps one of the most difficult and controversial aspects of dealing with criminal behavior is determining what is criminal. The enactment of criminal laws has long been an area of debate. While there is common agreement among the diverse members of our society that acts such as rape, robbery, murder, arson, burglary, larceny, and automobile theft should be criminal, there is great disagreement about how to apply the law to offenses. In addition, numerous behaviors, such as sexual relations between consenting adults and the use of alcoholic beverages, tobacco products, and recreational drug use, cause great debate within society (Hancock and Sharp, 2000).

An important component in discussions of criminal law is the concept of *overcriminalization*. When one considers the great number of laws and ordinances that exist, and all the activities they affect, the question arises, what behavior will be next? Some argue that one reason there is so much "crime" is because there are so many laws that, in effect, our society is overcriminalized. People who in other behaviors are law-abiding therefore become violators. This can lead to disrespect for the justice system as a whole. A solution to this dilemma is decriminalization. Basically, *decriminalization* refers to redefining certain criminal behaviors and making them lesser offenses or lawful (Schmalleger, 1999). For example, making the possession of a marijuana cigarette a civil infraction rather than a criminal offense would lessen the sanction against it. An example of legalizing behaviors would be lifting existing sanctions against consensual sexual acts between adults.

Regardless of how many laws there are or what level of punishment they exact, the reality is that criminal law requires a criminal sanction. Therefore, the issue becomes what type of sanction. Four types of criminal sanctions are commonly used in the United States: fines, incarceration, probation, and capital punishment. Corporal punishment was once common but has not been used in the United States since the 1950s (Albanese, 2000). In fact, corporal punishment of adult offenders is banned in most states as cruel and unusual punishment. Interestingly, it is still permitted as a "reasonable means of discipline" for children. The types of sanctions applied will be discussed in the section on sentencing.

Arrest and Prosecution

As we suggested in our discussion of deterrence, a major weakness of the criminal justice system is that so few offenders are actually apprehended (Hancock and Sharp, 2000). Our purpose in this section is not to detail the process by which an individual is apprehended and later adjudicated guilty of a crime (for a detailed overview of this process, we recommend the reader to one of the many excellent introductory texts on criminal justice that are currently available). We do wish, however, to make several important points about this process. The first is that in order for an individual to be arrested, authorities must have a legal reason for doing so, that is, there must be probable cause that a crime has occurred and that the arrestee is responsible.

Following an arrest, a series of legal procedures must be observed. Failure to follow proper procedures may result in the case being dismissed as a result of violation of the individual's right to *due process* of law. If a person's constitutional protections are not observed during the police investigation, after the time of arrest, or during their prosecution, an argument can be made that his or her rights to due process have been violated. Violation of due process can be grounds for the trial judge to suppress improperly obtained evidence or even to dismiss the charges, or might serve as a basis of appeal to a higher court if the individual is found guilty by the trial court (Territo, Halstead, and Bromley, 1998).

Under the American system of justice, the accused is considered to be innocent until proven guilty. This means that a jury (or a judge, if a bench trial has been accepted by the defendant) must listen to the evidence and determine beyond a reasonable doubt that the defendant is guilty of the crime of which he or she has been accused. It is the burden of the prosecution to prove guilt to the jury or the judge.

In addition to the previous safeguards, an accused person may offer any of several defenses to refute the charge or excuse his or her actions. The first defense is to present an alibi. Quite simply, an *alibi* is verification from others that the accused could not have committed the crime because he or she was elsewhere or was physically incapable of committing the crime and can prove it. *Duress* is another defense. In this situation, factors out of his or her control caused the accused to violate the law to avoid a greater harm (such as breaking into a remote mountain cabin to escape a blizzard). *Coercion* is also a defense. In this scenario, the offense was committed because of threats or force applied by another person capable of causing the accused or the accused's loved ones harm. Yet another legal defense is *self-defense*. Here the accused argues that his or her actions were necessary for self-protection or to protect others from physical harm. *Youth* is still another defense when the age of the offender precludes him or her from being held accountable for the actions, requires more lenient treatment or requires transfer to the juvenile justice system. Still another legal defense is *entrapment*, which occurs when the police or their agents actually entice someone into committing a criminal act that he or she would not have contemplated doing on his or her own initiative.

The last legal defense that we shall discuss is *insanity*. In this situation the accused claims to have been insane at the time of the crime or claims to be incapable of assisting in preparation of his or her legal defense. Under the American system of justice an accused individual must be able to understand the charges against them and to aid in their own defense. The determination of insanity varies among the fifty states and the federal government. In many states, the so-called M'Naughton Rule—"was the defendant capable of knowing right from wrong"—is the standard. This is the standard under which it is most difficult to prove insanity as a defense. M'Naughton is sometimes augmented by the irresistible impulse test, which stresses that although the accused knew it was wrong, he or she could not keep from acting. This defense is particularly useful for crimes of passion. In the District of Columbia and New Hampshire the Durham Rule—"the action was the product of a diseased mind"—is used. This is the easiest standard by which to prove insanity. It was the standard under which John Hinkley was found not guilty by reason of insanity for the 1981 shooting of President Ronald Reagan and James Brady. Acceptance of the diseased-mind defense was based on Hinkley's history of irrational actions, including his excessive infatuation with actress Jodie Foster. Currently, a majority of the states and the federal courts are using the substantial capacity test, which is modeled on the American Bar Association's Model Penal Code. The substantial capacity rule defines a defendant who is "lacking the substantial capacity to appreciate the wrongfulness of the action that was taken" as legally insane. This is also known as the Brawner Rule after the case in which it was first applied by a federal court (Gaines, Kaune, and Miller, 1999; Schmalleger, 1999).

The controversial nature of the insanity defense has led several states to amend their statutes to provide for a "guilty but mentally ill" finding so that emotionally disturbed individuals, such as John Hinckley, can be held more accountable for their actions. Anyone contemplating an insanity defense should be aware that, if convicted, defendants often are confined longer in mental institutions than they would be in prison. Despite the outcry following Hinkley's trial in 1982, at this writing, he is still confined in Saint Elizabeth's Hospital in Washington, D.C.

Adjudication

Once a determination of guilt has been made either by a trial or a plea bargain, the next step in the process is the sentencing phase. *Adjudication*, as the term is used in relation to the criminal justice system, actually refers to determining a punishment. Historically, we have sentenced or punished individuals for their criminal behavior for any or all of the following reasons: retribution, atonement, incapacitation, deterrence, and/or rehabilitation. *Retribution* occurs when the punishment given supposedly satisfies the victim's and society's need for revenge. *Atonement* is the idea that an offender must "pay his or her debt to society" so that having atoned for the crime he or she can then reenter society with a clean slate. *Incapacitation* is the removal of the offender from society or the imposition of restrictions that negate his or her ability to commit a specific type of crime. *Deterrence*, as noted earlier, can be either general or specific and is meant to keep the individual and others from repeating the behavior. *Rehabilitation* is meant to treat the behavior in an attempt to prevent it from recurring.

The United States relies more on imprisoning individuals for criminal behavior than any other democratic nation in the world. Sentencing may meet one of three forms: mandatory, determinate, and indeterminate. *Mandatory sentencing* exists in several states and refers to the automatic imprisonment for a specified period of time of an offender convicted of a certain crime. *Determinate sentencing* is the assessment of a specific number of years in prison (e.g., ten years). In theory, the offender is to serve the exact amount of time for which he or she is sentenced. *Indeterminate sentencing* refers to a sentence within a range of years (e.g., five to ten years). The type of sentencing imposed is based on state statutes. For example, Minnesota uses determinate sentencing while the state of Texas is an indeterminate sentencing state. The actual release date is determined by a parole board that reviews the inmate's behavior during incarceration. It should be noted that despite the method used, the amount of time actually spent in prison usually ends up being considerably less than the actual imposed sentence because of credit awarded for "good time," that is, for compliance with prison rules while incarcerated (Territo, Halstead, and Bromley, 1998).

One of the most recent developments in sentencing are habitual offender laws, most often referred to as Three Strikes. Habitual offender laws require that an individual who is convicted of a third felony offense, regardless of what it is, must receive a mandatory sentence, which can be as severe as life imprisonment. These laws seek to remove from society hard-core offenders who are said to be dedicated to a life of crime. However, the application of these laws in some cases to lesser felons with histories of property crime has caused some criminologists to question their appropriateness (i.e., Skolnick, 2000). It has been argued that these laws, along with mandatory sentencing and the "war on drugs," have led to the excessive reliance on imprisonment in the United States (Currie, 2000).

The ultimate punishment in the United States is capital punishment. The most debated of sanctions, the death penalty has a long history of use, misuse, and abuse. One of the major issues accompanying imposition of the death penalty is concern as to its constitutionality. The Eighth Amendment to the United States Constitution guarantees the right to be free from cruel and unusual punishment. Opponents of the death penalty cite this clause in their opposition. However, it is the arbitrariness and capriciousness of the death penalty's use that has motivated the appellate courts to intervene. Such an intervention led to a moratorium of the death penalty in the United States from 1967 through 1976. Two landmark U.S. Supreme Court cases impacted both the beginning and ending of the moratorium.

In 1972, in the case of *Furman v. Georgia*, the U.S. Supreme Court ruled that the Georgia death penalty statute was unconstitutional on grounds of capriciousness and arbitrariness. This affected the death penalty statutes in thirty-four other states. However, in the 1976 case of *Gregg v. Georgia* the U.S. Supreme Court ruled that the newly written Georgia statute on capital punishment was acceptable. This ruling, which created a two-trial system (one to determine guilt and a second to determine the sentence), opened the doors once again for states to execute prisoners. Utah was the first to break the moratorium with the execution of Gary Gilmore in 1977. As of April 1, 1999, more than 3,200 individuals were sitting on death row awaiting execution (*Sourcebook*, 1999). However, in the year 2000 a movement to once again place a moratorium on the use of the death penalty gained support when Illinois Governor George H. Ryan placed such a hold in his state.

Sentencing Options

The sentence imposed by the trial court judge may be severely limited by mandatory sentences or restricted by sentencing guidelines that proscribe the range of sanctions from which he or she may choose. However, judges often have great latitude in the decisions that they make. The judge's decision is primarily based on the severity of the offense and the offender's past history of crime. In most cases, judges are aided in their decision making by a presentence investigation report compiled by a probation officer. The choices available to judges in routine cases include fines, incarceration, and community corrections. In recent years, judges have also used alternative sanctions such as restitution, community service, and restorative justice.

Although primarily used as punishment for ordinance violations, traffic offenses, and minor misdemeanors, fines may also accompany felony punishments. *Fines* basically consist of monetary value set by the judge that the offender must pay to the court. Usually this money is used to pay court-related costs. In the case of serious misdemeanors (e.g., driving under the influence) and felonies, the fines may be in the thousands of dollars. In a few sensational cases of white-collar crime (such as the Michael Milken insider trading case in the mid-1980s, the fines may be in the millions (Territo, Halsted, and Bromley, 1998).

Incarceration is a popular means of dealing with criminal behavior. Incarceration or institutional corrections sentences may be served in a variety of settings, including jails, prisons (maximum, medium, and minimum security), rehabilitation centers, boot camps, and work camps. Assignment to a specific type is based on the sentence of the judge and the correctional system's classification scheme.

Community corrections programs allow offenders to remain within the community under correctional supervision. The leading type of community correction is probation. *Probation* is a means of keeping a person under supervision without incarceration. Although often used for first-time offenders, it is not unheard of that repeat offenders receive probation. Probation usually requires the offender to follow certain restrictions imposed by the court. Such impositions may include attending a drug or alcohol program, being employed, going to school, staying away from certain types of people, and curfews. The person on probation must report to a probation officer who determines whether the individual is abiding by the rules of his or her probation. At the end of 1997, more than 3.2 million individuals were on probation in the United States (*Sourcebook*, 1999).

Other forms of community correction include residence in a halfway house, house arrest, electronic monitoring, intensive probation, and shock probation. These techniques place more restrictions and requirements upon probationers than does normal probation. Shock probation refers to when youthful offenders are sentenced to a boot camp or a short term in jail or prison to make them aware of the consequences of their actions should they fail to meet their probation requirements. House arrest, electronic monitoring, and intensive probation are used for higher-risk offenders. Halfway houses and parole are means of allowing inmates who have served prison time to be phased back into society. With the exception of parole and halfway houses, the type of sanction imposed is usually based on the judge's decision. Parole decisions are generally left up to a parole board or set by mandatory regulations.

Alternative Sanctions

Since the 1980s we have seen a return to sentencing designed to ease the burden that the victim has experienced because of the offender's actions. The following chapter discusses the issue of victim's rights. *Restitution* for the harm incurred is one of many victim's issues. Restitution is also seen as a means of benefiting the offender. Compensating the victim for his or her loss is a means of atonement on behalf of the offender. It is also seen as being rehabilitative in that it forces the offender to see the humanity of the victim and to realize the impact of his or her actions (Doerner and Lab, 1999). This is a particularly useful strategy for lesser offenders and youthful offenders.

Restorative justice is another strategy that is being used for many lesser offenses. This is a peacemaking approach that uses mediation in lieu of judicial sanctions to seek to restore both victim and offender to their precrime status (Fuller, 1999). In these scenarios, disputants agree to accept the resolutions offered by a trained mediator instead of seeking a criminal prosecution. This method is appropriate in disputes in which there is confusion as to who initiated the situation that led to conflict. Often a simple apology may satisfy the aggrieved party. Restorative justice is especially useful for dealing with disputes within a community.

Last, judges (or prosecutors) may use creative sanctions that do not involve fines or incarceration. Mandatory *community service* is a common sentence for lesser offenders. This compulsory service in public projects may involve menial tasks (e.g., picking up trash, washing police cars) or actually using job skills (carpentry, mechanical abilities) to benefit the community. *Diversion programs* that require the offender to receive counseling, attend school, obtain job training, acquire employment, or spend weekends observing emergency room arrivals are also common. Less common sentences may involve the public wearing of placards that declare the offender's culpability or the mandatory placing of/offenders' photographs in local newspapers (a return to ancient shaming rituals) or having the offender agree to leave the community in exchange for the charges being dismissed. During the 1980s, Utah judges banished several offenders to California when California authorities refused to extradite several wanted felons back to Utah.

We still have much to learn about how to effectively deal with criminal behavior. Whether it is a fine, probation, incarceration, treatment, or death, no one means has proven to be the answer. Obviously, review and research as to what is the best way to deal with criminal offenders will continue to be necessary.

SUMMARY

The imposition of criminal sanctions has historically been tied to a particular society's view of human nature. The American legal system is based on the precepts of the classical school of criminological thought. The main focus of the classical response to crime is that crime can be controlled by punishing identified offenders. However, during the sentencing and corrections phases, precepts of the positive school of criminology are often used. The main concept of the positive approach to criminal behavior is rehabilitation.

While there is agreement among the diverse members of our society that certain acts should be criminal, there is great disagreement about how to apply the laws to these offenses. In addition, there are numerous other behaviors for which there is no consensus as to criminality. Some argue that there are too many laws, which actually causes law-abiding citizens to become violators. Regardless of how many laws there are or at what level of punishment they exist, the reality is that criminal law requires a criminal sanction. Four types of criminal sanctions are commonly used in the United States: fines, incarceration, probation, and capital punishment. An accused may present several defenses to excuse their actions. These include presenting an alibi, arguing duress, coercion, self-defense, youth, or insanity.

Historically, we have sentenced or punished individuals for their criminal behavior for any or all of the following reasons: retribution, atonement, incapacitation, deterrence, and rehabilitation. The United States relies on imprisoning individuals for criminal behavior more so than any other demo-cratic nation in the world. The ultimate sentence possible in the United States is capital punishment. The major issues that have accompanied the use of the death penalty are questions as to its constitutionality and its application.

Judges often have great latitude in sentencing criminals. The judge's decision is primarily based on the severity of the offense and the offender's past criminal history. The choices available to judges in routine cases include fines, incarceration, and community correction. In recent years, judges have also used alternative sanctions, such as restitution, community service, and restorative justice.

DISCUSSION QUESTIONS

1. It has been said that we try to use classical methods to determine guilt and positive methods to punish offenders. Explain how this occurs.

2. Advocates of decriminalization argue that excessive laws create con-tempt for the criminal justice system that may actually result in more crime. Explain how you think this might occur or why you think it doesn't occur.

3. Discuss the pros and cons of decriminalizing the sale and use of marijuana.

4. Discuss the pros and cons of capital punishment.

5. Discuss the pros and cons of the insanity defense.

REFERENCES

Albanese, J. (2000). *Criminal justice, 2000 update*. New York: Allyn & Bacon.

Barlow, H. D. (2000). *Criminal justice in America*. Upper Saddle River, NJ: Prentice Hall.

Currie, E. (2000). The myth of leniency. In J. H. Skolnick and E. Currie, eds. *Crisis in American institutions*, 11th ed. Needham Heights, MA: Allyn & Bacon.

Doerner, W. G., and Lab, S. P. (1998). *Victimology*, 2nd ed. Cincinnati, OH: Anderson.

Fuller, J. R. (1999). *Criminal justice: A peacemaking perspective*. Needham Heights, MA: Allyn & Bacon.

Gaines, L. K., Kaune, M., and Miller, R. L. (1999). *Criminal justice in action*. Belmont, CA: Wadsworth.

Hancock, B. W., and P. M. Sharp (2000). *Criminal justice in America: Theory, practice, and policy*, 2nd ed. Upper Saddle River, NJ: Prentice Hall.

Johnson, H. A., and Wolfe, N. T. (1996). *History of criminal justice*, 2nd ed. Cincinnati, OH: Anderson Publishing Co.

Schmalleger, F. (1999). *Criminal justice today*, 5th ed. Upper Saddle River, NJ: Prentice Hall.

Skolnick, J. H. (2000). Wild pitch: Three strikes, you're out and other bad calls on crime. In J. H. Skolnick and E. Currie, eds., *Crisis in American institutions,* 11th ed. Needham Heights, MA: Allyn & Bacon.

Sourcebook of criminal justices statistics, 1998. (1999). Washington, D.C.: Department of Justice.

Territo, L., Halsted. J. B., and Bromley, M. L. (1998). *Criminal justice in America: A human perspective*, 5th ed. Boston: Butterworth-Heinemann.

Vold, G. B., Bernard, T. J., and Snipes, J. B. (1998). *Theoretical criminology*, 4th ed. New York: Oxford University Press.

CHAPTER

Dealing with Victims

■ KEY CONCEPTS ■

child abuse
crime prevention
dispute resolution
domestic violence
elder abuse
hate crimes
offender restitution
restorative justice
special populations

spouse abuse
victim assistance
victim awareness
victim compensation
victim impact statement
victimization
victimizer
victim's rights

■ LEARNING OBJECTIVES ■

After reading this chapter, the student should be able to:

1. Present and discuss the various means of determining the extent of crime victimization in the United States.

2. Present and discuss the individual and social costs of victimization.

3. Compare and contrast victimization by strangers, victimization in the workplace, and victimization by family.

4. Discuss the problems of victimization among special populations.

5. Present and discuss the issues involved in dealing with hate crimes.

6. Present and discuss three methods of responding to victimization,

7. Discuss the impacts of the Victim's Rights movement.

Chapter 11 focused on the criminal justice system's response to criminal offenders. This chapter discusses the impact of crime on victims. The study of crime victims and issues related to victimization were also discussed in chapter 10.

THE EXTENT OF CRIME VICTIMIZATION

As shown in chapter 1, there are several means of determining the incidence of crime. Uniform Crime Reports (UCR) provide information on crimes reported to law enforcement agencies within a given year. These reports are augmented by the National Incident-Based Reporting System (NIBRS), which gathers more specific crime data such as incidents of family violence. Hate crime statistics are also gathered by the Federal Bureau of Investigation. In addition, the Bureau of Justice Statistics conducts the National Crime Victimization Survey (NCVS), which surveys households to try to obtain information beyond that reported to police agencies. Despite these efforts, there is still a great deal of uncertainty among scholars as to the true extent of crime and the actual number of crime victims in America at any given time. Fortunately, we can track crime trends by reviewing the changes within the various methods of data gathering (UCR, NIBRS, or NCVS). The good news at the time of this writing is that crime rates for both property offenses and violent crimes continue to decline.

According to the Uniform Crime Reports (Federal Bureau of Investigation, 1999), 12,475,634 crimes were reported in 1998. Of these incidents, 12 percent were violent crimes and 88 percent were property crimes (see Table 12–1). The National Crime Victimization Survey (Bureau of Justice Statistics, 1999) yielded a much higher finding of 31.3 million crimes that were reported by victims in 1998. Of these, 26 percent were reported to be violent crimes and 73 percent were said to be property offenses. While these numbers in themselves may appear to be impersonal presentations, they represent individuals who have been harmed financially, physically, and/or emotionally as crime victims.

TABLE 12–1 UCR Crime Incidents for 1998 (in percentages)

Total Number of Crimes	12,475,634
Murder	0.1
Rape	0.7
Robbery	3.6
Aggravated assault	7.8
Burglary	18.7
Larceny/Theft	59.1
Auto theft	9.9

Source: Crime in the United States (Federal Bureau of Investigation, 1999).

To put the incidents of victimization in perspective, consider that the UCR crime figures in Table 12–1 reflect an average national incidence of 4,615 crimes per 100,000 persons. In particular, they yield the following victimization rates: 1 in 12 children aged 12 to 15; 1 in 357 elderly aged 65 and over; 1 in 24 blacks; 1 in 28 whites; 1 in 23 males, and 1 in 33 females are victims of crime. In addition, 47 percent of murder victims are black, 49 percent are white, and 2 percent are from other racial groups. Seventy-five percent of murder victims are male and 63 percent are under age 35, with 11 percent under the age of 18 (Federal Bureau of Investigation, 1999). It is obvious from these data that despite the decline in criminal occurrences, millions of Americans are victimized each year.

THE CONSEQUENCES OF VICTIMIZATION

According to the Federal Bureau of Investigation (1999), the cost of criminal victimization in the United States was said to have exceeded $15.8 billion in 1998. Of this amount, only about 35 percent was recovered by law enforcement officials. These costs reflect only the value of property taken and do not reflect the costs of medical treatment for victims of violent crimes. Nor do they reflect the costs of property and/or injuries in incidents not reported to the police. It is not unreasonable to assume that the financial consequences of crime victimizations in the United States could be several times higher.

Individual Costs of Victimization

Individual victims of crime suffer many costs. The financial losses due to theft, arson, burglary, robbery, fraud, and other economic crimes can lead to financial difficulties for victims and their families. Medical costs for those who have

been victims of violent crimes could run into thousands and even hundreds of thousands of dollars. In addition, families in which a wage earner has been incapacitated or lost to homicide may well face severe economic hardship. The financial aspects of victimization may be minor in relation to the pain and suffering experienced by victims and their families. The emotional turmoil of losing a loved one to homicide, or the trauma of being a victim of sexual assault or other violent crime can cause long-lasting grief and anguish. The physical harm from violent assaults may result in permanent pain, illness, or disability. Even the less painful experience of having one's privacy violated by a burglar can cause victims to become fearful of being victimized again. These fears may actually result in an individual's being unable to cope with the pressures of work or school, family life, and social activities. Depending on the nature of the crime, victims may lose confidence in society's ability to protect them from harm and may withdraw (Karmen, 2001).

Societal Costs of Victimization

In addition to the cost to individual victims, the cost of crime for society as a whole is great. The economic costs to victims are often passed on to others. Retail establishments pass the costs of employee theft, shoplifting, and robbery on to their customers in price hikes. Insurance companies do the same with rate hikes. In a like manner, governmental intervention in compensating victims, investigating criminal incidents, adjudicating accused offenders, and dealing with convicted offenders is funded by taxpayer dollars that must be taken either from other governmental projects or from increased tax revenues.

The social costs of criminal victimization are also high. The fear of victimization may affect citizens who have not actually been crime victims but who are nonetheless fearful due to knowledge of real or alleged criminal incidents. Such fear can lead to a curtailment in social activities, limitations on travel, withdrawal from community involvement, restrictions in job potential and earnings, as well as a loss of confidence in the criminal justice system or even in the society in which they live. If such fears become widespread among a community, it will become extremely difficult for government officials to maintain order and stability. Ultimately, the loss of citizen involvement and support will lead to further social disorganization with increases in crime and victimization (Karmen, 2001).

TYPES OF VICTIMIZATION

Chapter 10 included a substantial discussion of victim precipitation. Studies of victim precipitation generally focus on violent crimes in which there is, if only briefly, an interaction between victim and offender. However, the majority

of crimes are not violent but are property crimes. In these incidents, the victim precipitation may have been leaving flowers on a front porch or simply being away from home. Different strategies are required to avoid being victimized by property and violent crimes. Preventing property victimization is often straightforward. You wish to protect your home from burglary and arson, your car from burglary and theft, and your other valuables from theft. Most of these protections are provided by using crime prevention strategies, such as locks, security devices, lighting and other target-hardening techniques. We limit our discussion here to the complex issue of victimization by violence.

Victimization by Strangers

Criminologists used to stress that you were more likely to be a victim of violence by a friend or family member than by a stranger. While this adage continues to have some merit, many of today's violent crimes are committed by strangers. Robbery, home invasions, car jacking, serial killings, road rage, sexual assaults, aggravated assaults, and hate crimes are but a few examples of how one might be violently victimized by strangers. Taking safety precautions such as not walking alone on campus at night or not provoking other drivers are not only wise but necessary actions.

According to Robert Meadows (1998, p. 90), 52 percent of victims of non-fatal violence did not know their assailant; 45 percent of murder victims were related to or knew their killers, and 15 percent of murder victims were murdered by strangers. In 40 percent of murder cases, the correlation between victim and offender was unknown. Seven of ten robberies are committed by strangers as are three out of ten of reported rapes. The implications of these data are clear: In today's complex and diverse society one must be cautious of strangers and in one's dealings with strangers. Caution moderated with politeness and a nonconfrontational demeanor are good strategies to avoid victimization.

Victimization in the Workplace

Violence within the workplace has gained the attention of criminologists, victimologists, criminal justice practitioners, the media, and the public in general because of highly publicized incidents at post offices, office complexes, governmental buildings, shopping centers, and schools. Much workplace violence is committed by strangers against taxicab drivers, police officers, hotel clerks, gas station workers, convenience store clerks, security guards, stock handlers, store managers, and bartenders (to name the occupations

with higher rates of victimization). However, many incidents are the actions of disgruntled employees who take out their frustrations on co-workers, supervisors, and customers (Doerner and Lab, 1998).

Because of the increasing incidence of workplace violence, many organizations within the public and private sectors seek to reduce the potential for such incidents with proactive human resource programs designed to reduce tensions among employees. However, the pressures of modern society too frequently overwhelm these efforts.

Victimization by Family

Of 421,493 victims of violent crime reported to the National Incident-Based Reporting System in 1998, 27 percent were related to the offender (Federal Bureau of Investigation, 1999, p. 280). The impacts of family violence are more frequently associated within the areas of spouse abuse, child abuse, and elder abuse. Table 12–2 displays the family relationships of victims to offenders as shown in the 1998 NIBRS Report. Violence by family members outside the immediate family is not included in Table 12–2 but several hundred incidents by "in-laws" were also reported to the NIBRS in 1998.

Spouse Abuse

Traditionally *spouse abuse* meant an intentional assault resulting in injury to a married female by her spouse. Women living in common-law marriages (that is, partners who have never exchanged vows but live together as husband and wife; under the old English common law, after a specified period of cohabitation,

TABLE 12–2 Family Violence by Victim's Relationship to Offender

Spouse	49,089
Common-law spouse	10,544
Parent	11,100
Sibling	11,726
Child	12,570
Grandparent	573
Grandchild	762

Source: Crime in the United States, Section V, Incidents of Family Violence: An analysis of 1998 NIBRS (Washington, D.C.: U.S. Government Printing Office, 1999). Adapted from Table 5.6, p. 280.

they were considered to be married) were often not considered as spouses unless state statutes specifically included them. Likewise, individuals who were cohabitating did not qualify as spouses. Most certainly, individuals living in same-sex relationships were not covered by spouse abuse statutes. As societal practices have changed, so has the interpretation of spouse abuse. Many states have now changed the term in their statutes to *domestic violence* to cover individuals living together within a "familial environment."

Factors that influence the incidence of spousal abuse are many and which factor has more impact in which situation varies with each relationship. Some factors leading to spouse abuse are social stress, power struggles or assertion of power by the batterer, marital dependency (which prevents women from leaving abusive relationships), and the influence of alcohol (Wallace, 1998). The common-law tradition that permitted a husband to "discipline" his wife was also ingrained within many domestic relationships.

As the status of women within society has changed from subservience to equality, the tolerance of spousal violence has declined. Unfortunately, women's increased status and the changing relationship between men and women actually causes many batterers to intensify their efforts to assert their authority through violence (Karmen, 2001).

Child Abuse

Just as wives were historically viewed as the chattel of their husbands, children were often seen as the property of parents who were free to use and punish them as they saw fit. In today's society children's advocates argue that corporal punishment such as spanking is not to be tolerated and cite nations such as Denmark where spanking is prohibited by law. We will not take a stance in this debate except to point out that while parents in America have the right to use corporal punishment, there is a clear distinction between a spanking and a beating. Unfortunately for hundreds of thousands of children, their parents or guardians are not aware of this distinction. The continued use of corporal punishment does not mean that society has turned a blind eye to child abuse. Injuries to children that once brought clucks of disapproval now result in law enforcement or family service agencies investigating the incident.

Like spouse abuse, the family dynamics that lead to child abuse are complex, and there are no simple remedies. The problem is exacerbated in that physical abuse is only one type of *child abuse* (Doerner and Lab, 1998). Many children are mistreated and/or neglected by their parents and suffer from malnutrition and disease due to inadequate food, shelter, and clothing. Still others suffer from emotional neglect from absentee or inattentive parents. Educational neglect occurs when parents fail to ensure that their children's

educational needs are met. While less frequent in occurrence, the too common incidence of sexual abuse of children is a major concern of child advocates because of the severity of both physical and emotional harm the child suffers as a result. Last, the most common form of mistreatment is emotional abuse. Parents who would be horrified to be accused of any of the previous forms of mistreatment do not think twice when they berate, verbally abuse, and emotionally torment their children.

Elder Abuse

A problem that has only recently gained the attention of victimologists is that of elder abuse. The elderly experience victimization at lower levels than do other age groups, but the impact of the victimization is often more devastating. As the number of senior citizens within our society continues to increase, the number of offenses against them is also expected to increase. One by-product of longevity is that as senior citizens become less able to care for themselves, they must depend more on family members or paid residential care. This dependence can lead to *elder abuse* by caregivers.

The types of abuse experienced by the elderly include physical abuse, psychological abuse, material abuse, active abuse, and passive abuse (Doerner and Lab, 1998). Physical abuse ranges from slapping to sexual molestation. Psychological abuse includes verbal abuse, threats, and intimidation. Material abuse consists of theft of money and property. Active abuse is the intentional neglect or failure to meet a caretaking obligation. Passive abuse occurs when caretakers unintentionally, through incompetence or lack of concern, fail to meet the needs of their charges.

Victimization of Special Populations

In addition to the problems already discussed, some attention to of special populations is warranted. These *special populations* include women, young people, gays, and the disabled.

Women

Women deserve classification within a special population because of the large numbers of sexual assaults committed against women each year by both strangers and acquaintances. According to a 1992 study by the National Victim's Center, one in eight women will be raped at some time in her life (Wallace, 1998, p. 127). Often the rapists are not strangers but acquaintances, co-workers, fellow students, friends, and even family members.

Rape is a traumatic event that can leave lasting harm both physically and emotionally, but it is not the only type of victimization women must fear. Sexual harassment is a common experience for women of all ages and walks of life. Sexual harassment consists of demands for sexual favors, subjection to overtly sexual conversations and imagery, sex-based denigration and ridicule, as well as a superior's permitting a hostile work or school environment, and merchants or professionals charging more for products or services sold to women.

Young People

Young people are a special population because immaturity, dependence issues, and minority status make them vulnerable to abuse. As indicated earlier, young people have the highest incidence of victimization of any age group. In addition to abuse within the home, victimization of young people outside the home is a major concern for child advocates, parents, and law enforcement officials. The many changes that children experience during the teenage years and the desire to gain independence from adult domination make them particularly susceptible to victimization by adults as well as by other youths (Hunter, Mayhall, and Barker, 2000).

The Elderly

The fear of abuse within a residential setting is not the only one faced by the elderly. As they move into late adulthood, people become increasingly aware of their vulnerability to crime. Loss of physical prowess, health concerns, the constraints of reduced income, and feelings of powerlessness cause the elderly to fear victimization (Hunter, Mayhall, and Barker, 2000). While statistics show their victimization rates to be relatively low, some offenders selectively prey upon the elderly. Con artists in particular often target older citizens for their scams.

Gays

Whether gay people constitute a special population is a matter for debate. Despite stereotyping on the part of both straights and gays, sexual orientation is often not as obvious a characteristic as are race and gender. However, because of the highly publicized incidents of violence against gay people, this community warrants attention. As exemplified in the Matthew Shepard murder, which received national attention in 1998–99, people are often targeted for victimization due to sexual orientation.

The Disabled

Individuals who suffer from physical or mental disabilities also deserve special consideration by criminologists and victimologists. Despite the equal protections guaranteed by the Americans with Disabilities Act of 1990, many disabled people are disenfranchised within American society (Hunter, Mayhall, and Barker, 2000). Physical incapacitation, such as blindness or deafness, and limited mobility make these individuals susceptible to victimization both inside and outside the home. Likewise, people suffering from mental illness and mental retardation are also susceptible to victimization.

Hate Crimes

Individuals who make up special populations are often singled out for victimization because of their increased vulnerability. For example, according to his killers, Matthew Shepard was selected not because of hatred for gays, but because they thought he would be an easy target for robbery. Whether one accepts this argument or that of gay advocates, that Shepard was selected and viciously murdered because of his sexual orientation, is moot. Gay people are frequently victimized by those who have disdain for their lifestyle. Such acts, which are based not on situational factors but on animosity toward individuals who are "different," are classified as *hate crimes*.

In addition to sexual orientation, hate crimes often target members of ethnic or racial minorities (as seen by the dragging death of African American James Byrd Jr. by three white racists in Jasper, Texas). Disabled persons are also sometimes victimized by assailants who consider them unworthy, as in the case of the mentally retarded young woman who was brutally gang raped by teenage boys, in a New Jersey suburb. Members of religious minorities are also occasionally targeted, as was exemplified by the 1999 shooting of several young children at a Jewish child-care center in California.

Concern with the apparent increases in hate crimes have led to the gathering and publication of hate crime statistics by the Federal Bureau of Investigation. Several states have created hate crime laws that impose more severe penalties if the victim was selected on the basis of race, disability, sexual orientation, or religion. As this is being written, federal hate crime legislation originated by former President Bill Clinton has yet to be enacted, partly because of concerns by conservatives and civil libertarians about federal involvement in offenses that are normally the concern of the states. Such laws must not infringe on the constitutional protection afforded to individuals to express their views, no matter how unpopular or "politically incorrect." Also, the fair application of hate crime legislation must be carefully considered. If violence against special populations warrants more severe punishment, then hate-based violence initiated by members of special populations against nonmembers should be equally punished. Last, singling out members of specific groups may actually provoke resentment and therefore increase crimes against the groups that hate crime laws seek to protect.

RESPONDING TO VICTIMIZATION

Victims, concerned citizens, government officials, criminal justice practitioners, and scholars can respond to victimization in a number of ways. Some of these responses are specific to victims, others target offenders, and still others emphasize community or societal solutions.

Crime Prevention

Programs designed to reduce the vulnerability of citizens to victimization are frequently implemented by law enforcement agencies, governmental agencies, civic organizations, and community action groups. The various types of *crime prevention* programs that are available range from individual efforts through programs at every level of society. They may consist of educational/awareness programs and self-defense training at the local levels, special assistance programs at the local and state levels, or the enactment of prohibitive legislation at the state and federal levels.

Victim Assistance Programs

Victim assistance programs may be run by governmental agencies such as a district attorney's office, by private organizations that contract with the state or local governments to provide services, or by volunteer organizations. The nature and extent of assistance varies, but victims can often find counseling and support from individuals who have had similar experiences. They may receive free medical or mental health services, or they may find someone who will assist them in understanding and enduring the strain of the criminal justice process.

Victim Compensation

Most states and the federal government have programs in which victims of crimes who have filed police reports and indicated a willingness to cooperate in having their cases prosecuted are eligible for financial support from governmental agencies. Florida was one of the first states to implement a *victim compensation* program on a statewide basis when it created the Florida

Crime Compensation Commission in the 1970s. Depending on the circumstances, victims may receive support in paying medical bills and/or living expenses incurred due to injuries resulting from a crime. Regrettably, at the time of this writing, most of the compensation programs of which the authors are aware tend to be underfunded, so financial assistance to victims is often limited.

Offender Restitution

Resulting from enhanced awareness and/or legal mandate, many judges are requiring offenders to make restitution for the harm they have caused victims. Monetary *offender restitution* requires offenders to make financial reparations to their victim. These payments may be made directly to the victim or may be paid to the court or community correctional officials for transfer to the victim. Offender restitution is similar to a fine in that moneys are paid to the community by the offender, but differ from traditional fines in that they are paid into programs specifically designated to aid crime victims. Service-offender restitution requires offenders to perform a specified number of hours or specific services to the victim to compensate for the harm that they caused. Service-community restitution usually requires a number of hours of community service as payment to the community for the criminal's victimizing behavior (Doerner and Lab, 1998).

Victim's Rights

In the 1980s and 1990s, advocates of victim's rights pushed for victims to have more participation in the criminal justice system. They called for victims to be made aware of and have input into plea bargain agreements, sentencing outcomes, and the release of offenders from prison. In response to these demands, the Victims of Crime Act was passed by Congress in 1984. This legislation provided millions of dollars in funding that helped establish many state compensation programs. In 1990, the Crime Control Act contained the Victim's Rights and Restitution Act and the Victims of Child Abuse Act. Among other things, these acts provided for victims of federal offenses to be notified of court proceedings, to be allowed to confer with governmental attorneys, and to receive restitution.

As of 1997, 29 states had enacted victim's rights provisions within their constitutions (Doerner and Lab, 1998). In addition, many states and the federal government now require *victim impact statements* to be provided to courts prior to sentencing. Actions at the state and federal levels have also made it easier for victims of crimes to hold their victimizers accountable in civil court for the harm done to them. O. J. Simpson was acquitted in the infamous "trial of the century" murder trial, but the families of victims Nicole

Brown Simpson and Ronald Goldman were successful in their civil litigation against him. Unfortunately, a federal law allowing rape victims to sue their assailants in federal courts instead of state courts was struck down as unconstitutional by the U.S. Supreme Court on May 15, 2000 (*U.S.* v. *Morrison*, 99-5; *Brzonkala* v. *Morrison*, 99-29).

Victim Awareness and Empowerment

The Victims' Rights movement of the 1980s and 1990s helped educate the public on victim's issues, which also helped promote crime prevention and victim advocacy efforts. In addition to education on how to avoid victimization and counseling on how to cope with victimization, programs in dispute resolution were also initiated. *Dispute resolution* programs enable offenders and victims to meet with arbitrators to resolve issues outside (and sometimes instead of) criminal prosecution and/or civil litigation. Dispute resolution efforts that seek to help offenders and victims return to their preoffense status are termed *restorative justice* (Karmen, 2001).

▓▓▓ SUMMARY ▓▓▓

The costs of criminal victimizations run into the billions of dollars each year. The costs reflect only the value of property taken and do not reflect the costs of medical treatment. They do not reflect the greater costs of economic hardships, physical pain, and suffering, as well as the emotional trauma experienced by victims and their families. Nor do they indicate the costs to society resulting from the fear of victimization.

In understanding victim's issues, it helps to understand the various types of victimization. Whether victimization is imposed by strangers, occurs in the workplace, or happens within domestic situations, it influences both the impact and means of dealing with victimization. Special populations of individuals who are particularly vulnerable to victimization require specific attention from criminal justice practitioners and scholars. Hate crime legislation is one means of trying to deal with offenders who select their victims based on biases against certain groups or communities.

There are several means of responding to the problem of victimization in American society. These include crime prevention, victim assistance programs, victim compensation, offender restitution, and victim empowerment. The development of programs to aid victims is the direct result of the Victim's Rights movement and subsequent federal and state legal actions. Although there is still a long way to go, we have come far in a short period of time in understanding and coping with the problem of victimization.

■■■■ DISCUSSION QUESTIONS ■■■■

1. Explain why the costs of victimization are high not only for individual victims but for other members of society.

2. Contrast the various types of victimization that occur within the family with those that occur within the workplace or that are perpetrated by strangers.

3. Debate the pros and cons of enacting hate crime laws. If hate crime laws are enacted, should they be the province of the state or federal government? Justify your view.

4. Discuss the various programs available within your state and community to deal with victimization.

5. Discuss the accomplishments of the Victim's Rights movement. Describe what you think the future accomplishments in this area will be and why they will occur.

■■■■ REFERENCES ■■■■

Bureau of Justice Statistics. (1999). *The 1998 national crime victimization survey*. Washington, D.C.: U.S. Government Printing Office.

Doerner, W. G., and Lab, S. (1998). *Victimology*, 2nd ed. Cincinnati, OH: Anderson.

Federal Bureau of Investigation. (1999). *Crime in the United States: 1998*. Washington, D.C.: U.S. Government Printing Office.

Hunter, R. D., Mayhall, P. D., and Barker, T. (2000). *Police-community relations and the administration of justice*, 5th ed. Upper Saddle River, NJ: Prentice Hall.

Karmen, A. (2001). *Crime victims*, 4th ed. Belmont, CA: Wadsworth/Thomson Learning.

Meadows, R. J. (1998). *Understanding violence and victimization*. Upper Saddle River, NJ: Prentice Hall.

Wallace, H. (1998). *Victimology: Legal psychological and social perspectives*. Boston: Allyn & Bacon.

CHAPTER 13

Dealing
with the Law-abiding

■ KEY CONCEPTS ■

Americanization
compliance
conservatism
diversity
justice
law-abiding
liberalism
noncompliance
political correctness
politics

punishment
Social Darwinists
social engineering perspective
socialism
social justice
social problems perspective
social reality
social responsibility perspective
symbolic reassurance
vengeance

■ LEARNING OBJECTIVES ■

After reading this chapter, the student should be able to:

1. Explain why there is a need for justice within American society.

2. Discuss how politics influence the administration of justice.

3. Present and discuss the social responsibility perspective of criminal justice.

4. Present and discuss the social problems perspective of criminal justice.

5. Present and discuss the social engineering perspective of criminal justice.

6. Describe why society must exact vengeance on behalf of crime victims.

7. Explain what is meant by punishing noncompliance of law-abiding citizens.

8. Explain how the compliance of law-abiding citizens is rewarded.

9. Explain the concept of symbolic reassurance.

Throughout this text we have examined the different approaches to the study of crime and criminality and have presented different perspectives on the nature of crime and criminal behavior. Chapters 11 and 12 revisited those earlier discussions by assessing responses to offenders and victims. This chapter focuses on how these diverse views apply to members of society who do not commit criminal acts.

JUSTICE IN THE EYES OF THE LAW-ABIDING

The purpose of government is to maintain order and promote stability within society. All other governmental activities are derived from this primary function (Burns, Peltason, and Cronin, 1997). Criminal justice systems were created as governmental components to facilitate this basic obligation of government. While there are many forms of government (ranging from democracy to tyranny), each must have a means of making and enforcing law in order to continue to exist.

According to Frank Schmalleger (1999), social reality is interpreted according to the cultural experiences and personal interests of the observer. How people view the relationships among society, offenders, victims, and the justice system influences their belief in the justice system and ultimately their commitment to society. Just as the influences or lack of social bonds, strains, and social controls may explain criminal behaviors (Hirschi, 1969; Reckless, 1967), so, too, do they explain law-abiding behaviors.

THE POLITICS OF JUSTICE

The United States is a nation bound by political traditions rather than ethnic or cultural traditions such as those found in many nations. This does not mean that issues such as ethnicity and culture are not important. Rather it means that according to our governmental institutions, issues such as race, creed, color, religion, and national origin are not supposed to factor into public decision making (Cummings and Wise, 1997).

Whereas a nation such as Sweden is comprised of a relatively small homogeneous population, America has great diversity in ethnicity, cultural traditions, religious perspectives, socioeconomic status, and political ideologies. What this means for the criminal justice system is that we not only do not have the common ethnic or cultural heritage that helps bind other nations, but our common bonds of democracy and personal freedom are often disputed as well. The result is that justice in America is extremely political in nature.

Pause for a moment and think about the myriad of political views held by those with whom you associate. Each of the approximately 280 million people thought to reside in the United States has his or her own individual perspective on how their governments (local, state, and federal) should operate, what should be lawful, how laws should be enforced, and how lawbreakers should be treated. Those who view America from an elitist perspective have very different views from those who view it from the perspective of political pluralism (the reader may wish to refer back to the social conflict discussions in chapter 7). Partisan politics influences how the different levels of government are perceived and how they function. Sexism, racism, and classism (all of which have differing definitions depending on who is doing the defining) impact the political process (Greenberg, 1999).

Determining what the balance will be between promoting crime control and protecting individual freedoms is difficult. A group that argues for personal liberties may see governmental involvement as abusive while another group may see those same governmental actions as ensuring such liberties (Hunter, Mayhall, and Barker, 2000). Throughout this text, we have presented many different theoretical perspectives on why people become criminal. Chapter 12 presented differing means of dealing with criminal offenders. There are just as many disagreements on how government should deal with the law-abiding.

The product of diversity is disagreement. No matter how tolerant individuals may claim to be, they tend to think less of those with whom they disagree than they do of those who share their views. Ensuring social stability requires that citizens have confidence in their governments (Greenberg, 1999). Defining acceptable morality is even more complex (Montague, 1995). For these reasons, the administration of justice in America will continue to be highly politicized.

The Social Responsibility Perspective

The last quarter of the twentieth century saw an increasing conservatism of the American public and governmental entities in regard to crime control and dealing with offenders. Jerome Skolnick (2000) represents many liberals, and perhaps the majority of criminologists, who assert that this "get tough on crime mentality" is creating large prison populations and that the policies are both economically and socially costly, as well as being ineffectual in preventing crime. John DiIulio (2000) represents conservatives, and quite a number of criminologists, in his support for policies that have gotten dangerous criminals off the streets, lowered crime rates, and allowed the public to express their condemnation of criminal acts.

At the heart of this disagreement among respected criminologists, as well as within the American citizenry, is their perception of accountability. These disagreements hark back to the classical school's focus on the law and punishing those who knowingly violate the law (Barlow, 2000). This view is compatible with political conservatism in which a smaller, less intrusive government that holds people individually accountable for their actions is preferred (Cummings and Wise, 1997). Political conservatives tend to promote individual responsibility.

Schmalleger (1999, p. 26) refers to this emphasis on an individual's accountability for his or her actions as *social responsibility*. This outlook stresses accountability in civil and noncriminal matters. While acknowledging that social forces may impact decision making, social responsibility proponents argue that people still must be held accountable to society. In addition, criminals are punished to enforce system values. While social programs may help remove some factors that might lead to crime, they are seen as having little impact on deterring criminals from committing crimes. Therefore, strict law enforcement and harsher penalties reassure law-abiding citizens who hold to this perspective (Hancock and Sharp, 2000).

The social responsibility perspective is popular not only with political conservatives, but also with moderates and some liberals who believe that punishment is the only means of obtaining compliance from certain offenders. Indeed, the view of social responsibility advocates is based on punishment not just as deterrence, but as a means of atonement so that offenders may regain entry into society. At the very least, society is seen as being safe from victimization while the offender is incapacitated and/or incarcerated.

Perhaps the greatest benefit of this perspective to ordinary citizens is that it gives them a "sense of justice," that is, they believe that evildoers will be punished for their crimes. Victims of criminal acts, as well as the whole of society, find comfort in the belief that the governments they pay their taxes to will enact vengeance on their behalf (Montague, 1995). By exacting vengeance, government promotes stability not only by deterring criminals or would-be criminals from future crime, but by preventing citizens from "taking the law into their own hands" by seeking personal vengeance.

Another major benefit of this perspective is that it reinforces within the citizenry the idea that they as individuals are accountable to society for their actions. This emphasis serves to ensure compliance to governmental edicts and social norms, as well as to criminal codes. In addition, accountability promotes self-reliance and self-worth, which are seen as enabling individuals and groups to achieve success within society.

The Social Problems Perspective

Just as positive criminology challenges classical criminology in regard to individual responsibility and punishment, so do proponents of the *social problems perspective* challenge those who support social responsibility (Schmalleger, 1999, p. 25). Social problems such as poverty, discrimination, poor education, family violence, the breakup of traditional social institutions, and poor socialization are seen as leading to crime. Since these are social problems, society, not the individual, should be held accountable for criminal behavior.

Instead of strict law enforcement and harsh penalties, social programs designed to ease the burdens of the poor and of other groups who have previously experienced social injustice are preferred. Many advocates of the social problems perspective are political liberals who support government intervention because they believe that society as a whole is responsible for the actions of individuals within that society. These advocates prefer promoting social mores and norms, as well as sharing in the responsibility for society and the community by creating government-sponsored programs to address perceived social ills (Burns, Peltason, and Cronin, 1997). Strict law enforcement is seen as being counterproductive to developing a just and equitable society (Skolnick, 2000).

Proponents of the social problems perspective call for more governmental intervention to ease the burdens on the poor and protected classes. Critics of the social problems perspective argue that its supporters are seeking to punish the law-abiding by infringing on individual rights (such as gun ownership) of the law-abiding and view these efforts as "coddling criminals" and promoting immorality. Some conservative political activists have gone so far as to accuse advocates of gun control of using crime issues to promote their political agenda. Proponents respond that any inconveniences to the middle class and the affluent are necessary concessions to social well-being and should therefore be tolerated.

The greatest benefit of the social programs perspective is that it seeks to prevent crime before it occurs by addressing societal issues that may promote crime. While the poor and members of disadvantaged social groups are usually targeted by these programs, the advantages are believed to extend to all members of society. Those who support the social responsibility perspective tend to approve of programs such as Head Start, Social Security, Medicare, and Medicaid. Indeed, highly criticized programs such as welfare are usually attacked based on perceptions of mismanagement, abuse, and corruption rather than on the premise of whether society should help those in need.

Critics of social programs usually do not object to governmental efforts at addressing social ills; it is the perceived inequities in the methods in which the programs are applied that rankles. Providing help is sanctioned as long as it does not create dependence or reward irresponsibility (Greenberg, 1999). Defenders respond that it is better to have a humane system with some flaws than to neglect those who are needy. They argue that individual accountability cannot be imposed on all members of society if all of its members are not able to fully participate in society. Therefore, the social ills (poverty, homelessness, hunger, inadequate medical care, racism, sexism, homophobia, religious intolerance, elitism, etc.) must be addressed by governmental programs supported by the tax dollars of those who can afford to pay for them. Critics respond that such interventions are intrusive and place undue burdens on the working class and lower-middle class (Cummings and Wise, 1997).

Depending on one's religious, political, and personal ideologies, choosing between the two perspectives may be very easy or quite difficult. Just as it is difficult to decide what correctional technique should be applied to an offender, so it is difficult to decide what obligations members of society should have toward other members. Ultimately, both perspectives promote individual responsibility and accountability to society: The social responsibility perspective does so by calling for good citizens to comply with the law and do their part. The social problems perspective does exactly the same. It is not the intent or the caring that differs; it is the process by which they are applied.

The Social Engineering Perspective

The debate over social responsibility and social problems is further stirred by those who believe that neither perspective adequately addresses the problems of American society. Critics of these perspectives believe that stressing individual accountability only exacerbates the frustration and feeling of injustice experienced by the poor and the oppressed. In like manner, trying to fix social problems by enacting governmental programs such as Equal Employment Opportunity and welfare are but minor efforts that do not address the underlying problems inherent to capitalism. Instead, they believe *social engineering* is called for to ensure that society is properly structured. Social engineering is the view that society is so badly flawed that it must be reworked by those best equipped to do so.

Critical and radical criminologists, as well as adherents of the political far left, argue for stronger measures than those found within welfare capitalism. Some social engineering advocates urge that America must become more socialistic by using governmental intervention to redistribute wealth and promote international egalitarianism. Others see communism as the only fair solution to eliminate the legacy of greed, corruption, and oppression that capitalism has created (Bohm, 1997). Less extreme proponents of social engineering do not call for adopting socialism or communism as an economic system but do see the need for increased government intervention and the increased use of social institutions to bring about social changes (see the social control arguments of chapter 7).

Such ideas of using education and governmental pressures to impose social changes on the law-abiding masses are not new: During the 1800s, Native Americans and immigrants were forced to become "Americanized" or suffer harsh consequences from the government, social institutions, and private citizens. In the late 1800s, *Social Darwinists* encouraged poverty and governmental neglect as a means of eliminating the unfit from society. In the 1950s, McCarthyism sought to rid the nation of leftists who were believed to threaten the moral decency and economic stability of American society. Today voices from both the left and the right seek to impose their views on the majority (Hunter, Mayhall, and Barker, 2000).

Calls for equitable treatment of women, gays, and minorities have received support throughout the nation. Cultural diversity has been recognized as an integral aspect of American life. While there has often been disagreement over the methods to use (such as reliance on Equal Employment Opportunity enforcement versus maintaining affirmative action), the disagreements are mostly over process and anticipated effects rather than against fairness and equality. However, despite a "confused consensus" among Americans in general, many on both the left and the right are dissatisfied.

Political correctness, religious conservatism, and civil rights activism are but some of many issues that are argued across the country. The nature and role of government itself receives endless scrutiny. In election years, Democrats, Republicans, and a multitude of smaller parties cajole voters with promises of what will happen if they are elected and threats of what will not if they are defeated. Regardless of party, politicians and political pundits are increasingly concerned about the indifference and skepticism of the electorate, without realizing that it is they who have created that alienation. As our society continues to develop, many Americans will continue to be unhappy with the directions that are or are not being taken, and this unhappiness will impact the administration of justice.

ADMINISTERING JUSTICE ON BEHALF OF THE LAW-ABIDING

This section describes various activities on the part of government that are designed to influence the opinions and behaviors of the law-abiding. While these events are characterized within the American system of justice, they are not unique to the United States but may be found in any nation regardless of the political structure.

Condemning and Punishing Crime

When nation states came into being, the government accepted responsibility for exacting vengeance on behalf of those who had been harmed by criminal actions, which not only enables government to administer justice uniformly, but also keeps citizens from having to achieve their own revenge (Roshier, 1989). As we discussed in chapters 10 and 12, it is a basic human emotion to strike back at those who have done harm to us or our loved ones. If governmental agencies (police, courts, or corrections) are not perceived as exacting justice on behalf of their constituents, there will most assuredly be those who will feel a need to impose their own justice on those who have offended against them.

The act of condemning and punishing crime is a fundamental responsibility of government (Packer, 1968). It is through punishment that government demonstrates to the victims, their friends, their family, and the public in general that the government can and will exact vengeance on their behalf (Montague, 1995). This support from government is also displayed in public calls for sympathy for victims, as well as calls for new criminal sanctions. The responses to the Oklahoma City bombing in 1995, the Jasper, Texas, dragging death of an African American by white racists in 1998, and the Columbine High School massacre in 1999 are examples of how government can show support for crime victims. Despite criticisms of President Bill Clinton on other justice issues, he was always quick to offer his personal support and the more important figurative condolences of the nation to victims of sensational crimes. While some may criticize such actions as political posturing, they also send a message of compassion and sympathy that benefits the victims as well as concerned citizens across the nation.

Wooing Constituents

Seeing lawbreakers punished is also a means of maintaining citizen support for criminal laws and government in general (Packer, 1968). While we have stressed that punishment is a classical approach that is more appropriate to a conservative political ideology, that does not mean that moderates and liberals do not sanction its use. Indeed, the current effort on the part of liberal Democrats to enact federal and state hate crime legislation exemplifies such support. Conservative Republicans also do the same, as evidenced by federal carjacking laws that were enacted despite the fact that every state in the union has laws against auto theft, robbery, kidnapping, and murder that would cover any carjacking incident. In these cases, the goal is not to necessarily correct a void in the law, but to make points with political constituents. Another motive may be to extend governmental influence into areas that were previously considered to be outside government's sphere of influence.

Promoting Social Change

In addition to showing constituents that they are tough on a particular category of crime, politicians use the criminal justice system to maintain control over the population (Packer, 1968). An unspoken message is, "Do what we feel to be appropriate voluntarily or we will enact a law that makes compliance mandatory." Federal hiring regulations, protection of voting rights, and sexual harassment prohibitions are illustrations of governmental interventions to halt social wrongs that were not being addressed.

Governmental intervention in a behavior that has previously been considered to be lawful may come about because of technological advancements such as the development of the Internet; social movements such as civil rights; less dramatic changes in the social mood such as increased fear of victimization; or through the efforts of "moral entrepreneurs" who successfully lobby for new laws to halt a behavior that they consider to be evil or inappropriate. Regulations of pornography and nude dancing, limitations on the sale of alcoholic beverages, restrictions on tobacco, and regulation of firearms are examples of this strategy (Siegel, 1998).

In short, just as lawbreakers are punished if they do not conform to the legal codes imposed by government, the law-abiding are punished with new legal codes if they do not yield to governmental pressures to change. Enacting criminal codes is not the only means by which the law-abiding populace is pressured to change its behavior. Civil procedures and administrative rulings may serve the same purposes. But perhaps the most successful means that political, social, and economic leaders have in imposing their wills on the populace is through media exposure.

Despite denials by the news and entertainment media, they are instrumental in shaping Americans' outlooks on what is and is not socially acceptable behavior. Social change may be more readily accomplished by statements and actions on the political stage and in the media than through the enactment of laws. In fact, the successful application of law often involves a great deal of public debate and media coverage (consider the debates over gun control, school prayer, and abortion) both prior to and after the passage of the law. Politicians may not have to use legal codes, they may be able to use social condemnation of opponents and the support of their allies in the news and entertainment media to accomplish the same purposes.

Rewarding Compliance

The rewards to law-abiding citizens that are provided by the criminal justice system are many: public safety, which enables us to conduct our daily business and to let our children play in our neighborhoods with only minimal concern; an orderly society, in which despite diverse opinions on a myriad of political, social, and economic issues, we are able to participate in social activities with only limited fear of terroristic activities; low crime rates compared to other Western democracies; and, despite minimal amounts of crime, protection of individual freedoms. Indeed it is not the acts of justice (i.e., punishment of offenders) but the *idea* of justice that unites society.

SYMBOLIC REASSURANCE

For several years, Ronald Hunter (1995, 1996) has been advocating an alternative explanation for how and why justice is administered. He refers to this perspective as symbolic reassurance. The concept of *symbolic reassurance* builds on the concluding statement from the previous section about the importance of the idea of justice. The basic premise of this theory is that the criminal justice system not only provides guidelines for society to follow, it also punishes evildoers to affirm the law-abidings' belief in the system. The mass citizenry are law-abiding not because they fear the law, but because they believe in it. Therefore, universal conformity is not attained through threats of prosecution, but by reassuring the law-abiding that the system of justice is working.

This principle may even be taken to the extreme by asserting that to a large degree, it does not matter what is being done as long as the public perceives that *something* is being done. Symbolic reassurance asserts that the criminal justice system exists not to deal with lawbreakers, but to reassure the law-abiding public. As long as a few offenders get occasional punishment (the more severe the better), the public, especially the middle class, will remain compliant, even if they are not totally satisfied.

There are many means of dealing with criminal and deviant behavior. No one theory will emerge as being the miracle solution to the problem of crime, which is a normal social phenomenon. What is truly important is that law-abiding citizens believe that they are being served and therefore do not have to take the law into their own hands. Serious social unrest—societywide distrust that threatens the existence of governmental entities, not the isolated and short-term threats exemplified by urban riots or actions of fringe groups—will occur only if governmental institutions fail to symbolically reassure the general populace.

SUMMARY

America has great diversity in ethnicity, cultural traditions, religious perspectives, socioeconomic status, and political ideologies. What this means for the criminal justice system is that we not only lack the common ethnic or cultural heritage that helps bind other nations, but our common bonds of democracy and personal freedom are often disputed as well. The result is that justice in America is extremely political in nature.

Political conservatives place emphasis on an individual's accountability for his or her actions. This social responsibility outlook stresses accountability in civil and noncriminal matters. Strict law enforcement and harsh penalties are seen as reassuring by law-abiding citizens who hold to this perspective. The social problems perspective holds that it is society, not the individual, that should be held accountable. Instead of strict law enforcement and harsh penalties, social programs designed to ease the burdens of the poor and other groups who have previously experienced social injustice are preferred. The debate over social responsibility and social problems is further stirred by those who believe that neither perspective adequately addresses the problems of American society. Social engineering is the view that society is so badly flawed that it needs reworking.

The act of condemning and punishing crime is a fundamental responsibility of government. While there is considerable disagreement among politicians, criminal justice practitioners, and citizens as to how the criminal justice system operates, government must demonstrate to the public that it will exact vengeance on behalf of victims and society as a whole. Government also uses legal sanctions (or the threat of new legal codes) to encourage citizens to comply with changes that those in power wish to create within society. The greatest reward for compliance on the part of law-abiding citizens is social stability. Therefore, it is not specific actions of the justice system but the idea of justice that unites society.

The concept of symbolic reassurance asserts that in addition to providing legal guidelines for citizens to follow, lawbreakers are punished to affirm the law-abidings' belief in the system. Rather than obtaining compliance through general deterrence, compliance is gained by reassurance that the system is working for them.

■■■ **DISCUSSION QUESTIONS** ■■■

1. Describe how political disagreements impact on the administration of justice in the United States.

2. Compare and contrast the three perspectives on criminal justice.

3. Describe how law-abiding citizens are influenced by governmental and social institutions to conform to social policies and norms.

4. Describe the premise of symbolic reassurance, and explain how it may be applied within American society.

■■■ **REFERENCES** ■■■

Barlow, H. D. (2000). *Criminal justice in America.* Upper Saddle River, NJ: Prentice Hall.

Bohm, R. M. (1997). *A primer on crime and delinquency.* Belmont, CA: Wadsworth.

Burns, J. M., Peltason, J. W., and Cronin, T. E. (1997). *Government by the people*, 17th ed. Upper Saddle River, NJ: Prentice Hall.

Cummings, M. C., and Wise, D. (1997). *Democracy under pressure: An introduction to the American political system*, 8th ed. Fort Worth: Harcourt Brace College.

Dilulio, J. J., Jr. (2000). Instant replay: Three strikes was the right call. In J. H. Skolnick and E. Currie, eds., *Crisis in American institutions*, 11th ed. Needham Heights, MA: Allyn & Bacon.

Greenberg, E. (1999). *The struggle for democracy*, 4th ed. New York: Addison-Wesley.

Hancock, B. W., and Sharp, P. M. (2000). *Criminal justice in America: Theory, practice, and policy*, 2nd ed. Upper Saddle River, NJ: Prentice Hall.

Hirschi, T. (1969). *Causes of delinquency.* Berkeley: University of California Press.

Hunter, R. D. (1996, October). Symbolic reassurance: How and why the system really works. Paper presented at the Southern Criminal Justice Association Annual Meeting, Richmond, VA.

_____. (1995, March). Symbolic reassurance: Why we punish. Paper presented at the Academy of Criminal Justice Sciences Annual Meeting, Boston.

_____, Mayhall, P. D., and Barker, T. (2000). *Police-community relations and the administration of justice*, 5th ed. Upper Saddle River, NJ: Prentice Hall.

Montague, P. (1995). *Punishment as societal defense*. London: Rowman and Littlefield.

Packer, H. L. (1968). *The limits of the criminal sanction*. Palo Alto: Stanford University Press.

Reckless, W. (1967). *The crime problem*. New York: Appleton-Century-Crofts.

Roshier, B. (1989). *Controlling crime: The classical perspective in criminology*. Chicago: Lyceum.

Schmalleger, F. (1999). *Criminal justice today*, 5th ed. Upper Saddle River, NJ: Prentice Hall.

Siegel, L. J. (1998). *Criminology: Theories, patterns and typologies*, 6th ed. Belmont, CA: West/Wadsworth.

Skolnick, J. H. (2000). Wild pitch: Three strikes you're out and other bad calls on crime. In J. H. Skolnick and E. Currie, eds., *Crisis in American institutions*, 11th ed. Needham Heights, MA: Allyn & Bacon.

Index

WARNER MEMORIAL LIBRARY
EASTERN UNIVERSITY
ST. DAVIDS, 19087-3696